The Education of Adults in Britain

**The Open University Press Series
in Adult and Continuing Education**

General Editors:

H. A. Jones   formerly Vaughan Professor of
Education, University of Leicester

G. Normie   Special Assistant to the Vice-
Chancellor, The Open University

Titles in the series:

*Education and the Challenge of Change : A
recurrent education strategy for Britain,*
R. Flude and A. Parrott

*Philosophical Concepts and Values in Adult
Education,*
K. H. Lawson

*Strategies for Adult Education : Practices in
Western Europe,*
C. J. Titmus

The Education of Adults in Britain
C. D. Legge

The Education of Adults in Britain

Derek Legge

The Open University Press
Milton Keynes

The Open University Press
A division of
Open University Educational Enterprises Limited
12 Cofferidge Close
Stony Stratford
Milton Keynes MK11 1BY, England

First published 1982

British Library Cataloguing in Publication Data

Legge, Derek
  The education of adults in Britain
  1. Adult education—Great Britain
  I. Title
  374'.941   LC5256.G7

  ISBN 0-335-00267-6

Typeset by
R James Hall Typesetting and Book Production Services
and printed by The Anchor Press Ltd, Tiptree

To my daughter Angela
and
to all my former students

Contents

Foreword

The author of this book has for much of his life been teaching students in pursuit of advanced diplomas and higher degrees in adult education. Indeed, the department at Manchester University which he helped to found was the pioneer among British universities in this field.

Now everyone who has ever taught adults knows that he has learnt at least as much from his students as they from him. So Derek Legge is uniquely qualified to approach the task attempted here of giving an overview of the education of adults in Britain; and I am sure he would be the first to acknowledge his debt to his students, who are now to be found in most countries of the world.

The task is no simple one. The education of adults in Britain is a complex field of study. Its components derive from a variety of social and educational traditions and the relationships between the parts are constantly changing. For example, there are the powerful traditions of liberal adult education, examplified by university extra-mural education and the Workers Educational Association, whose roots lie in nineteenth-century movements of social emancipation that pre-date the local education authorities by whom almost all other forms of education are now provided. There are the increasingly varied opportunities for adults to acquire new vocational qualifications following the burgeoning of technical education in the third quarter of the present century, a process that must become stronger and more comprehensive under the pressures of technology and economics. In the last decade the discovery of large numbers of adults with imperfect command of those skills of reading, writing and number that a modern society demands has led to a movement of basic education that is only now beginning to gain momentum. Leisure has turned out to be a less simple commodity than the mere respite from labour and has created both demand and opportunity for education, as well as much voluntary activity for the benefit of others in our communities. There are, in truth, few aspects of adult life in the modern world that do not carry a latent educational dimension.

By a fortunate coincidence, just as this book appears the Advisory Council for Adult and Continuing Education has produced its major report on a strategy for continuing education, a term that is now coming into general use in this country to denote the whole range of the education of adults. The report argues for a coherent plan that will link together all post-initial education in a structure that is relevant enough and flexible enough for the needs of an informed, responsible and creative population in a twenty-first century democracy. Major international agencies such as UNESCO, with its advocacy of lifelong education, and OECD, with its strategy of recurrent education, are sounding similar challenges.

To understand how such desirable destinations might be reached, it is necessary to know clearly where we start from. That is the purpose of the present volume. It offers, in a form not hitherto available, a comprehensive survey of the education of adults in Britain, whatever the providing agency and the tradition from which it has arisen. To map a terrain of such complex topography is a difficult undertaking, but one which students of adult education have long wished to see.

Moreover, the British have been sufficiently innovative in many forms of adult education — in the university connection, through voluntary bodies, in political and trade union studies, in literacy, in outreach work, in community education, in new opportunities for women, and so on — that it is not chauvinistic to suggest that readers in other countries will find matter for reflection in Derek Legge's study. Educational practices do not readily transfer to different environments and the colonial record has perhaps too many examples of inept attempts at such transfer. But what Derek Legge has done here is to describe provisions in enough detail for them to be viewed as case-studies with accompanying critical comment on the concepts that have infused them. This clarification of our ideas is particularly welcome at this time of scrutiny (sometimes hostile scrutiny) of what is implied by the term 'education of adults'. Because Legge is interested in ideas and their influence on practice, and because statistics of adult education are notoriously difficult to establish soundly even over a short time, there is little attempt at quantification beyond general indications of orders of magnitude.

The final impression is of rich variety, as in one of those Breughel village scenes where work, play, social interaction, personal contact and community activity are all separately identified, but within a frame that is the whole of human life. That is what the education of adults ought always to be, if only the political will were strong enough to make it so. Nowhere has the realistic potentiality been more clearly presented than in this account by Derek Legge.

H A Jones
lately Vaughan Professor of Education
University of Leicester.

CHAPTER 1

Problems of definition:
some open questions

One of the problems of writing about 'the education of adults in Britain' is a general failure to agree what that term should include. There has been a strong tendency to divide the provision into packages, each carefully given a separate name, and those actively involved argue lengthily and with passion about the exact delimitation of territory. A cataloguing of categories may be of value in identifying differences, but it can equally be argued that the sectarian battles considerably weaken the public image and reduce support, both financial and non-financial. To the outside observer the education of adults must often appear as a jigsaw of unrelated pieces. Not surprisingly, he may be tempted to view them with indifference and condemn them as irrelevant. To the adult educator, therefore, it is of vital importance to get the terms of reference clear and to gain an understanding of the disputed issues. In general, the three main issues have been those of types of subject, the meaning of 'adult' and the type of activity.

Types of subject

It is clear that in Britain, though not in all parts of the world, there developed in the late nineteenth and early twentieth centuries an emphasis on a radical division between 'vocational' and 'non-vocational' subjects, and within the non-vocational, an exaltation of 'liberal studies' as something special and superior to all others. The origins of this view lie partly in the concept of education necessary for 'gentlemen', contrasted with that required for artisans and others who needed only technical know-how to produce goods and services. Liberal studies, it was said, are concerned with the ends rather than the means of living: in a twentieth century catch-phrase, they help one to 'learn to live rather than to earn one's living'. Subjects such as history and politics, economics and government, philosophy and religion, psychology and sociology, together with the appreciation of literature, music and the arts, and a few 'human' sciences such as biology were thought to be those which above all enabled a student to develop values and judgement, and to interpret life experience in ways which enriched its quality. In the late 1950s Roby Kidd declared that liberal education 'is an education that seeks for meanings, is concerned about relationships and values, formulates principles and solves problems'.[1] A little earlier the Association of Tutors in Adult Education produced a *Statement* which claimed Ministry of Education support for a view

1

that 'these studies are essential to meet the needs of civilization'.[2] Many others have talked about their importance in terms of insight, the use of reasoning power and the development of moral values. Technical and craft education, on the other hand, was 'merely' concerned with cognitive knowledge, with facts and processes, with job performance — necessary for some, but limited, mechanical and blinkered.

Perhaps inevitably, these concepts were associated with a hierarchical view of the relative importance of subjects. Some subjects were held to be more worth while than others and at the top of the pyramid were the liberal studies. Their elevation gained considerably from the fact that, for the general public, they had become the major provision of the universities and the allied, though independent, Workers' Educational Association. The distinction was also sanctified by special Board of Education regulations, issued after the First World War, which became an almost codified article of faith justifying the special position in which the teachers of such subjects tended to be paid much more highly than others. It provides the basis for what is sometimes described as the 'traditional' or 'narrow' British definition of adult education in which the teaching of the liberal studies is the only element. Many books still keep to this definition and support for it can be found in many quarters, including government circles. Even so, the Russell Report[3] cautiously declared that 'no academic subject or social or creative activity is superior to another provided that those engaged in it develop a greater awareness of their own capacities and a more certain knowledge of the totality of their responsibilities as human beings'.

Since the Second World War, however, many have felt the need to widen the definition and there has been a growing acceptance of the view that adult education should include all non-vocational studies such as music, art and drama, arts and crafts of all kinds, languages and physical education, a range at one time classified in the Ministry of Education as OFE (Other Further Education). This view retains the division of further education into 'Preparation for Work' and 'Learning for Leisure', as the 1947 Ministry pamphlet put it.[4] On the whole, the distinction between vocational and non-vocational education is widely held and perhaps most still think of adult education as defined in the United Kingdom contribution to the 1951 UNESCO *Directory of Adult Education:*

> Adult education is taken to mean forms of study and other activities which are undertaken voluntarily by mature people (i.e. over the age of 18) without *direct* regard to their vocational value.

It is not surprising, therefore, that the terms of reference of the Russell Committee appointed in 1969 were 'To assess the need for and to review the provision of non-vocational adult education in England and Wales'. The rationale for the distinction rests mainly on asserted differences in student motivation, shown particularly in voluntary commitment, in the age and maturity of the students, in the ethos of the class as co-operative rather than competitive, and in the objectives as being related more to 'personal development and citizenship than to examinations and job-advancement'. The definition is wider than the first one but still carries echoes of the pre-eminence of liberal studies.

More recently there has been considerable criticism of this distinction

2

between vocational and non-vocational as the basis for a definition of adult education. It is asserted that the division is a nonsense, that so-called vocational studies influence personal development, attitudes and values as much as the so-called non-vocational studies, which at times may be very narrow and limited. Training for a job, it is said, involves the whole person. Moreover, what for one person is a non-vocational study is for another entirely vocational. Amid the controversy a third definition has emerged which seeks to be all embracing, and inclusive of all types of education for adults. As the Education Committee of the OECD put it in 1975:[5]

> Adult education refers to any learning activity or programme deliberately designed for adults. Its ambit is taken as spanning non-vocational, vocational, general, formal, non-formal and community education and it is not restricted to any particular level.

Although the number of supporters of this view is growing, British adult educators as a whole have been reluctant to accept it; opposition comes from all sectors, including those labelled 'technical education' and 'higher education'.

The meaning of 'adult'

Different opinions are just as marked in the second disputed area: that of the meaning of 'adult'. It is generally assumed that 18 is a suitable minimum age for the education of adults, though inconsistently there has been a tendency to exclude undergraduates of 18 to 21 and 18 to 20-year-olds on day release courses. The age question is bedevilled by thoughts about 'maturity' and 'citizenship'. The writer of the UNESCO 1951 definition felt that he had to define 'mature people' by 'over 18', and others have tried to link adult education with being old enough to 'work, vote, fight and marry'. Phrases such as 'soundly and professionally adult', 'with a commitment as a householder', 'independent of guardianship', 'having achieved an agreed role in society', 'accepting social responsibility' are frequently used but they do little to clarify. There are varying marriage ages, earlier and increasing mobility, changing roles and commitments, and some young people are more 'mature' by some definitions than many 50 or 60-year-olds. It has been suggested that the minimum school leaving age should be used as the basis for adulthood, and indeed some voluntary organizations such as the Women's Institutes, take 16 as the age at which membership becomes possible. On the other hand, Harold Wiltshire limits an adult to a person over the age of 20 who is first of all free — 'no longer under tutelage and able to do what he likes and to make his own judgements and choices'; second, mature — 'with some experience of life, whose personality, attitudes and social roles are becoming fixed, though they may not be irrevocably fixed'; and third, a full citizen — 'with all the rights and duties of a citizen'.[6] Perhaps we should ask how much need there is for a precise minimum age for adult life or for sharp dividing lines between 'child' and 'adult'.

Linked with the age question is the view of 'adult education' as something that takes place after the completion of a first stage of full-time education; as a National Institute report[7] puts it, 'people who have completed

3

the cycle of continuous education commenced in childhood', a statement similar to that given in the Interim Report of the Advisory Committee set up to survey adult education in Ireland: 'people who have broken with full time continuous education'. Although there have been increasing numbers of older people in university undergraduate courses, teacher training and institutions for higher technical studies, this exclusion of 'higher education' and of initial training for jobs still seems to be acceptable to most people. Looking ahead, however, this may be increasingly difficult to maintain as the need for retraining throughout life becomes greater and possibilities emerge of radical changes in ideas about educational needs and structures. Certainly there will be queries about the continuity of education and possibly a development of part-time study, or a mixture of part-time and full-time education, for everyone over the age of 14 or 15 which will then be recurrent throughout life. The 1944 Education Act divided education into the three stages of primary, secondary and further, the latter meaning all post-school education, i.e., all over what is now the age of 16. Although in some quarters 'further' has since acquired a more limited connotation and is even by some restricted to just vocational training for young people, the original intention seems to have been near to the third, wide, definition of 'adult education'.

Types of activity

The definition of adult education in terms of types of activity is also subject to dispute. Obviously all experiences can lead to learning, and people are 'educated' by their daily life at home, at work and in the community. Human beings learn informally about attitudes, values and action, and it is often difficult to separate this from more formal education. Most young mothers, for example, acquire their information, ideas and attitudes about the treatment of babies not from formal education but from chance conversations with relatives and friends, incidental reading of magazines, broadcasts and the many agencies of community views. Some years ago a librarian commented:

> A man's effort in making a garden, decorating a house or taking apart an internal combustion engine; a woman's in making a cake, sewing a garment or training a child . . . is as much a creative and educative experience as attending a class in economics or musical appreciation.[8]

With the women's liberation movements, we may regret the implied role differentiation, but the central idea of the value of informal learning experience remains valid.

Nevertheless, for practical purposes it is not particularly helpful to define adult education in such wide terms, and most people wish to restrict the definition to the provision of distinct opportunities which are planned to have an educational purpose. At the UNESCO World Conference in Tokyo in 1972, adult education was defined as:

> A process whereby persons who no longer attend school on a regular or full time basis, undertake sequential and organised activities with the conscious intention of bringing about changes in information, knowledge,

4

understanding or skills, appreciation and attitudes: or for the purpose of identifying or solving personal problems.[9]

This interpretation excludes casual learning which is incidental to other activities, for example the normal tasks of one's job or home life, travel, playing games and shopping, and stresses those activities whose primary purpose is to educate. In recent years there has been some challenge to this by those who extol the virtues of 'informal education', defined by Philip Coombs of the International Council for Educational Development as

> The truly lifelong process whereby every individual acquires attitudes, values, skills and knowledge from daily experience, and the educative influences and resources in his or her environment — from family and neighbours, from work and play, from the market place, the library and the mass media . . . for the most part this process is relatively unorganised and unsystematic . . . yet it unquestionably accounts for a very high proportion of all that any person accumulates in a lifetime.[10]

Within the provision of deliberate activities it is possible to distinguish two main types. The first consists of fairly formalized teaching and learning activity characterized particularly by the part-time evening class or the full-time course in a technical college or similar institution. Implying the presence of a teacher and a group, to some this is 'adult education' *par excellence* and perhaps it is the image most readily conjured up when the words are used. Yet there are also purposeful groups without a teacher, somewhat on the lines of Scandinavian study circles, and groups who work hard each week but are visited by a teacher only once a month. Correspondence education and home study have become more respectable, as will be discussed later, and this implies an individual rather than a group, and a teacher at a distance. The individual autodidact who sets out to 'teach himself', following a study programme organized by himself, clearly belongs to the category of deliberate activities.

The second type of deliberate activity is organized and planned but may well have less continuity than a class, and certainly often a less than clear view of educational objectives by those taking part. A visit to a factory, like those frequently carried out by the women's organizations, may be planned as 'education' by the organizers but viewed by the participants as entertainment, an afternoon out, however much they may have gained educationally in developing attitudes and values as well as in receiving information. A regular listener to a series of broadcasts such as Alistair Cooke's 'Letter from America', or a viewer of a television series such as Bronowski's 'The Ascent of Man' or Sir Kenneth Clark's 'Civilization' may think of the activity as pure entertainment. Should such programmes, however, be classified as organized adult education? Is there a clear line to be drawn between the education of adults and 'adult entertainment', or are these just points on a continuum? In which category are to be placed the exhibition, the film show, the one-off panel discussion or debate? How 'continuous' or structured must an activity be before it can be called 'education'? Does the definition rest solely on the motives of the participants? Purists often find it almost too easy to make clear distinctions. 'Call things by their right names', wrote Charles Kingsley long ago, 'recreations are not education. Don't say people must be educated when you only mean amused, refreshed, soothed, put into good spirits and good humour, or kept from vicious excesses'.[11] Indeed, it has been asserted that the identification of adult education with recreation is responsible for the low status it is sometimes given. On the other hand, it may be argued that the dividing line is too thin to be tenable and likely to exclude, for instance, the educational activities of many voluntary societies and community development projects. Must the definition of adult education be restricted just to a fairly formalized teaching and learning activity?

Terms and definitions

The problems of definition are further clouded by the advent of words and phrases which in one way or another seem to be put forward as alternatives to the words 'adult education'. In the international field at an earlier date there arose a series of words such as 'fundamental education', 'mass education' and 'out-of-school education' which is still popular in some UNESCO circles. At the moment it would seem that the most popular phrases in Britain are 'recurrent education', 'community education' and 'continuing education', with 'lifelong education' a rather less popular foreign import. Thus there is an Association for Recurrent Education, a Scottish Council for Community Education, an Open University Committee on Continuing Education and a Trades Union Congress pamphlet entitled *Priorities in Continuing Education.*[12] Drawing perhaps not very clear distinctions, the Association for Adult Education has chosen to become the Association for Adult and Continuing Education, a phrase which also appears in the title of the new body set up by the government in 1977: 'The Advisory Council for Adult and Continuing Education'. Using the sadly literal but misleading translation adopted by the Council of Europe, the Russell Committee in its 1973 Report refers to 'permanent education', although most people nowadays follow Paul Lengrand in preferring the phrase 'lifelong education' as a translation more equivalent to the French *'éducation permanente'.*

Often, of course, many of these words are used without precision and appear almost as synonyms. The TUC Statement, indeed, begins by talking about 'the area traditionally known as adult education but increasingly being termed "continuing" or "recurrent" education'. Ideological fanatics will no doubt fight to secure more exact limits to their chosen territories, but it seems questionable if these battles to secure the adoption of a favourite term really produce much clarification. If they become vested interests they may even harm the general cause of education for adults. The contenders do, however, make a number of points which can be noted as a possible help to find a path through the jungle.

Recurrent education

In the preface to a book entitled *Recurrent Education,*[13] published as early as 1974, there is the comment that 'the term "recurrent education" has been used synonymously or interchangeably with others having similar connotations, such as *"éducation permanente"*, "continuing education" and "lifelong learning" ', but that in this book 'recurrent education means much more than a paraphrase or an amalgam of these three ideas.' It then proceeds to suggest that recurrent education is 'a revolution', 'a shift in the current constellation of beliefs, values and technologies', and that it stresses 'human adaptability' as an aim and 'learner centred' as the central idea. Kenneth Lawson, in the first monograph of the Association for Recurrent Education,[14] draws attention to the various schools of thought and the different interpretations of 'recurrent education' which exist. These, he says, vary from the more radical which want devolution of decision making, a rejection of 'curriculum teaching' (as in the ideas of Paulo Freire) and a 'democratization of knowledge', to the more moderate views in which some value is attributed to some publicly-validated education even if the emphasis is still on education 'built upon the perceived needs of individuals and of social groups — perceived by them rather than by educationalists'.[15]

Lifelong education

Some of these ideas appear also in the writings of the advocates of 'lifelong education'. They too suggest the need for a new educational philosophy and the link with a radical change of regime. They see education as being 'planned as something which will be experienced by people in an individually on-going, though discontinuous way, over the whole of their lives — and which will correspond with their emerging vocational, social and personal aspirations'.[16] They believe that radical changes are necessary in all branches of education — the 'very concept of school is put in question' said Henri Janne[17] — and that lifelong education is a 'master' concept, a 'guiding principle'[18], a reinterpretation of education. It is said that it 'includes formal, non-formal and informal patterns of learning throughout the life cycle of an individual for the conscious and continuous enhancement of the quality of life, his own and that of his society'.[19] Despite Illich's view that lifelong education implies institutionalization — being 'imprisoned in the global classroom'[20] — it is generally viewed as producing great flexibility and freedom of choice of means. Besides 'formal' education, there will be 'non-formal' education, defined by Philip Coombs as 'any organised educational activity outside the established formal system — whether operating separately or as an important feature of some broader activity — that is intended to serve identifiable learning clienteles and learning objectives'[21], and 'informal' education, regarded as the relatively unorganized and unsystematic process of learning from daily experiences. The Russell Committee thought that 'permanent' education implied that 'the education system would be re-made to meet people's lifelong but discontinuous needs, which might recur in personal, social, academic or vocational life'.[22] As the 'traditional notion of a terminal age for education somewhere between sixteen and twenty-five would be abandoned', the Committee staked a claim for adult education as 'an integral part of the total provision, not as something for the less fortunate or more studious, but as something to be expected and experienced by the whole nation'. One is reminded of the view of the *1919 Report* that 'Adult education is national necessity . . . and therefore should be both universal and lifelong.'

'Lifelong education' has been attacked as a 'fuzzy, shorthand, politically expedient term, offered as a solution to a clump of ill defined problems which would be thought about more usefully if they were kept separate',[23] but it provides a useful stress on the need to consider the unity of education from cradle to grave, and on the need to integrate more formal types of education with the great variety of non-formal ways of learning in the home and in the community.

Community education

The word 'community', of course, is open to a multitude of interpretations. The Scottish Alexander Report[24] wanted to use 'community education' in a 'wide and comprehensive sense' as a description of 'the wide spectrum of educational opportunities' made available by both statutory and voluntary agencies. It declared that 'social, cultural, recreational and educational activities for adults are so interrelated that any attempts to distinguish between them or to deal with one without regard to the others would be undesirable even if it were possible', and therefore recommended that adult education — meaning 'the more academic side . . . the more traditional classes and courses' — should be regarded as an aspect of community education, part of a 'community education service' which would also embrace the youth and community service. In practice, however, in Scotland a clear division seems to have developed between 'further education' in which teachers are trained as teachers and belong to teachers' unions, and 'community education' in which the educators are local government officers, belonging to the National Association of Local Government Officers (NALGO), and trained for 'youth and community work', 'social work' or 'community education'. Mee and Wiltshire note seven ways of using the term 'community education' but want to restrict it to a 'narrower connotation', for example in Community College or Community School, 'where it implies a view of education as a totality continuing throughout childhood, adolescence and adulthood, involving a commitment to participation in all aspects of the life of the catchment population'.[25] This seems very close to the broad concept of 'lifelong education'. Lawson, in fact, commented in 1977 that the term 'community education' had been inadequately defined and suggested that the values and assumptions underlying it could be questioned, in particular the rather vague implied use of adult education as an instrument of social control, and the shift of resources away from the 'traditional role of general cultural and personal development'.[26]

Continuing education

'Continuing education' seems sometimes to have reference to some kind of retraining when needed, for example, by a new job. It certainly presupposes that something has gone before, presumably initial education, which has first to be completed. The Department of Education and Science Paper proposing the setting up of the Advisory Council for Adult and Continuing Education, however, referred to the inclusion of the word 'continuing' as taking account of 'the developing appreciation of adult education as part of a process which extends from the immediate post-statutory education period throughout life'.[27] Reviewing the Council's first year's work, the Secretary, John Taylor, spoke of 'both adult education and the much more widely conceived continuing education',[28] which seems to indicate both a limited definition of 'adult education' and a tendency to move towards the broad Scottish view of 'community education'. The Open University Committee under the chairmanship of Sir Peter Venables also took a broad view: 'Continuing education,' it said, 'is understood . . . to include learning opportunities which are taken up after full-time compulsory schooling has ceased. They can be full or part-time and will include both vocational and non-vocational study'.[29] The ACACE Discussion Paper on 'Towards continuing education' returned to a view that continuing education meant the same as "*éducation permanente,* lifelong learning, recurrent education'[30] even though the first two and possibly the third of these terms clearly include the education of children as well as that of adults. Later the document pleads that the 1944 Act should be amended so that the third stage of further education should have 'specific reference to adult and continuing education'. However, as it says earlier, there is a 'cardinal need, in the Eighties, for a coherent philosophy towards what is coming to be called, all embracingly, "continuing education". The phrase so far used somewhat loosely and *faute de mieux,* is growing up and beginning to find its true and clear physiognomy.'

The education of adults

No doubt the search for an all-embracing phrase will go on. However pleasant it would be to envisage a time when 'adult education' would mean all forms of education for adults, it is perhaps too late to hope for this to happen, and no doubt the arguments and verbal ambiguities will continue. Happily most ordinary men and women know little of them; for those involved, however, all the terms seem to bring out three useful points: first, they all stress the importance of education for all adults, and the futility of limiting it to children; second, they all point to education in the adult sector as an ongoing process in which attention should be paid to people's real needs, whether personal or social, rather than to what is thought 'good' for them; third, they all tend to move towards a concept of education as including a great variety of activities other than strictly formal teaching. It is a pity that these common elements cannot be carried over into a universal agreement about the term to be used. More unity would give strength and remove confusion.

This book will, therefore, be wide in scope and will include reference to all the rich variety of activities and opportunities which in some way or another help the education of adults. The aim is to provide as full a picture as possible, without fragmentation. No doubt some of the activities will be viewed as recreational entertainment rather than education, but the reader is asked to look closely at the evidence before making decisions of this kind. The only limitation, in fact, is the omission of full-time education taken end-on to children's full-time education. This follows the definition, quoted earlier, which was accepted by the UNESCO Tokyo Conference, and also partly that of J.A. Simpson who declared that 'by adult education we mean the provision which a society consciously makes, either publicly or through approved voluntary organisations, of facilities for learning, by anyone, of whatever age, where the initial education in schools, colleges, universities, apprenticeships and initial professional training has been terminated'.[31] There seems no point, however, in attempting to determine a precise age division between child and adult; there is a child—adult continuum and each individual passes along it at his or her own pace.

The concern, therefore, is with the totality of formal, non-formal and informal opportunities. To avoid unnecessary misunderstandings the term 'the education of adults' will be used as far as possible even though it may be a little cumbersome.

References

1. KIDD, J.R. 'Liberal education for business leadership', *Adult Education*, XXX/2, Autumn, 1957.

2. Association of Tutors in Adult Education: Statement on 'Liberal Studies in Adult Education', *Further Education* Vol. I, No. 11, Feb., 1948, pp. 243—4.

3. Department of Education and Science: *Adult Education: A Plan for Development*, 1973, HMSO, (the Russell Report) para. 6.

4. Ministry of Education, Pamphlet No. 8, *Further Education*, 1947, HMSO. The titles are those of chapters 2 and 3.

5. OECD Paper of 28 April 1975.

6. WILTSHIRE, H. Inaugural lecture on 'The nature and uses of Adult Education' (1966). Also printed in *The Spirit and the Form*, ed. A. ROGERS, 1976, p. 136.

7. National Institute of Adult Education: *Adult Education — Adequacy of Provision*, March 1970, p. 10.

8. LIGGETT, MARY, 'The library service and adult education', *Adult Education*, XXIV/2, Autumn, 1951, p. 152.

9. See UNESCO/CONFEDAD 4, p. 24 *A Retrospective International Survey of Adult Education*, 1972. The definition originated in *The Exeter Papers* edited by LIVERIGHT and HAYGOOD in 1968.

10. See COOMBS, PHILIP H. *New Paths to Learning for Rural Children and Youth* I.C.E.D., New York, 1973, pp. 10—11.

11. CHARLES KINGSLEY: Letter to *The Spectator*, 1851.

12. Trades Union Congress: Statement — 'Priorities in continuing education' (1978).

13. HOUGHTON, V. and RICHARDSON, K. (eds.) *Recurrent Education: A Plea for Lifelong Learning*, 1974, Ward Lock Educational.

14. LAWSON, K.H. *A critique of recurrent education* ARE Discussion Paper No. 1, 1975.

15. FOWLER, G. Chapter 11 in Houghton and Richardson, op. cit. p. 124.

16. SIMPSON, J.A. Chapter 10 in *Permanent Education*, 1970, Council of Europe, p. 343.

17. JANNE, HENRI. Chapter 1, Ibid, P. 16.

18. UNESCO *Learning to Be* (the Faure Report) 1972, UNESCO Chapter 8, p. 182.

19. DAVE, R.H. (ed.) *Foundations of Lifelong Education,* 1976, Pergamon, for UNESCO Institute for Education, p. 11.

20. ILLICH, I. and VERNE, E. 'Imprisoned in the global classroom' *Times Educational Supplement,* 21.3.75, pp. 21–24.

21. COOMBS, P.H. Op. cit. pp. 10–11.

22. The Russell Report, para 50.

23. RICHARDSON, PENELOPE l., 'Lifelong Learning and Politics', *Convergence,* XII/1–2, 1979, p. 96.

24. Scottish Education Department *Adult Education: The Challenge of Change,* (the Alexander Report), 1975, HMSO, p. 34.

25. MEE, G. and WILTSHIRE, H. *Structure and Performance in Adult Education,* 1978, Longmans, p. 15.

26. LAWSON, K.H. 'Community Education: a critical assessment', *Adult Education,* 50/1, May 1977, pp. 6–13.

27. Department of Education and Science Discussion Paper: 'Setting up a national advisory council for adult and continuing education', 1976, para 6.

28. TAYLOR, J. 'The Advisory Council for Adult and Continuing Education' *Adult Education,* 51/4, Nov. 1978, p. 210. Also available as a separate pamphlet from ACACE.

29. Open University *Final Report of the Committee on Continuing Education,* (the Venables Report), Dec. 1976, p. 6.

30. ACACE Discussion Paper: 'Towards continuing education', 1979, para 12.

31. SIMPSON, J.A. *Today and Tomorrow in European Adult Education,* 1972, Council of Europe, p. 28.

CHAPTER 2

Objectives and needs:
why educate adults?

In a relatively unchanging society it may be difficult to make a case for the education of adults. In the isolated rural villages which still exist in some parts of the world, and existed for long periods in pre-industrial Britain, the seasons come and go but the life of the community proceeds on its way with little being changed from one generation to the next. People in such a society can learn as children almost all the knowledge and skills required in adult life. They acquire the agricultural techniques and routines practised in the village and develop the ability to care for crops and animals, to use standard tools, to prepare food and clothing and to undertake whatever jobs may fall to their lot. Moreover they learn the attitudes and values that prevail in the community, its customs and taboos, its hierarchy, its relationships and its behaviour patterns. By puberty, or soon after, the process can be completed, and in many societies this completion is signalled by ceremonies initiating the young person into adulthood.

Such an 'education' is conformist, seeking to ensure that the young person becomes of service to the large group, helping to maintain its security and to preserve its way of life. It is also protective in a world in which natural disasters may threaten the food supply or the health of the community, and it tends to be limited in that it is concerned with clearly-defined needs, thought to be static and unchanging. It relies a good deal on informal learning, on 'learning by doing', on imitation of adult actions, although at times there may be some group learning under a 'teacher' who may have a particular role assigned to him or her. Of course it is made much easier by a small close community network, and probably by an 'extended family' system in which there is easy daily contact between the generations. Few communities are entirely unchanging but the rate of change, of the introduction of new methods, inventions and ideas is so slow as to be imperceptible to those living in the community. Except for certain specific needs which are met during adult life such as the knowledge needed by the new mother or that required on the assumption of special responsibilities of leadership, education can therefore be a matter for childhood, a preparation for adult life, short though the latter sometimes is. In a real sense what is learned under such circumstances is a kind of 'package', a definable entity, a survival kit for life within that community. In an agricultural community it is important that everyone plays a full part as soon as possible, and 'education' therefore is seen as having a terminal date, however much incidental learning might continue.

The education 'package'

These concepts persist in Britain today though conditions in most areas are very far removed from those in an isolated rural village. Most people still view education essentially as an affair of childhood, a preparation for adult life and a fixed 'package' to be obtained as soon as possible, after which a person can be said to have 'finished his education'. Just how big the package should be and what it should contain depends on social, economic and political beliefs and there are many varying answers. After the coming of the new industrial towns had shattered the old community learning system of the village, new ideas about the 'package' began to emerge. In early nineteenth century Britain, most of those in power thought that any education for the masses was highly dangerous unless rigidly controlled and kept as limited as possible, just enough to secure obedience to the masters, efficient workmanship and less violence. Literacy was at first suspect and when reading came to be accepted as a need to be met by 'education', writing was still viewed with doubt. Today, when literacy is thought by most people to be essential in modern Britain, arguments rage about other 'unnecessary' subjects or so-called 'frills'. Should the 'package' include only the 'useful', basic' subjects or should it be much more extensive? How far is competence in a second language, or a knowledge of art and music, part of the education which all must have? Should there be different packages for different sections of society? Probably most people think of education as being concerned with factual matters, with cognitive skills and knowledge to be assimilated, rather than with affective objectives and personal, emotional development — preferably, indeed, with something which is 'measurable'. Aware that knowledge is increasing at an ever-expanding rate, some schools make almost superhuman efforts to cram as much factual knowledge as possible into the curriculum before the boy or girl leaves school and 'finishes' his or her education. Values, relationships, attitudes and behaviour patterns create more difficulty. They can no longer be inculcated in the old village way and are now beset with uncertainties. Though some schools still seek to impose their own particular views, others react against such 'propaganda', and 'leave it to others', to parents, or to peer groups. In the mills and mines of early industrial Britain, children received a moral education as well as minimum job training from their employers and this was supplemented by religious teachers in church, chapel or Sunday school, and by parents who perhaps had folk memories of what had been thought 'right' in the villages from which their forebears had come. On the whole such 'education' was given with a degree of certainty which has now gone. What persists is the concept of the fixed entity and the belief that it should be acquired when young.

Adult education as a 'remedial' activity

In these terms any education undertaken by adults is entirely remedial, filling gaps which somehow have been left in the child's education. Literacy can be taught to children: if an adult is unable to read and write then it is because he or she has 'missed out'. If other items are thought to be essential in the package then any adult without them is 'underprivileged', perhaps 'disadvantaged', and steps must be taken to help the poor unfortunate person 'catch up' by means of a 'second chance'. Historically, making good the deficiencies of childhood education was of great importance in Britain, just as it still is in some other parts of the world, and as a purpose of the education of adults it still dominates the thoughts of many committees. Of course it does provide the rationale for part of the provision although, as will be indicated later, only a minor part in modern Britain. Some children have missed out because their schools offered only a limited range of subjects and they were therefore deprived of opportunities enjoyed by other children. Some were unable to use existing opportunities because of ill health, parental mobility or parental opposition to some subject areas. In some schools the size of over-large classes has militated against the assimilation of the whole 'package' on offer, and in others individual opportunities may have been limited by a stress on early specialization, or by late development. If education is viewed in this way, then many of us have gaps to be filled and some of the most marked deficiencies may receive special attention, such as that provided by the various literacy and basic education agencies and units since the mid-1970s. Logically, however, if the ideas are valid, it should be possible by improvement in children's education to reduce, if not remove, the need for the education of adults, the latter being an abnormality, a marginal process.

Education for a long time may just reproduce or echo outworn ideas and former social states, but the whole range of views on which the remedial view of education for adults is based can be challenged as being quite inappropriate in modern industrialized, urban Britain. The situation is now vastly different to that in the period before the Industrial Revolution. The whole content of the individual's environment, both physical and mental, has changed and continues to change at an accelerating rate, so that ideas about a fixed entity for education and about its preparatory nature are now invalid. The persistence of these ideas may in fact be harmful, however much the population at large and governments of all shades of political opinion cling to them. The real case for the education of adults lies not in gap filling but in its contribution to the needs first of individuals and second of the community as a whole in the modern world. The argument that it is essential because of these two major purposes can be developed in the following terms.

Adult education for individual needs

The individual in employment faces a highly disturbing, changing world today. New knowledge and new skills arrive to replace the old ones with alarming rapidity and both methods of work and methods of organization change. Mechanization, automation and changes in, for example, the size of the production unit all create new demands not just for new skills but also for new attitudes and behaviour. Changes in human relationships on the factory floor are paralleled by new changing relationships between trade unions, management and government, and at all levels there seems a clear need to learn how to communicate in a world of new specialisms and new phraseology. Many can expect to be displaced as manufacturing industry moves to a smaller, highly-trained labour force, and there is no guarantee that there will be growing numbers employed in the services sector. There is thus a strong case for regarding retraining and the development of adaptability as permanent needs. Similarly, if industrial democracy is ever to grow on the lines recommended by the Bullock Committee, there is a need for education to help workers participate in management. All require a working knowledge of new technologies — the current particular need is to appreciate the potential application of micro-electronics — and since these are likely to arrive at an increasing rate, it is not enough to give some understanding of the existing ones to young people in schools and colleges. Just how much formal education is needed or how much can be left to informal methods of 'learning to cope' depends a good deal on the nature of the changes as well as upon the rate of change which cannot be foreseen, but it is clear that both are likely.

Childhood education cannot be relied upon to prepare an individual for life other than work, especially in a situation in which the amount of leisure or non-work time is likely to grow. As the 1978 Conservative Party discussion paper on 'The Arts — the way forward' put it: 'We are moving, indeed to a certain extent have already moved, towards a leisure society, in which time spent at work occupies a diminishing proportion of people's lives.' Just as a 'steady job' is becoming a thing of the past, so there are changes in value systems and attitudes. Surrounded by new gadgets, new forms of entertainment, more mobility and varying degrees of affluence, and faced by changing ideas about status, role and relationships, it seems the modern urban dweller lives surrounded by instability. The response to these 'shifting sands' may be apathy, indifference and the search for superficial pleasures; or it may be violence, or a wanton waste of 'expendable' goods; or it may be a search for understanding and control perhaps through educational means.

One of the major purposes of the education of adults, therefore, is to enable individuals to achieve their full competence and status, and some control over a complex world. In all aspects of life — at work or at home, in isolation or in a group — human beings need educational help and the increasing tempo of change requires that this help must come throughout adult life. It cannot be given solely in childhood because the needs cannot be forecast. Childhood, anyway, is too short to allow human beings adequately to reach up to the full development of their abilities and capacities which now lies within their grasp. By continuing education, adults can be helped to find more meaning in life, to gain some sense of security, self-respect and independent significance, in the mass society in which too often they seem but numbers on a file. For people just to submit to being mindless cogs in a machine and to wandering their way blindly through life in an indecipherable universe is an inexcusable waste of human resources. Whether the education of adults could empty all the hospital beds which are filled with mentally ill patients is certainly open to question but it is arguable that it could lead to a better mental equilibrium in a world where too many seem unconsciously to echo Housman's phrase 'I alone and afraid, in a world I never made'. Older people may look back with nostalgia to a previous age in which they think they perceive more stability. According to their outlook on life, it may be a backward gaze to 'cheap' goods bought in 'real' money, to home entertainment in the family circle, to a time when 'people knew their place', or a condemnation of new-fangled gadgets, of decimalization and metrication, of modern cars and motorways, of 'too much money' in young people's pockets, or of the 'independence' of 'workers'. It is not to be expected that the education of adults will remove these feelings and the expression of them, but it can help the individual to understand and assess the changes in a more balanced way and so live life more competently. In this sense, although stability is not to be had, human beings have a better chance of contributing to their own happiness and to that of others.

These are large claims and indicate the vast distance still to be travelled by most people who have not considered the education of adults in this way. Conditioned to the belief that the package of childhood education will enable them to cope with the rest of life, they grumble when it fails to do so, but as yet do not find an answer in the education of adults. There are exceptions. Vocational recurrent retraining is now more common and in some types of occupation people regularly 'go on courses'. Marriage guidance courses as well as counsellors are increasingly used to give the help which once was given by the extended family or by the community. More and more people have tended to go to evening classes in which they find greater stability as well as pleasure in reaching a tangible, identifiable achievement in, for example, pottery or other crafts. Whatever the subject they often find status and significance in the small groups in which 'they count', and they learn the arts of communication through which to create and strengthen more satisfactory human contacts and relationships. Much has been written about what the education of adults has achieved for those taking part and among the devotees the validity of the statements above has been almost unchallenged. No doubt for each individual some objectives, like motives, are more important than others, but the general strength of this case for the education of adults lies in the needs created by the circumstances of life in modern industrial urbanized Britain: it is vital for everyone if individuals are to live life to the full and enjoy it more abundantly.

Adult education for community needs

The second major justification advanced for the education of adults stresses its value in meeting community needs. This can mean just the sum of individual needs, a good community being just a collection of competent 'happy' men and women. 'We must plan for a balanced community of well-balanced men and women,' declared the Ministry of Education in 1947.[1] There are those, however, who believe that the education of adults has a role to play in developing technical and organizational skills for the good of the community as a whole. It is urged that education could ensure economic growth and maximize the increase in national wealth. Others, however, think of community needs more in terms of general citizenship and advocate the education of adults as the only way of ensuring satisfactory government and communal life at all levels. Whether economic or political, the argument depends very much upon concepts of the nature of the state, of freedom and equality, of democracy and justice. In very broad terms, there seem to be two main types of interpretation.

The first interpretation of 'good citizenship' can be seen in the wishes of those in power in nineteenth century Britain. To them it meant conformity to their own ideas and practices, adjustment to their concept of a desirable, existing society, fitting people to the behavioural patterns, values and attitudes which they thought beneficial. The education of adults was advocated, if at all, as a way of conditioning the masses to be sober, obedient, hard-working members of the community, who would preserve the structure of the 'model'. Education was to be supported as a conditioning agency in a world which was being transformed by the industrial revolution. As a member of the rising élite, the manufacturer wanted his factories to proceed without strikes or riots, his workpeople to accept the hours, wages and conditions he laid down and the whole country to be peaceful so that his trade would be undisturbed. Education was to reinforce the 'new society' because in the long run this would be beneficial to all. In many parts of the world this view of 'civic competence' prevails and there are many echoes of it in modern Britain. Many of those in power at local and national levels, as well as newspapers and other media, advocate the use of education to secure better citizenship in terms of better productivity, fewer strikes, the restoration of 'old values', less vandalism, more harmony between sections of the populace, more obedience to the law, less drinking and drug taking, more conformity to the norms, whatever these are alleged to be. As the Final Report of 1919 put it; 'The main purpose of education is to fit a man for life, and therefore in a civilised community to fit him for his place as a member of that community.'[2]

The problem, of course, is what kind of a 'place'? The 1919 Report went on to say that 'the goal of all education must be citizenship', and to talk of the rights and duties of the individual. Mannheim thought that there was an alternative to conformity: 'The task of education', he declared, 'is not merely to develop people adjusted to the present situation, but also people who will be in a position to act as agents of sound development to a further stage.'[3] This is the second type of interpretation of education for citizenship. Earlier Bernard Shaw had declared that: 'Civic education does not mean education in blind obedience to authority, but education in controversy and in liberty, in manners and in courage, in scepticism, in discontent and better- ment, tempered by the fear not of artifically manufactured punishments, but of genuine natural consequences.' Ivor Brown talked about 'the training of critical powers, the creation . . . of a healthy scepticism.'[4] Since change is inevitable in the modern world, and a democracy implies that all share in government, education should be used to assist the process, to develop the adult individual's competence to criticize and control, and to attack acqui- escence and unthinking acceptance. In a world increasingly dominated by the conformist pressures of the mass media, and of television in particular, the education of adults should help people to be really interested in affairs, to think for themselves, to consider all views and then to take individual decisions on which to base responsible actions. As Richard Hoggart declared: 'The case for adult education is basically what it always was . . . It is to assist a responsible questioning of the quality of our social and personal lives . . . to help more people to question, more radically and imaginatively, the nature of their democratic society and to help them to see how far they can each try to make it work better.'[5] The Workers' Educational Association in its 1939 *Statement of Policy* looked on education 'not only as a means of developing individual character and capacity, but as an equipment for the exercise of social rights and responsibilities'[6] — a point which R.H. Tawney elaborated after the war in the *WEA Handbook* with a statement that 'our business is not to make up his mind for him but to aid him to make up his mind with greater confidence for himself. It is not merely to impart knowledge, important though that is. It is to confer the power to use it.'[7]

This case, therefore, is for the use of the education of adults to develop 'active, democratic citizens' who will evaluate the plans and policies of experts instead of being dominated by them, who will effectively control their own lives and discharge their democratic responsibilities within the community. This is not necessarily an easy role for most ordinary members of the community and from time to time special efforts have been made to develop the interest, knowledge and mental equipment needed for it to be accepted. Examples of these are the work of the Association for Education in Citizenship formed in the 1930s and that of the Hansard Society concerned to awaken the civic spirit and the sense of social commitment. The National Union of Townswomen's Guilds states in its Constitution that its first objective is 'to encourage the education of women to enable them as citizens to make their best contribution towards the common good',[8] and when it was felt desirable to reprint most of the 1919 Report, it was given the title "A Design for Democracy".

It remains a difficult task and the case itself is not without its challengers. Though lip service is paid to the view that 'education should be a means of fighting social disease not an innoculation against it', there is unease when active, democratic citizens become 'too' active and begin to take 'community action'. Criticism and challenge are sometimes viewed as a form of neurosis, and individual convictions, passionately held, may be regarded as mental instability. The problem shows itself particularly acutely in the so-called 'depressed' or 'disadvantaged' areas in some of which in the 1970s there were community development projects. Should the inhabitants be led to 'exercise their rights and responsibilities' in ways which could only be uncomfortable to those in power? How far should the education of adults be used, in Keith Jackson's words, to 'assist the poor to break out of the poverty cycle'? Should education be used to try to provide greater equality in society? Could it do so or would greater educational opportunities in adult life merely result in greater inequalities? Would such education tend more to rationalize a meritocratic class structure? Can the education of adults really help to secure the active participation of all in community life? Will the results of education to produce imagination, insight and resourcefulness be agreeable, or even predictable? For those who feel uneasy, conformity is more comfortable.

It is often said, however, that only the second interpretation of education for citizenship is valid in a democracy, and Churchill[9] gave this support when he commented on the importance of education for adults in this 'age of clutter and buzz, of gape and gloat'. In fact, both interpretations are to be found in Britain and the conflict between them is part of the background to the education of adults and a key to some of its problems. What is clear is that people need help in the art of living together and that in the absence of old-style community influence, this has to be specially provided. Recurrent re-education in values, attitudes and ethical judgement about life is needed if people are to survive and play a fully human part in the affairs of the community. 'An uneducated democracy cannot be other than a failure'[10] is a phrase of particular importance to modern Britain. Are we to secure the continued education of just an élite in power, whether this is composed of the more traditional middle and upper elements, or of trade union leaders, or are we to attempt to create a greater degree of democracy by the education of all the people throughout their lives? Such civic education is not particularly popular with those it is meant to benefit but perhaps there is a vicious circle of feelings of insignificance and frustration which lead to cynicism and to a rejection of education for adults. Perhaps to many it seems easier to conform, to accept the decrees of a ruling élite, and then just to enjoy the delights of spectator sports or television viewing. Though screened by grumbles, and lip service to other ideas, is there still some acceptance of the old military view of 'Yours to do and die, and not to reason why'? Part of the argument for the education of adults rests on the need for more than grumbles if democracy is to survive and grow. The case is that democracy requires a knowledgeable, active and responsible citizenry, and that in a world of rapid change only the education of adults can secure this. 'Civilisation', said Tawney in his book *Equality,* 'is not the business of an élite alone, but a common enterprise which is the concern of all.'

To this argument is added that which states that the education of adults is an essential means of 'improving the quality of life' a phrase which, however, seems capable of as many interpretations as the word 'democracy'. Usually it seems to mean a widening of interests, the development of greater curiosity and awareness, and the enlargement and enrichment of experience. In its 1947 pamphlet, the Ministry of Education stressed the value of education for adults in providing men and women with opportunities 'to develop interests which will enrich their leisure'.[11] Ruskin College at the turn of the century said that the aim was 'to widen the horizon of a man's mind',[12] and the Adult School Movement declares that the objective is for its members 'to learn together and to enrich life'.[13] Because it has seemed a long way from life in an industrial factory and from modern employment in general, this aspect of the education of adults has tended to be associated with leisure. Sometimes it is linked to a fear that people may 'misuse' the increased amount of leisure that the future is likely to bring, a fear usually expressed, of course, by those who feel competent to use their own leisure satisfactorily but who are reluctant to trust others to do so. There are, however, problems about work as well as leisure which are real enough and which can find in the education of adults an instrument to provide answers. There have, for example, been courses concerned with human relations in industry and with working conditions and methods of production: courses which may be designed just to increase production or as real attempts to secure improvements in the quality of working life. For the end of that life, there has developed a considerable provision of pre-retirement and retirement courses, in which attention is paid not just to financial and health matters, but to the widening of interests and the planned use of the increased amount of free time expected at any rate for men. Sometimes the adult provision of education has been directed to the removal of what are thought to be the causes of alienation. More often, however, the emphasis is on helping people to enjoy life more fully in courses which are concerned with the widening of interests or the creation of new ones, with the promotion of studies related to hobbies and with leisure activities in groups. Happy evening classes in a good evening centre reflect the pleasure experienced in such provision and the contribution it can make both to the enlargement of experience and to self-fulfilment.

'Improving the quality of life' may be interpreted differently in middle class suburbia and in working class housing estates, and perhaps the present provision reflects the needs more of the former than of the latter. Even so, there is plenty of evidence that some individuals in all sections of the community believe that their education as adults has contributed very greatly to their enjoyment of life. To some it has meant intellectual pleasure or a greater understanding and grasp of human affairs. Others have found new friendships and improved relationships, or have felt, perhaps for the first time, that their ability and capacity have been recognized. Certainly many declare life to be 'better' or 'happier' because they have acquired new skills or knowledge, or emotional strengths, and so are able both to do things which they could not do before and to experience a fruitful sense of fulfilment, of creativity. Waller wrote that the education of adults is 'the travellers' friend, guide and companion, beguiling his vacant hours, clearing and fortifying his purpose, interpreting the surrounding landscape and keeping him on his road happy in his journey and confident of reaching his destination'.[14] This may be much too fanciful for many people, and certainly would gain few recruits in urban renewal areas, but it emphasizes the important contributions the education of adults can make to the quality of human life in Britain far beyond the literacy, technical production and elementary hygiene which still seem to be the main objectives in so many parts of the world.

Why educate adults?

The main case for the education of adults in Britain is to be argued in terms of individual competence to cope with a rapidly changing world, of the quality of a person's life within it, and of the ability of democratic citizens to play a full part in human affairs at local, national or international levels. This has nothing to do with 'gap filling' or remedying the defects of early education, but a statement that the education of adults is demanded by the dynamic situation of life today. It is not a question of 'a second chance', which always carries with it a flavour of patronage, and of the view that only poor unfortunate failures 'missed out' on an assumed first chance. The education of adults is needed in fact by everyone, not just by a select few; everyone has to continue to learn throughout life in order to survive and evolve in a world where each has to adapt to change probably more in the next twenty-five years than in the past 25,000.[15] Some would like to view the education of adults as a commodity to be bought and sold according to the whims of the market; others want to use it to foster a 'social purpose' or their interpretation of a 'better world', and perhaps more now think of it as a service which ought to be provided in a civilized community. Whatever the view, the education of adults now requires a central rather than a marginal place. 'The necessary conclusion', declared the 1919 Report, 'is that adult education must not be regarded as a luxury for a few exceptional persons here and there, nor as a thing which concerns only a short span or early manhood, but that adult education is a permanent national necessity, an inseparable aspect of citizenship, and therefore should be both universal and lifelong.'[16] Over fifty years later, in 1975, the Alexander Report said much the same: 'The education of adults must be accepted as an essential component of national policy. The view of adult education as a marginal enterprise serving the interests of a relatively small proportion of the population can no longer be justified.'[17] The chapters which follow examine how far this country has so far acted on these conclusions.

References

1. Ministry of Education, *Further Education* Pamphlet No. 8, 1947, HMSO. para. 1 page 5.
2. Adult Education Committee of the Ministry of Reconstruction. *Final Report,* 1919, HMSO. Covering letter Page 4, section (xi).
3. MANNHEIM, K. *On the Nature of Economic Ambition and its Significance for the Social Education of Man,* 1930.
4. BROWN, I. *The Meaning of Democracy* 1920, (revised 1950) p. 159.
5. HOGGART, R. *On the Nature and Quality of Mass-Communications,* 1959.
6. Workers' Educational Association, *Statement of Policy,* 1939, Section 1.
7. *WEA Handbook,* 1945. Preface facing p. 1.
8. N.U.T.G. *Constitution,* Section III, para. 6.
9. CHURCHILL, WINSTON S. Letter dated March 1953 to Sir Vincent Tewson, General Secretary of the Trades Union Congress.
10. *Final Report,* 1919, op. cit., page 6, para. (xii).
11. Ministry of Education, 1947, op. cit., para. 102.
12. *Ruskin Hall News and Student Magazine* Vol, I, No. 1, December, 1899.
13. National Adult School Union. Education Committee Minutes 1948.
14. WALLER, R.D. *Learning to Live* Art & Educational Publishers 1946, p. 6.
15. See the Faure Report, *Learning to Be,* UNESCO 1972, pp. 157–8.
16. *Final Report,* 1919, op. cit. page 5, para. 5 of the covering letter.
17. Scottish Education Department. *Adult Education: the Challenge of Change* (the Alexander Report) 1975, HMSO, para. 63.

CHAPTER 3

An overview: the providers and their finances

Before looking in detail at the provision in Britain, an overview of the general situation and of its legal and financial basis may be helpful, if only to provide some framework to which the many strands may be attached. Any framework is, of course, artificial because the complex of educational provision for adults has developed not by planning but by a series of pragmatic responses. The result is great richness but no system or order.

Statutory provision

A first key, in fact, to understanding the complex provision is to recognize that one of the main characteristics has been decentralization. This contrasts sharply with those countries where the whole of the structure is determined, planned and controlled by the central government. In terms of the statutory provision of education for adults, ultimate power in Britain, of course, rests with the central government, but detailed planning and management have been devolved to local level. On the whole, the work of the central government is confined to 'grants, arbitration and advice', as was once stated by a former Permanent Secretary in the Welsh Department.[1] Advice and guidance is offered by means of administrative memoranda, circulars or circular letters. These do not carry the force of law, but are unlikely to be disregarded by the local authorities. Often, indeed, they have been drawn up in consultation with local authorities and rely more on argument and compromise than on power. Even so local authorities can only do what an Act of Parliament says they can do; their powers derive from central government which can wield considerable financial sanctions if it so wishes, especially as it has often contributed about 60% of local authority expenditure.

Before 1944 there was no statutory obligation to provide any education for adults in Britain. Even in the late nineteenth century, however, some local authorities had used permissive legislation to foster quite large developments. Some, for example, had used the Technical Instruction Act of 1889, or the 1898 Code for evening continuation schools to create a substantial number of technical or other classes, and later some of the new local educational authorities used their 'higher education' options to reorganize and develop art and technical education. Nevertheless, there were great variations in the pattern of provision, and whether a man or woman had any local facilities available depended very much upon where he or she lived. In 1927–8 over a million students were to be found in local authority evening courses in England and

Wales but their distribution was very uneven. In London and in many of the industrial cities, for example, the provision was reasonably extensive but in some of the rural agricultural districts the amount was negligible and in some instances non-existent.

The Acts of 1944 and 1945 changed the permission granted to local authorities into a duty and a responsibility. They had 'to contribute towards the spiritual, moral, mental and physical development of the community' by securing 'that adequate and efficient provision is made throughout their area of all forms of primary, secondary and further education'.[2] 'Further education' was thus given the same status as child education, a considerable step forward, especially as stress was laid on provision being made for all members of the community and not just for a selected few.

Local education authorities

Under the impetus of the Acts, the local education authorities (LEAs) have everywhere become the major providers of education for adults. After the Second World War, as might be expected, most LEAs felt that in the adult sector priority should be given to technical, vocational education, and they developed a full network of colleges, many being purpose built and well equipped. There are now about 600 of these 'major establishments' and thirty-one polytechnics. Adults also benefited from the building of new day schools for children, many of which are used for evening classes, and in some areas, multipurpose establishments based on a school have been created taking the title of 'community college' or 'community campus' as well as the earlier 'village college'. In 1980 the LEAs provided over 85% of the courses available for adults, with the necessary buildings and equipment and human resources in the form of teachers and organizers. About 80% of the part-time teacher force of about 165,000, and an even higher proportion of the full-time staff, are LEA employed. The number of full-time staff in grant-aided, vocationally-oriented establishments has increased very considerably in the period since the Second World War, and at one time was expected to reach a total of more than 90,000 in Britain in the early 1980s. Full-time staff in the LEA non-vocational sphere were almost non-existent in 1950 but by 1980 numbered over 2,000, employed mainly as organizers, advisers or heads of centres but some as subject specialists. Overall about 3½ million adults attended courses provided by the LEAs in 1979–80, many on a part-time basis. LEAs also possess most of the forty or so short-term residential colleges, where attendance is normally for a period of a few days, though some of these, for financial reasons, are now under threat of closure.

The interpretations of the duties imposed by the Acts, however, varied and still vary a great deal. This is partly because each local authority places its own interpretation on the requirements laid down, and on subsequent regulations, so that instead of one system there are over a hundred. Despite the reduction caused by the reorganization of local government in 1974 and 1975, there are still 116 local authorities in Great Britain concerned with education.

In the local authorities the whole council is responsible for education but each council acts on the recommendations of its education committee which consists of elected councillors but may also include co-opted members with a special interest in education and knowledge of local conditions. Often there are sub-committees to consider particular sections of the educational provision, for example, community centres or evening centres, and separate governing bodies may be established for particular institutions. There is no uniformity: except for the obligation to have an education committee, each council devises its own arrangements and the whole picture is influenced by the particular traditions and characteristics of educational administration in the various parts of Britain. Scotland in particular, with its own long tradition of local democratic control of education, differs considerably from the rest of the country.

The main variations in the provision, however, are the result of somewhat unclear drafting of legislation, and indeed, although no one perhaps envisaged the extent of the variations, some of the key sections seem deliberately to have lacked precision.[3] In the Acts of 1944 and 1945, 'further education' was used to mean all post-secondary education, but in many authorities it came to be restricted to attendance at mainly vocational establishments, with sometimes a speculative indication that this could be differentiated from 'other further education' (OFE) which was not so job-orientated. In the ensuing years, the Ministry of Education (England and Wales) and the Scottish Education Department tried to help with circulars and other advisory publications, but in accordance with tradition and custom much freedom was given to the local authorities. Though the Acts required them to prepare and submit for approval schemes of further education, this was not too rigorously applied even though repeated in the Education Acts of 1962. Section 41 of the 1944 Act decrees that: 'It shall be the duty of every local education authority to secure the provision for their area of adequate facilities for further education', but the word 'adequate' may have many interpretations and 'secure the provision' does not necessarily mean 'provide'. The Section went on to define 'further education' in terms of:

(a) Full-time and part-time education for persons over compulsory school age; and
(b) leisure-time occupation, in such organised cultural training and recreative activities as are suited to their requirements for any persons over compulsory school age who are able and willing to profit by the facilities provided for that purpose.

Similar phrases were used in the Scottish 1945 Education Act and in the 1962 Act which replaced it. This definition appears to permit almost anything. What exactly are 'cultural training and recreative activities'? What is meant by 'suited to their requirements', or 'able and willing to profit'? In 1947 the Ministry of Education for England and Wales issued a 200-page pamphlet on the scope and content of the opportunities for further education[4] which, although not greatly clarifying the position, gave an imaginative stimulus to LEAs and stressed their vital importance. 'The immediate task of the authorities in regard to further education is indeed a challenging one,' said the pamphlet. 'It is to assume leadership in the co-operative enterprise of community education'.[5]

They were not, therefore, to go it alone. The Acts made it a duty for the authorities to 'have regard to any facilities for further education provided for their area by universities, educational associations and other bodies' and, moreover, they 'shall consult any such bodies as aforesaid and the local education authorities for adjacent areas'.[6] In Scotland they had to 'have regard to the expediency of co-operating with any voluntary societies or bodies whose objects include the provision of facilities or the organization of activities of a similar character'.[7] Some LEAs have perhaps been tempted to preserve their control over the whole range of educational provision and to go ahead with their own plans without much consideration of the availability of similar provision elsewhere, or, having consulted, to refrain from co-operation. Yet, however much councillors and their officials may have experienced an understandable irritation with what appeared to them to be the slow, inward-looking and muddle-headed approach of some voluntary agencies, the intention of the government was clear on this point. 'The first need is co-operative action . . . generosity and trust . . . a close and confident relationship . . . There is an opportunity to advance, if we march together'.[8] What is sad is that some have marched very slowly and out of step with their neighbours.

It may be argued that decision making has been brought closer to the grass roots but the result is still that little has been done to remove the great variations in the amount of educational opportunity available to adults in different parts of the country. Whenever there has been a period of financial stringency, the varying interpretations of the imprecise word 'adequate' have also led to severe cut-backs in provision, especially in non-vocational courses for adults. Until recently most LEAs have tended to keep the fees charged to students at a low level, but wide variations have now arisen, some LEAs arguing that adults should pay the whole cost of classes while others wish to continue large subsidies. The amount of the student fee thus varies considerably even between similar types of area, a situation which causes confusion, especially as some authorities have refused to continue the former system of 'free trade' which allowed people living in one area to attend classes at subsidized rates in a neighbouring area. Where fees have been sharply increased there has been a considerable effect at first on the numbers attending and, more importantly, on the type of student, only the richer sections of the population finding it possible to attend. How far this is 'adequate' in terms of the Acts is a matter of dispute; the meaning has so far not been tested in the law courts or clearly defined by any Secretary of State so that LEAs are left to use their own judgement. It seems likely that the vocational sector of education for adults, up to now relatively untouched, might soon be subject to similar pressures, anomalies and fee increases.

The State's direct role

The State, in the form of the Department of Education and Science, while not in general directly owning institutions or employing teachers for the education of adults, does make a few direct interventions. A specific ear-marked grant, for example, has been made for adult literacy work and basic education each year since 1975; at first this was £1 million a year, and later £500,000. Grant aid is also given directly to mature students attending universities and, since 1975, to those in long-term residential colleges. It also seeks to influence development by the employment of H.M. Inspectors. Originating from the nineteenth century system of payment by results (when schools had to be inspected to see if they were efficient and hence worthy of grant), H.M. Inspectors do not in theory belong to the Department of Education and Science, as the former Ministry of Education is now called in England and Wales, or to the Scottish Education Department. They are appointed by the Queen and their duty is to advise both central and local government. Their work now is ideally that of cross-fertilization in which they carry new ideas and techniques from one place to another, and of oversight in order to help the development of a more efficient educational service. Some of the advisory work has now been somewhat supplanted by special bodies such as the Schools Council, and some questions have been raised about the future purposes and effectiveness of this relatively small band of fewer than 650 people. Their width of first-hand experience in a great range of educational activity, together with their freedom to make personal judgements place them in a unique position to be valuable consultants and stimulators. However, in recent years they have been able only to visit a much smaller proportion of the provision because of changes in the pattern of their work, such as the assumption of more direct responsibility for training.

As will be indicated in later chapters, several government departments other than the Department of Education and Science and the Scottish Education Department are also involved in the education of adults. An important development has been the setting up, under the 1973 Employment and Training Act, of the Manpower Services Commission which took over a good deal of responsibility from the Department of Employment. Through its Employment Services Division and its Training Services Division, a considerable amount of public money has been fed annually into industrial training. Of other government departments, the Department of Health and Social Security is concerned with health education and the Home Office has responsibility for education in prisons and for the training of the police. Similarly, the Ministries of Transport, Agriculture and Defence each look after training relevant to their own fields. Questions have been asked about the need to consolidate such responsibilities and relate them more directly to the Department of Education and Science, but little has been done and the involvement of many branches of government therefore still adds further complexities to the picture.

The main contribution of the State is undoubtedly financial. Local authorities raise their own income in part by local taxation, the 'rates', but they also receive a generally larger contribution from the central government in the form of a rate support grant (a block grant assessed on a somewhat complex formula) which local authorities use as they wish. Education is the major item of local expenditure, especially as the levels of teachers' salaries and capital costs rise, and at one time it had an earmarked, specific, grant. This was changed in 1958, however, and the education committee in an authority has therefore to compete with the other services, such as environmental health, roads, planning, fire service and police, for its share of the available finances. Local authorities are responsible for about 85% of all public expenditure on education. The allocation of resources between the sectors of the educational service is, however, very variable, reflecting both local and national ideas about their relative importance. In 1974–5, for example, the total cost of all education for adults in the United Kingdom, including vocational courses and basic education but excluding full-time higher education, was about £160 per student per annum.[9] This may be contrasted with an expenditure of approximately £1,500 per annum per student in full-time higher education.

Universities

The State in England, Wales and Northern Ireland also makes direct subventions, usually in the form of annual block grants, to universities. Since the late nineteenth century, universities, none of which are state owned, have provided courses for the general public 'outside the walls', and from the 1920s onwards they established extra-mural departments to conduct their contribution to the education of adults. These differ from the extension departments, for example, of American universities in that so far they have been little concerned with degree courses, and have traditionally concentrated on the provision of liberal adult education. As will be discussed later, there have been some signs of change in recent years, but most of the work is still non award (non credit) bearing. At first mainly administrative in nature, the extra-mural departments have developed staffs of full-time tutors who now number in total about 500. They continue to employ part-time teachers, of whom nearly half are drawn from the internal staffs of universities. As each university is independent under a separate Charter, there is a strong tendency for extra-mural policy to vary from place to place, just as does the title of the extra-mural department itself, even though they consult together in a Universities Council for Adult Education. The basic pattern, however, is much the same: the universities organize and administer courses for the general public or for special groups who are not undertaking study for undergraduate or postgraduate awards. They also undertake activities such as summer schools, and may own or sponsor adult centres or short-term residential colleges.

Over the years, geographical spheres of influence have gradually been defined, a pattern into which some of the newer universities do not easily fit. At present there are nineteen such areas in England, four in Wales, six in Scotland and two in Northern Ireland, but this may change in the near future if some of the newer universities develop more traditional extra-mural departments, or if there is a radical alteration of the system. On the whole, the most recently founded universities have not created extra-mural departments but are experimenting with alternative types of machinery. In all universities many internal departments are also directly providing courses for the outside public, without reference to the extra-mural departments, especially those of a refresher type for professional groups. About fourteen universities have also developed an interest in the study of the education of adults as an academic discipline, in the conduct and supervision of appropriate research, and in the provision of professional training courses for adult educators. Following their involvement in the Regional Committees for Education in H.M. Forces during the Second World War, a few universities also continue to make special

27

provision for education in the armed services. Some too have been responsible for the development of training for university teachers.

The Russell Committee suggested that 'a realistic costing of the universities' services in (non-vocational) adult education would show at present the contribution in the form of grant from the Department [of Education and Science] amounts to no more than some 35% of the total cost'.[10] For the remainder university extra-mural departments look elsewhere, partly to local education authorities which at times have given grant aid for both teaching costs and administration, but more to a share of the general university funds which are drawn mainly from the University Grants Committee (UGC) which serves as an intermediary for substantial funding from the State. From time to time there are suggestions that the whole cost should come from the UGC which does in fact finance the London and Manchester Business Schools and Birkbeck College which are exclusively concerned with mature age students. General university funds also finance the internal departments concerned with the study of education for adults and with training, although these have also obtained additional resources from charities and trusts, and, where there are overseas students, from the Ministry of Overseas Development. With pressure for sharply rising fees charged to students, direct government aid may well play a lesser part in future arrangements although it can be argued that the work is too important to be left only to those who can afford to pay the full cost. Internal departments in general, however, make their external courses either self-financing, or from time to time obtain funds from sources such as the Department of Health and Social Security, the National Health Service or professional societies, with occasional contributions from LEAs. Extra-mural support for education in H.M. Forces is funded directly by the Defence Ministries.

Workers Education Association

The extra-mural departments provide courses of many types either directly or in association with other bodies, particularly the Workers' Educational Association (WEA), an independent voluntary organization founded in 1903. Non-sectarian in religion and non-party in politics, the WEA's objects are both to promote and to provide education for adults, especially for members of workers' movements, and generally to develop a more adequate system of equal educational opportunity for all throughout life. The WEA has been concerned particularly with liberal adult education, has no entry tests, and tends to be hostile to the idea of examinations and awards. Following the recommendations of the Russell Report, however, the Association has put more stress on work in an industrial context and on political and social education of the socially and culturally disadvantaged. Essentially it is a students' association, organized in about 900 autonomous local units or 'branches' which in turn are linked to twenty-one district federations and to the national centre. Districts employ full-time district secretaries to assist the work and most have a small number of full-time tutor—organizers, of whom there are rather fewer than 150 in the whole of Britain. At national level there is a staff of three paid, full-time national officers, but the elected president, vice-presidents and treasurer are honorary appointments. The

'Russell type' work has led to the development of some 'industrial branches', in addition to the older branches which were based on a town or village, and much of the work of the tutor—organizers is now directed to these. Before 1939 most extra-mural work was concerned with the provision of joint courses with the WEA and in most areas Joint Committees were set up to oversee this work. These remain with some modifications, despite a great increase in extension courses run by the universities alone, and separate provision by the WEA. In all, over 10,000 classes were provided in 1979—80, attended by about 300,000 students. The most substantial class provided jointly has been the three year University Tutorial Class, first started in 1908, but this has had a considerable decline in recent decades and in some areas has faded out altogether. The WEA directly provides the shorter and more elementary courses in subjects selected by the members, of whom there are about 170,000.

WEA districts do receive financial grants from central government, but must look elsewhere for part of their finances and tend to rely on LEA contributions, student efforts or special grants. Though changing year by year, the general picture can be examplified by the position in 1973—4 when the total budgets for the WEA districts in England and Wales showed contributions of approximately 20% from the LEAs, less than 60% from the State and the remaining 20% or so met by student contributions, affiliation fees, voluntary fund-raising efforts and some help from universities and individual supporters. In 1977 the regulations were extended to allow the Secretary of State to pay an extra grant to a district committee of the WEA and these special grants were particularly welcomed by some WEA districts at a time when rising costs were pushing them close to bankruptcy. It would seem, however, that all such grants have now been terminated. In general terms, branches provide much unpaid voluntary service and, having collected the student fees, they retain only a relatively small amount, often as little as 30%, for publicity, stationery, postage, telephone bills, room rent if applicable and any other miscellaneous costs. The rest they forward to districts to meet the costs of administration and, in England and Wales, any deficit on teaching costs. Districts forward an amount to the national office as a contribution to expenditure not met by fees from affiliated societies or grants from the central government or elsewhere. The central national office has had frequent financial difficulties and has exhausted most of the reserves built up just after the Second World War. As districts often tend to take a critical view of the national centre and have a fierce tradition of autonomy and independence, they are not always willing to give enthusiastic help. Moreover, some of the work with the trade unions and the disadvantaged ('Russell type' work) has proved to be more expensive than the older type of class provision, and this has restricted the ability of districts to pay more to the centre.

Responsible Bodies

In England and Wales, the extra-mural departments, the seventeen English and Welsh Districts of the WEA and the Welsh Council of Young Men's Christian Associations are designated as special 'Responsible Bodies', able to receive direct financial grants from central government under special conditions. Special regulations have been issued from time to time to administer these grants, which are quite separate from those to local authorities. Originally they were given for teaching costs only and this is still the legal position, although they are now given as an annual block grant. In the 1975 Further Education Regulations for England and Wales, the Secretary of State may therefore 'pay a grant to a "responsible body" towards the cost of providing tuition in any course of liberal adult education included in a programme approved by him'. (Regulation 28(1).) Recommendations for approval are normally part of the task of Her Majesty's Inspectors but the amount of grant is determined by a somewhat complex formula prescribed as:

> reference to the general standard of the courses in the programme (having regard to the syllabuses, the quality of teaching, the length of courses and the arrangements for written work, reading under guidance and other forms of private study to be carried out between meetings), the needs of the area, the activities of other bodies providing further education in the area and the fees paid by students. (Regulation 28(2))

In receiving state grants the Responsible Bodies preserved their right to determine their own independent policies and, in the case of the WEA, the right of the students to select their own tutor and choose their own syllabus. Earlier in the century, grants had been paid on a basis of 75% of the teaching costs of all qualifying classes, and it is perhaps not surprising that this tends to persist as a notional concept. Student fees were originally kept very low so that no one should be excluded, but there were sharp increases in the late 1970s. Responsible Body student fees tend to be comparable with LEA non-vocational class fees in most areas, although occasionally there are wide discrepancies. Despite the increases, student fees have until recently remained at a relatively much lower level than in many countries of Western Europe or North America. Fees to tutors have tended to be higher in the Responsible Body sector than in the LEA provision as a result of a different historical background, and ideas about the academic levels of both teachers and subjects.

Northern Ireland

In Northern Ireland, the former Joint Committee on Adult Education of Queen's University and the WEA dominated the scene as a Responsible Body for a long period. After the Morris Report of 1963, however, each part has had direct funding from the Northern Ireland Department of Education, the extra-mural department of Queen's University, Belfast, receiving a grant of 75% of approved teaching costs, while the WEA Northern Ireland district receives 75% of approved teaching costs and 65% of approved administrative costs. The WEA was much overshadowed by Queen's and took some time before it appointed any full-time staff. Similarly LEA work was slow to develop, although in the last quarter of the twentieth century it has assumed a central position, under the five Area Education and Library Boards on whom the statutory duty to 'secure adequate provision' was laid in April 1973. These Boards work mainly through the colleges of further education, of which there were twenty-seven in 1979, with some smaller associated units. Since the 1963 Act the New University of Ulster in Londonderry, with its Institute of Continuing Education, and the Ulster Polytechnic, with its Department of Continuing Education, have come into being. Their substantial programmes of continuing education are funded from their overall budgets and are not based on the older Responsible Body basis, although the New University has had some direct government grants to help with staffing. Like many English and Welsh universities, they have also extended their programmes with a good number of self-financing courses.

Scotland

In Scotland there are major legal differences reflecting the distinct educational system that it has had for centuries. The local authorities have held to their dominant position in the provision of education for adults and there is no 'Responsible Body' system of direct funding of teaching costs by the Scottish Education Department. For teaching costs the universities and the WEA are much more dependent on the LEAs which determine all fees for teachers and students and provide all the necessary funds as employers. For administrative and organizational costs some central government money is available through extra-mural committees established with bases in the universities of Aberdeen, Dundee, Edinburgh and Glasgow. These are composed of representatives of the LEAs, the appropriate university and the WEA and are recognized by the Secretary of State for Scotland as 'approved associations' eligible for grant under the Further Education (Scotland) Regulations of 1959. The Secretary determines the amount 'after consideration of the nature, efficiency, extent and estimated cost' (Regs Pt II, 10). The universities of St Andrews, Stirling and Strathcylde have no extra-mural committees of this type, although they have various kinds of consultative machinery not funded by the Secretary of State or by the Scottish Education Department, and Herriott-Watt University, with no extra-mural department but an Adult Education Committee is in much the same position. For their own full-time staff, Scottish university extra-mural departments depend upon UGC resources. There has been a considerable development of self-financing courses and of a successful search for finance from sources other than the education authorities, notably from trusts. The Alexander Committee received pleas for a change to something nearer to the English and Welsh 'Responsible Body' method of finance, but decided firmly in favour of the established Scottish system.[11] The LEAs, now on a regional basis, are the major providers of education for adults and draw their funds from rates and the rate support grant.

The Open University

The Open University provides a special kind of education for mature adults. In contrast to the traditional universities which demand rigorous entry qualifications, the Open University does not require previous educational qualifications, although, confronted by a greater number of applications than resources available, it has had to make some selection based broadly on 'first-come, first-served'. Courses lead mainly to ordinary or honours degrees at

31

undergraduate level and there are some advanced degree courses. The basis of the work is a credit system, and study is home based, the method being correspondence courses supported by linked television and radio broadcasts and face-to-face tutorials at local centres. The latter are often situated in LEA premises. One organizational difference between the Open University and other universities is the degree of centralization, detailed planning being carried out at the centre, despite the development of regional offices, each with its director and professional staff. Beginning in 1971 with 24,000 students, there are now nearly 70,000 undergraduate students. The average age is in the mid-thirties and there are rather more men than women students though the proportion is changing. A series of non-degree courses is also offered which are designed to provide updating or entry to a new field of knowledge. Though autonomous like the other universities, the Open University is financed directly by the Department of Education and Science and by fees paid by students for each credit course. The cost per undergraduate appears to be lower than at a conventional university, but even so there is regular pressure to increase student fees. There is no obligatory financial support for these from LEAs although some contribute to the cost of students from their area attending Summer Schools arranged by the Open University.

Voluntary agencies and non-formal education

As indicated, the LEAs have a supreme and at present unchallenged place in the general provision of courses and classes, while the university extra-mural departments and the WEA have a special role in the area of liberal adult education. A considerable contribution of a non-statutory kind is made, however, by a great range of voluntary organizations other than the WEA. These are diverse and numerous. In even a moderate-sized town, there are often over a hundred such organizations, although, as there is no system of registration or reporting, the exact number can only be estimated. In the country as a whole some are large organizations on a national scale, such as the women's institutes and the townswomen's guilds, while others are very local and small, such as a village photographic or local history club. The women's organizations have a structure not unlike that of the WEA with local units, district federations and a national federation. The women's institutes, for example, have a membership of over half a million, with paid district-federation level officers as well as a national staff, a regular monthly magazine and their own residential college. There are also independent community associations and educational centres linked to the important National Federation of Community Associations and the Educational Centres Association respectively. The National Councils of YMCAs and their local units promote the education of adults as part of a programme of general activities. Some of these organizations receive direct government grants to help their work and some also attract local financial support for special activities. On the whole voluntary organizations like to keep their membership fees to a minimum so that all can join, and until recently in some areas many have had free or low-cost accommodation provided by the LEA. The vast majority of voluntary organizations, however, receive no grants and continue on a basis of unpaid voluntary work carried out by annually elected officers and committees. Apart from membership fees they rely on special money-raising efforts. They include many religious and political groups, societies meeting specific hobby interests such as gardening or pigeon fancying, or providing for amateur activities in music, art, drama or dance, and societies concerned with educational travel. There are also professional associations bringing together those in the same kind of employment, such as those for bankers, butchers, engineers, doctors, teachers or accountants, and societies with particular functions such as working men's clubs or Rotary. Recently there has been a rise in groups concerned with parent education and the needs of the more disadvantaged sections of the population, in particular immigrants or those in need of basic education. Some of the associations and institutions stem from creations of the fairly distant past — the Adult Schools, for example, have an unbroken history since 1798 and the independent London Working Men's College was founded in 1854.

Much education of a non-formal type is provided by these thousands of voluntary organizations, organized on a democratic basis. Almost all have programmes of talks, discussions, visits and other activities with an educational objective, arranged as their members wish. The broad picture is kaleidoscopic, with new groups forming, developing, and then weakening to be replaced by other groups as interests and needs change and as the quality and characteristics of the voluntary workers in them change. Although sometimes they seem to be a sort of thicket of tangled growth obscuring the main outlines of the provision, their value in terms of stimulus, information giving and democratic training is not to be underestimated. Among them the citizen can often find the means of satisfying his needs and interests; if not, and if he can find people of a like mind, he can go off to form a new voluntary organization. Regrettably, perhaps, many people do not share in this hive of activity; they are 'non-joiners' as Joseph Trenaman showed in his research carried out in the 1950s.[12] The evidence then was that half the population at least was resistant to the idea of sharing in what was on offer, and indifferent to educational resources however informal. It also appeared that the facilities on offer were taken up mainly by those who were already well endowed educationally. This finding has been echoed in many enquiries since then in Europe and North America.

Industrial provision

Of considerable importance is the independent educational provision of industry and commerce, and of the trade unions and the Co-operative movement. In-service training courses are provided for employees in many of the larger industrial concerns, some of which have residential establishments of their own, and, especially after the Industrial Training Act of 1964, a considerable amount of money has been fed into industrial education and training. Commercially activated educational providers are particularly prevalent in the provision of correspondence courses and home study related to language learning and to shorthand, typewriting and book-keeping. They also organize some full-time and part-time courses. The Trades Union Congress has a special Education Committee, its own training college and a postal course service, while a network of educational work is carried out by its regional divisions and, locally, by independent unions associated with it. Under the auspices of the Co-operative Union, to which the retail co-operative societies are affiliated, there is a National Co-operative Education Association and a Scottish Co-operative Education Association. These seek to meet the educational needs of the 10½ million or so members either directly in local classes, summer schools, and correspondence courses, or indirectly by arrangement with other agencies. The movement has its own Co-operative College and a number of voluntary organizations such as the Co-operative Women's Guilds.

Mass media

Part of the framework also consists of the organs of mass communication — broadcasting and the press. Some of these have expanded enormously and reach out to almost everyone in the community. Despite a public tendency to associate them exclusively with entertainment, both the British Broadcasting Corporation and the Independent Broadcasting Authority have a charter obligation to provide education and information, and besides the direct provision of educational courses, they contribute a great deal of educative material in their supposedly non-educational programmes. Potentially they are able to contact those who are unlikely to join any other form of education for adults, especially as they have access to at least 97% of homes. Broadcasting can be particularly helpful to those living in the more remote areas of the British Isles, for example in the Scottish Highlands or the Hebrides, or in the more mountainous areas of Wales or England. Its educational influence is clearly now greater than that of the Press, as about a fifth of the population do not even buy a newspaper.

Libraries and museums

Membership of the public libraries, which are perhaps the most extensive in the world, is about 30% of the population. On the whole, however, they are used by the members of the community who have had the most education, the same people in fact who read the more serious newspapers and watch the most educative programmes on television. Education therefore reinforces education. Similarly museums and art galleries are available in increasing numbers and are becoming more educationally orientated, but they are still not attended by the mass of the population. The libraries and museums are largely funded by the local education authorities, despite a central government grant which in 1977—8 was just over £200 million.

Conclusion

In summary, part of the provision is formally organized in classes and courses, some full-time but mostly part-time, sometimes residential but usually not. These may be related to work or leisure, and attended by people of any age, but in either case the major statutory provider is the LEA. Other providers include the universities and the WEA, industry and the trade unions, and a host of voluntary organizations and commercial agencies. Study may be undertaken at home either in courses provided by commercial correspondence schools or by the Open University, or in self-directed learning, drawing upon the resources of books and libraries, and of broadcasting. There is also a very wide range of less formal opportunities for learning in membership of the multitude of voluntary organizations. Finally there are all the stimuli, the surrounding influences of the mass media, and the incidental casual learning which takes place by living together in the community. It will be noted that the same provider can fulfil a number of different functions.

Freedom to experiment has produced a multiplicity of both programmes and providers. On the whole the rich diversity is the result of attempts to respond to locally expressed demand from all sections of the community, sometimes professionally stimulated, but, perhaps inevitably, there are considerable gaps, and problems of segmentation, in various parts of the country. Little attempt has been made to give central direction, except in the broadest of terms, and the response from the local areas has been patchy. Sometimes there is more discussion than action: in the 1970s for example there was much talk and writing about extending educational opportunities for adults, but comparatively little was done, despite some interesting experiments such as the 'Brain Train'.[13] Much, however, takes place which is unrecorded, and statistics even of the major types of provision are often fragmentary and uninformative, despite pleas to the Department of Education and Science for more complete and comprehensive collection and some response to these by the central government in recent years. Inconsistency in the provision of public money for the education of adults perhaps matches the lack of clarity about definitions and purposes to which attention has been drawn in previous chapters. The only common factor seems to be the general inadequacy of subsidies, without which it is not possible to expect all adults to share in the educational opportunities that are available.

References

1. Sir Ben Bowen Thomas. See WEA *Jubilee Addresses on Adult Education,* 1953, p. 26. Speech on 'The tradition of co-operation in adult education'.
2. Section 7 of the 1944 Education Act and Section X of the 1945 Education (Scotland) Act. The 1962 and 1969 Education (Scotland) Acts particularly emphasize the breadth of definition to be given to 'further education'.
3. In the Ministry of Education pamphlet No. 8 of 1947 on *Further Education,* para 20, there is a declaration that 'the Education Act allows great freedom for initiative and experiment and it is the Minister's hope that this freedom will be used in any direction which offers promise'.
4. Ministry of Education, Pamphlet No. 8 *Further Education,* 1947, HMSO.
5. Ibid para 20. 'Community education' had not then acquired a more specialized meaning.
6. Section 42 (4) of the 1944 Education Act.
7. 1945 Education (Scotland) Act, Section 3 (2). Section 2 (7) also applies.

8. *Pamphlet* No. 8 Ibid Para 76.
9. *Basic Education Statistics for the United Kingdom,* DES, Jan. 1978. The figure excludes on-the-job training.
10. *Russell Report,* para 222.
11. *Alexander Report,* paras 211—213.
12. TRENAMAN, J. *Communication and Comprehension,* 1967, Longmans.
13. Le PELLEY, PAMELA. *Go to Work on a Brain Train,* 1979, Mutual Aid Press.

CHAPTER 4

Work-related studies

Against this general background of decentralization and lack of uniformity, the only point of fairly general agreement in recent decades seems to have been the importance given to vocational, or work-related, education. 'Our fortunes tomorrow,' said the Ministry of Education in 1947, 'depend upon the extent to which our plans for technical and commercial education are placed today in the forefront of our reconstruction programme, and the vigour and vision with which they are carried through'.[1] Implementing this idea, however, has been a far from simple matter in the decades that followed, mainly because of the rapidity of change within industry, agriculture and commerce. The uncertainties of the modern world, the increasingly fragmented nature of many types of work and the disintegration of previously accepted beliefs have all raised questions about the purposes and nature of work-related education. Some argue that all that is needed is to equip people with limited mechanical skills as required, while others feel that a much broader educational task is called for. This is not just an argument about 'training' and 'education' but rather about the educational needs of the modern world. 'Training' is frequently used without any clarity of meaning, and despite the protests of purists it often refers as much to personal development, judgement and attitudes as to skills appropriate to a particular job. The real question for the future is what sort of work-related education and training is needed in a world where mechanized, automated processes are increasingly displacing the human use of repetitive skills. Behind this is the more difficult question of what sort of work, if any, is likely to be undertaken by human beings in a world in which the whole concept of the value of work may be radically changed.

The employers' role

For the present, two of the most vexed questions about the provision of work-related education are: who should be responsible for these studies, and where should they be located? Should the local education authorities be the providers or should it be carried out by industry and commerce? Should the state make financial resources available or should employers foot the bill entirely? In fact, a recent DES document has asserted that employers should be financially responsible for this provision.[2] Should, however, a current financial contribution (or long-term commitment to the particular employer providing the training) be expected from the employee?

Traditionally, much of industrial training in Britain has been regarded as the responsibility of the industry concerned. People have learned their job skills at their place of work by watching others carry them out. 'Sitting by Nellie', as it is often called, is still a characteristic of work-related education in many occupations, although it may be extended a little to the 'copy me' system in which there is a more deliberate attempt to instruct. Apprenticeships, first given legal recognition in the reign of Elizabeth I in the sixteenth century, involve a process of direct handing on by the master craftsmen not only of skills but also of attitudes, values and behaviour patterns. To some extent, the apprenticeship system was dislocated and weakened by the Industrial Revolution with factory mechanization, but the twentieth century did bring some revival. At its best it can bring improving standards of workmanship but in recent years it has again been under attack, especially because of the tendency to insist on rather rigidly defined periods of five or seven-year apprenticeships and to establish barriers to the entry of older people. Other difficulties threatening apprenticeships have developed from the progressive raising of the school leaving age and from the general uncertainty of a world in which skilled trades may rapidly become out of date. Nevertheless they are still part of the picture.

Some industrial firms had early developed their own Works Schools, the one at Mather and Platts in Manchester dating from 1873, while at Metropolitan Vickers a large training department for a time almost dominated the whole vast works. These works schools usually have a full-time head assisted by full-time or part-time staff drawn from the factory. Many of them in their original form have now disappeared but where they still exist they provide an opportunity for a close correlation between theoretical knowledge and practical work on the shop floor. They tend, however, to be provided only by large firms where the management exhibits an enthusiasm for training. At its best the training is not limited to the inculcation of skill needed just for particular machines or processes but may include a large amount of general education for the young worker. Some kind of induction training is usual in most industrial firms, whether a works school exists or not, especially in those concerned with craft work or repetitive mass production processes, but these vary according to the nature of the work and the type of firm. Some last for six weeks or more, while others are barely a week in duration.

Various other kinds of in-service provision may be made by the larger firms. Some, for example, provide summer schools for refresher training and several now have residential colleges of their own as well as hiring other premises for residential work. Nationalized industries such as the National Coal Board, the Gas Board and the Electricity Board have, for example, acquired their own colleges. Even so, most industries also use the resources provided by the LEAs especially for in-service education to meet the needs of young people. Some LEA colleges are thus heavily dependent on the supply of students from firms in their area, either for day-release or block release courses. Day-release from employment, however, continues to present problems. Successive reports, including the Carr[3] and Crowther Reports[4] and the Report of the Henniker-Heaton Committee[5] in the late 1950s and early 1960s recommended extension of the system. For example the Henniker-Heaton committee said in 1964 that 'for the year 1969–70 a national target should be set of at least an additional 250,000 boys and girls obtaining release from employment for further education. Our aim involves an average increase of the order of 50,000 a year during the next five years.' But in fact attendances slightly declined and in the commercial and clerical occupations, in which there are many women employees, there is a very poor record. The peak seems to have been about 40% of the young men and 10% of the young women in the age groups concerned. Partly there has been some substitution of 'block' release to short full-time courses, but much depends upon the attitudes of both employer and young worker, and upon the amount of information and understanding available. Some industries, such as engineering, give great encouragement, and in general it is the larger firm that provides opportunities for day-release. For the numerous smaller firms, indeed, the whole question of provision is more an issue of feasibility than of principle. They do not have the resources in manpower or the general facilities to meet their technical education requirements, and even the induction training they provide is of very variable quality. Some students as well as teachers and employers have also questioned the value of day release because of the stress it can create by constant readjustment problems in family and social life as well as at work.

Industrial training boards

To try to remove some of the unevenness in industrial training, both of quality and of quantity, which resulted from the uncoordinated decisions of a large number of individual firms, the Industrial Training Act of 1964 set out to share the cost of training more equitably between firms. The method was to create an Industrial Training Board (ITB) for each industry which would be responsible for ensuring that the quality and quantity of training were adequate. Each Board would impose a financial levy on employers within that industry to provide an income from which to pay grants to those who provided training directly or indirectly in accordance with the Board's requirements. A firm which did not provide training would thus pay a levy but get no grant while one that did a great deal of good training might well receive more in grant than it paid in levy. The Boards make an important contribution by focusing attention on training and by stimulating new thinking and new initiatives. New programmes have been developed, as, for example, the modular system for training apprentices, craftsmen and technicians that was pioneered by the Engineering ITB. Special training centres have been established by some Boards and a large number of firms now have specialist training officers and training instructors. The general impact has been to increase substantially the amount of systematic off-the-job training.

By 1972, however, there were doubts about the levy/grant scheme and about various limitations which appeared to be inherent in the scheme. Separate Boards for particular industries made it impossible to include some millions of workers who were in industries composed of large numbers of small firms each with very dissimilar training needs. There were also problems arising from the requirements of the local labour market and from the need to train those in declining industries for work in other industries. As a result of the problems, a discussion document *Training for the Future* (the Carr Report) was issued in 1972 by the Department of Employment,[6] to be followed by the Employment and Training Act of 1973. This established the Manpower Services Commission in 1974 and provided new arrangements under which the ITBs no longer have a duty to raise a levy although they still have the power to do so. For firms with adequate training standards, a system of levy exemptions in fact replaced the levy grant system as from April 1975, and on the whole the upper limit of a levy has been fixed at no more than 1% of payroll. Today the Boards vary in size and importance according to the nature of the industry they serve, and they may, in fact, decline in number. Some employ training officers, most issue publications often giving advice and guidance, and a few such as the Construction Industry Training Board provide national training centres. They continue their work of stimulus, recommendations and overseeing, although on reduced budgets.

Manpower Services Commission

The real responsibility for running the public employment and training services, however, is in the hands of the Manpower Services Commission. Technically separate from the government but accountable to the Secretary of State for Employment, its main executive functions are to help employers find suitable workers, and to help people train for, and obtain, suitable jobs. The Commission itself has ten members but works through divisions, one of which is the Manpower Intelligence and Planning Division which undertakes the task of advising the government on manpower policy issues and conducts research with a view to improving the planning. Another is the Employment Services Division (ESD) which is responsible for about sixty Job Centres, issues a useful series of *Choice of Career* booklets and provides an Occupational Guidance Service available in the larger centres of population. The Training Services Division (TSD) has a particular concern with the Training Opportunities Scheme (TOPS) which is designed to help individuals over the age of 19 who wish to learn new skills. This was described by the Trades Union Congress as 'a major breakthrough'. The Special Programmes Division is responsible for the Youth Opportunities Scheme (YOP) and the Special Temporary Employment Programme (STEP). Courses take place either at Skill Centres which concentrate mainly on engineering, construction and commercial skills, or in educational institutions provided by the LEAs or in employers' establishments. Over 300 different training courses have become available under TOPS, and up to 90,000 trainees a year have taken part in them, about 40% of these being women. There have been recent proposals to widen the range of courses, to include, for example, training for people to start new businesses, and higher level courses for scientists, technologists and engineers. There is also an experimental programme to develop courses for women who wish to take up employment after some years at home – the 'Wider opportunities for women' scheme (WOW). This follows various special courses pioneered elsewhere, for example, in the 'Fresh horizons' courses at the City Lit. from 1966, and the 'New opportunities for women' (NOW) courses at Hatfield Polytechnic from 1971. All this work, of course, is likely to be greatly affected by cuts in education budgets and by 1980 some ten thousand TOPS places had already disappeared. There had also been a reduction of £172 million in the allocation to the Manpower Services Commission in 1979—80.

While some training has thus been opened up for older workers, priority continues to be given to the needs of young workers. An MSC working party under the chairmanship of Mr Geoffrey Holland examined the feasibility of a new coherent programme to deal with the mounting numbers of young unemployed and in 1977 reported in favour of a scheme which would double or treble the existing opportunities. The resultant Youth Opportunities Programme (YOP) offers both first-hand work experience and training courses to prepare young people for work. The latter may take the form of employment induction courses or short industrial courses related to a specific though broad occupational area. The Holland Report estimated that the programme would ultimately cater for up to 234,000 young people a year. For such a programme it was clear that large numbers of instructors would need to be trained and the City and Guilds of London organized a pilot project to develop a suitable course for instructors and supervisors, a 'Holland instructors course' in which unemployed craftsmen would be trained for work with young people. Some have criticized the whole YOP scheme on organizational grounds and in particular would like to see more local representation and control. There have also been some threats that the government would radically reduce or abolish the scheme and it is clear that the problems of the relationship of the government to education and training are far from being resolved. There is a view that YOP courses should be available to all unemployed school leavers but there is disagreement about whether the content should be narrow skill training or a broader education. Alternatively the whole scheme could be left to private enterprise and the employers; or secondary schools could help more by enabling the unemployed young person to go back to school ('Return and learn') rather than use the further education institutions, both public and private.

Management education

Employers have thus varied a great deal in their response to the educational and training needs of their workforce, and similar variations can be seen in ideas about management education. Before the 1950s there was very little formal education for management in Britain and indeed the first real developments came only after the introduction by the Ministry of Education in 1949 of a national diploma in management studies. Those successful at the end of a part-time course could be admitted to graduate membership of the British Institute of Management (BIM), a body established in 1947 which began running its own 'executive development courses' for promising young managers. Employer interest in management training has also been shown by the Confederation of British Industry (CBI) founded in 1965 to bring together a number of earlier employer organizations. It produces a useful quarterly journal entitled the *CBI Education and Training Bulletin*. A lead has also been given by the British Association for Commercial and Industrial Education (BACIE) which is a national voluntary organization founded as early as 1919, with ten Regional Groups and a Scottish Branch. In membership of BACIE are the Industrial Training Boards, nationalized industries and private industrial

41

and commercial firms, together with representatives of local and central government, universities, technical colleges and some trade unions. The association organizes special courses for training officers and educators as well as conferences and seminars, issues a regular *Journal* and other supportive publications, has a specialist library and a model training centre, and runs an advisory service on training. Other interested organizations are the Foundation for Management Education (FME) and the Council of Industry for Management Education, a body created by the FME in association with the CBI and the BIM. The Industrial Society, founded in 1918, also issues many publications with particular reference to management education. The Administrative Staff College was opened in 1946 at Henley to try to do for industry what the Staff Colleges do for the armed services. It is an independent organization which offers courses on the principles and practice of management and administration. Candidates must be nominated by their employers and normally be between the ages of 33 and 42. The basic qualification is declared to be 'practical experience not academic distinction' and admission is by competitive interview. The college is financed mainly out of fee income and partly by voluntary subscriptions. A typical feature is the sandwich course leading to the degree of Master of Business Administration. Some individual companies have established their own staff training centres and an increasing number of courses for management, usually of a post-experience kind, have grown up in the major establishments of further education. These often lead to a CNAA degree. In some areas co-operative action has developed; in the north-west, for example, a Regional Management Centre brings together the various Area Schools of Management in Cheshire and Merseyside, Lancashire and Greater Manchester.

In the past managers took decisions on the basis of previous experience, hunches and 'common sense', but it seems to be more and more believed that the complexity of the present inter-dependent economy now requires managers to have a sound theoretical background and knowledge of specialized techniques such as systems analysis and operational research. As a result several universities offer post-experience management courses as well as a more limited number of undergraduate level courses. Durham University, for example, has an M.Sc. in management studies and Strathclyde University an M.Sc. in marketing, as does the Cranfield Institute of Technology.

Trade unions

Work-related education is clearly very much a concern of the trade union movement which, with nearly 13 million members, represents over 50% of the labour force. Besides its interest in general membership education, to which reference will be made later, the Trade Union Congress (TUC) has shown a particular concern for the training of full-time trade union officers and of the voluntary workplace representatives who have key organizational and representative roles. The TUC Education Committee, a standing committee of the General Council, looks after all aspects of educational provision and has devised a modular programme of courses for workplace representatives mostly on a day-release basis. These cover the subjects required by shop stewards in their representational duties, such as industrial law, health and safety matters, work study, job evaluation, company finance etc. For the 300,000 shop stewards, and the more recent 200,000 union safety representatives, about 20,000 places a year are provided in co-operation with public educational bodies. The aim is to provide a comprehensive service to ensure that members understand trade union aims and activities and that representatives function efficiently. There are now nine Regional Offices to ensure co-operation with other agencies. The TUC also has its own non-residential Training College which concentrates on the design and development of teaching materials, and on making a contribution to the training of both professional and union tutors. Over 900 full-time union officers, for example, have been trained in the use of specialized materials produced by the College. There is also a modular programme of one week, updating, courses for full-time officers, of whom there are now about 4,000. Regionally there has been a fairly extensive provision of weekend courses on subjects such as trade union structure, communications, collective bargaining, the role and functions of trades councils, workers' participation etc. Sometimes these are organized on a linked basis with an extended study over three weekends on, for example, 'Trade unions and economic policy', 'Management techniques' or 'Statistics for trade unions'. In its 1977 Annual Report the TUC estimated that by the early 1980s about 180,000 trade unionists a year would be attending courses connected with union work, and that an additional 500 full-time tutors would be required to cope with such an expansion. It therefore asked central government to provide adequate funds to meet these needs and help establish a national trade union education centre. So far this has not had a favourable response, although in 1976–7 the Department of Education and Science made a grant of £400,000 to the TUC specifically for trade union education. This was, however, only a fraction of the amount made available by most other European governments: in the same year the Swedish government, for example, provided a grant of £5½ million.

Individual trade unions also make a substantial educational contribution. Part of the functional training of officers and representatives is carried out independently in the union's own weekend courses and summer schools, but a good deal is also done in co-operation with bodies such as the Workers' Educational Association, some university extra-mural departments, some colleges of further education and polytechnics and with the BBC. The WEA Districts have long provided special weekend schools for trade unionists and more recent years have seen further development of shop steward training as well as of special industrial branches. An early example of co-operation with universities came in Nottingham where special day-release courses were developed for miners, particularly from 1957.[7] These brought together a limited group of trade unionists to study economics and the mining industry, and to improve the general union efficiency by training in communication. Similar developments have taken place in other universities, such as Sheffield and Manchester, and this special type of course provision has been extended to other industries.

LEA colleges have contributed to trade union education particularly with skill and information courses dealing with matters such as health and safety regulations, communications and work study. In the public sector over 1,100 courses for about 16,000 students have been held regularly. The BBC has also assisted and in 1975 a three-year course was launched, in conjunction with the WEA and the TUC, to help shop stewards, branch officials and others to understand the role of the unions in industry and society as a whole. The project consisted of three series each of ten television programmes linked to special publications, TUC correspondence courses and tutorial services provided by the WEA in short, residential courses.

Like some of the large industrial employers, individual unions have been opening their own colleges to help the training of their own officials. An early example was the college at Esher set up by the Electricians and Plumbers Trade Union in 1952. Similarly the General and Municipal Workers Union opened Woodstock College in Surbiton in 1964 and nine years later established another residential centre near Hale, Manchester. In 1976 the Association of Scientific, Technical and Managerial Staff opened Whitehall College in Bishops Stortford, and the Transport and General Workers Union opened a large centre in Eastbourne which can accommodate up to 280 students. One of the later colleges is that provided by the National Union of Railwaymen in a Sussex mansion in 1977. This kind of development has raised questions both outside and within the unions about the amount of money a union can afford for education and training, and also the direction the expenditure should take. If there are developments in industrial democracy as proposed by the Bullock Report[8] it is argued that individual unions will need a good deal of financial help from central government sources. The type of vocational training needed by shop stewards also remains a somewhat open question; should it be confined to fairly narrow skills training, particularly in communications, or should it seek to give a broad understanding of economic and social questions?

Co-operative movement

Faced with considerable changes in retail selling practices and the challenge from supermarkets and hypermarkets, the Co-operative Movement has found it necessary not only to undertake a considerable reorganization but also to plan for improved management and general efficiency. Committed to education from the pioneer days in Rochdale from 1844 onwards, Co-operators have looked upon membership education as a means of achieving the kind of just and well-ordered society the movement desires. In recent years, however, perhaps more attention has been placed on staff training and education while at the same time attempting to preserve the distinctive character of the Co-operative store. The number of autonomous retail societies has been reduced by amalgamation but in 1980 there were still 209 with over 10,000 retail outlets, a total membership of almost 11 million people, and about 140,000 employees. At local level each retail society uses part of its trading surplus for educational purposes but the position is very variable and the statistics show that in many of the smaller societies, the amount is negligible. In the larger societies which now predominate, however, short-term courses both for induction training and for continued in-service training are regular features, particularly for salesmen, provision assistants and branch managers. These are often organized in, or with the co-operation of, the LEA colleges, although they usually follow syllabuses prepared by the Co-operative Union. Local activities are stimulated and supplemented by the activities of seven regional sections which, especially in Scotland, have provided district and group training for managers and senior staff, for dairy supervisors and for other officials. The Education Department of the Co-operative Union provides syllabuses, examinations and awards for a range of studies in salesmanship and management, and in clerical work and secretaryship. It also issues publications. Under the auspices of the Co-operative Union there is a National Co-operative Education Association for England, Wales and Ireland and a Scottish Co-operative Educational Association; their work is to help meet all the educational needs of both employees and members. Postal courses are offered in all the subjects required for certificates and diplomas with some special provision for directors of societies and education secretaries. For long-term residential courses and occasional short courses, the movement has its own Co-operative College, first established in Manchester in 1919 and transferred to the more magnificent Stanford Hall, near Loughborough, in 1946. Open to men and women, and able to accommodate 110, the College offers courses leading to various diplomas and certificates, such as the Diploma in Co-operative Management and the Certificate in Distributive Management Principles. A full management training scheme is, in fact, available. Students may also take the Diploma in Political, Economic and Social Studies awarded by the University of Nottingham for external students or the Diploma in Co-operative Development and Management awarded by Loughborough University. The latter is taken usually by the overseas students, of whom there are usually about thirty in the college. Scholarships are available from all levels of the Movement for employees who wish to attend. In Scotland there is usually an annual weekend school for chief officials and accountants, and various short courses are arranged with Strathclyde University. In general the Co-operative Union, the national federation of consumer co-operative societies which was established in 1869, has made staff training a major priority.

Private institutions

Many privately run, mainly commercial, institutions contribute to education for paid employment.[9] These are very diverse and vary from the very small, often just one man or woman, to large commercial corporations employing several hundred people. Many are short lived and the whole situation is in a constant state of flux. Anyone can establish a private, educational institution and it would seem that the only control is that of the fire and building regulations. The exact number of students in such establishments is not known but it has been estimated that in 1970–1 there were over a million and a half in the United Kingdom following courses in some sort of proprietary establishment, including perhaps 900,000 in driving schools.[10] Another estimate suggests that the number of students in private colleges represents about 15% of all adults taking vocational education and training or over 20% if the correspondence colleges are included.[11]

Correspondence courses will be discussed more fully in a later chapter. The other types of provision can be divided into institutions which offer short, flexible courses, and a rather smaller number of specialist institutions which offer long, formal courses in subjects such as electronics, occupational therapy and architecture. Particularly strong are the contributions of courses in office skills and languages but the subject range is wide and includes driving (both private cars and heavy goods vehicles), accountancy, law, beauty therapy, hairdressing, diving, flying, floristry, marine communications, various paramedical subjects such as physiotherapy, pharmacy and osteopathy, nursery nursing and agriculture. There are also Schools of Music, of Drama and of Art, and within the range of private institutions must also be included the various theological colleges which prepare people for work as priests and ministers of religion. Of the profit-making institutions, Pitman's College, established in 1898 in London, is the largest of its kind in the world with its special provision of secretarial courses at various levels for older women as well as young girls. Commercial education seems to be becoming more and more a private industry, and almost every town has at least one private commercial college, drawing its income from fees charged for courses in shorthand and typing. Of the 180 or so language schools, some are concerned with the teaching of foreign languages – the Goethe Institute, for example, has a range of courses in German – but many offer English, particularly to foreign students, and are concentrated in the south-east of England. The length of commercially provided courses is very variable; correspondence courses last an average of twenty weeks, but the average length of a management course is two weeks and of a driving course, fifteen hours.

Of the students, just under half are from overseas, or if correspondence courses are excluded, about one-third. The teachers, especially in correspondence courses, are mainly part-time, and even outside the correspondence schools part-timers are over 40% of the total. A 'full-time' teacher in a small establishment such as a hairdressing salon, is often the proprietor, and it is not easy to draw clear lines between off-the-job and on-the-job training, 'tuition' sometimes being little more than learning by experience under the eye of the master craftsman. There are, however, training centres run by professional or trade associations such as the Building Societies Institute or the College of the Institute of Marketing which provide more organized, if short, courses for the in-service training of member firms.

Inevitably in this heterogeneous type of provision there are questions about quality. There is no legal requirement for Department of Education and Science approval or inspection, and often the provision appears to be just a simple exploitation of demand. It is said, for example, that some 'cowboys' have moved into the lucrative language school industry, providing courses without adequate accommodation and equipment, or a properly qualified staff. Some steps have been taken by the private providers themselves. An Association of Recognised English Language Schools (ARELS) has been formed, for example, with its own code of conduct, while the leading correspondence colleges have established a Council for Accreditation (CACC). The Council for Legal Education has 'approved' four tutorial establishments, while the Law Society has its own College of Law. But most subject specialisms are without associations or any degree of control. Some are charitable trusts, but predominantly they are profit making, or profit seeking, and even in 1971 the turnover was over £100 million per year, excluding the private driving schools. Their virtues would seem to be flexibility, convenience and responsiveness to the apparent needs of students. On the whole the alleged 'degree mills' and other forms of fraudulent operation, seem to be a very small element within the whole provision, and public response suggests a good degree of student satisfaction and cost effectiveness.

Universities

As has already been indicated many universities have developed joint activities and courses with both the trade union and the Co-operative movements, and assist employers with management training. Two universities in England have fully established Business Schools while the Scottish Business School has three divisions within the Universities of Glasgow, Edinburgh and Strathclyde. Within university undergraduate courses, however, the increase in the intake of mature students still remains painfully slow and the statistics show that they are still less than 6% of the total. It can be argued that there is an undue emphasis on the full-time nature of the first degree course taken end-on to school, and that what is needed is the provision of a varied pattern of recurrent opportunities, including sandwich courses, with possibly more stress on the suggestion that universities should admit more people over the age of 35 than under the age of 25. Even in the postgraduate courses, which have increased considerably in recent years, only about 20% of the entrants are mature students. These courses, however, do offer some opportunities through which people can acquaint themselves with new developments and gain knowledge and practice in new fields of work open to mature persons. These may be related to areas such as electronics and communications engineering, or the design and manufacture of equipment for the automatic control of industrial processes. Some occupations have more opportunities than others. In-service postgraduate refresher courses for teachers have become almost a standard provision of most universities, although now tending to be part-time rather than full-time as local education authorities reduce the number of secondments. Other professions for which work-related postgraduate courses have developed are architecture, town and country planning, social administration, medicine, nursing, occupational health, law and engineering. Some special provision is made in the limited number of university Departments of Agriculture for postgraduate schools; for example, Bangor is concerned chiefly with animal husbandry while Oxford specializes in agricultural economics and plant physiology.

Reference will be made in a later chapter to work-related correspondence courses and to the Open University which provides the major university contribution for mature students taking first degrees. Most other universities have special regulations for the entry of mature students but there are still considerable obstacles, especially the lack of adequate financial support for older candidates and the failure of departments to adjust courses designed for the 18 to 20 age group. It has been argued that more part-time provision should be made, or a combination of part-time and full-time study. Birkbeck College in London has made such provision for some time and in the 1967 Report on the future of Birkbeck College the hope was expressed that the example might be followed in other large university cities. Similarly the Robbins Report[12] hoped that special consideration would be given to the establishment of university evening courses for first degrees. University extramural departments, however, have shown a reluctance to follow the American example of developing as extension divisions administering the university programmes of part-time study for degrees. Nevertheless, a few moves have been made as, for example, the experimental part-time course for a degree in psychology arranged by the Department of Adult Education in collaboration with the Department of Psychology in the University of Hull. Some of the internal departments in the newer universities are also showing signs of developing more flexible arrangements for part-time undergraduate study. The University of Stirling, for example, has created a structure of part-time courses leading to B.A. or B.Sc. degrees and this has proved attractive to a wide cross-section of mature adults. As the number of potential young undergraduates straight from school declines, so more universities are likely to turn to the provision of alternative arrangements in order to attract the older person.

Polytechnics

Polytechnics are those thirty institutions in England and Wales, and one in Northern Ireland, which were formed from over seventy existing institutions. Most came from the amalgamation of a college of technology and a college of art, with the possible addition of specialist institutions such as a college of commerce and teacher training establishment. Some, as in Oxford and Plymouth, consisted of only one college, while Liverpool put together four institutions. Sometimes, the institutions were geographically dispersed – up to ten miles apart in some instances – and, naturally, each institution brought its own distinct tradition to the new polytechnic. It was, in fact, anticipated that the polytechnics would fulfil three main functions. First, they were to provide, for students of 'university quality', full-time and sandwich courses more vocationally based than university degree courses; second, they were to provide similar courses at sub-degree but still advanced level; and third, they were to meet the needs of 'the many thousands of students who, being already in employment, can find time only for part-time day and/or evening courses, whether they lead to a degree or to a qualification below that standard.' The centres should be 'comprehensive in the sense that they plan their provision of courses to meet the needs of students in all three categories' and be 'mixed communities of full-time and part-time teachers and students' having 'closer and more direct links with industry, business, and the professions'.[13]

The above suggests comprehensive, multi-opportunity, work-related centres of adult education. In fact, most of the polytechnics have tended to reduce the amount of lower level work and to stress the needs of the full-time rather than the part-time student, but the emphasis does vary, Birmingham and London having relatively large numbers of part-time students, while others have reduced them to a mere 15% of the total. In fact, the polytechnics seem to have moved closer to the universities in terms of their student intake, their courses and structures. Nevertheless, they have forged closer links with industry and commerce, and have demonstrated greater flexibility, particularly in terms of opportunities for student transfers between courses. However, a number of polytechnic teachers would prefer the original vision of 1966 rather than a drift toward university status; they would prefer to present distinct alternatives to universities, to be, in fact, comprehensive, multi-opportunity, work-related centres of education for adults.

In Scotland it should be mentioned that although there are no polytechnics, the colleges at Aberdeen and Paisley play similar roles. Instead, there are fourteen 'Central Institutions' which are responsible through the Scottish Education Department to the Secretary of State for Scotland. The main features of these institutions is their preparation of students for a particular career. Five have a wide remit, but the others specialize in agriculture art, music and drama, textiles and marine engineering. The independent governing body of each includes representatives of professional, industrial, commercial and educational interests. In recent years there has been a significant growth in degree courses offered at these institutions.

Colleges of education

In the 1950s and 1960s teacher training was one specialized form of vocational education which saw a considerable rise in the provision for mature students. Special arrangements were made for the entry of older students either attending as day students in the residential colleges provided for the immediate post school age range, or in the sixteen separate day colleges which came to be established. At one point mature students came to nearly one-fifth of the total number of students, a figure which reflects particularly the desire of married women to take up a new career when their children have become more independent, but also the wish of some men to change jobs in middle life.

The first training colleges for teachers were established early in the nineteenth century by voluntary agencies, especially the churches, in order to staff elementary schools, and a few voluntary colleges still continue. The LEAs in England and Wales were permitted to enter the field by the 1902 Education Act and after the Second World War they took the lead. In 1944 they had 29 colleges, but within twenty years they had 119 including eight specialist colleges for housecraft, seven for physical education and twelve for art teachers. There were also four for technical subject teachers. The standard course became one of three years' duration and much stress was given to a college being a close-knit, preferably residential, community. The course comprised personal higher education, usually in one or two main subjects, as well as professional pedagogical studies in the philosophy, psychology and sociology of education, and in teaching methods. To this was added observation in schools and teaching practice, and the whole course led to a certificate of one of the twenty, university-based, area training organizations (ATOs) established after the McNair Report of 1944 and often called Institutes of Education. Success also led to 'qualified teacher status' granted by the Department of Education and Science. The ATOs were made redundant in 1975 and new machinery is still awaited.

After the publication of the James Report[14] in 1972, many of the colleges moved to a more varied programme, which included a two-year Diploma in Higher Education and a B.Ed. degree. The economic problems of the late 1970s and the decline in the school population then led to decisions to reduce the teacher training capacity. As a result the total number of institutions with teacher training has been approximately halved and instead of the 110,000 or so places, by 1980 only about 60,000 were available in

England and Wales. In Scotland teacher training has long been in the hands of ten colleges of education with a large measure of autonomy in academic matters and the whole pattern of teaching qualifications is controlled by a General Teaching Council (GTC), the majority of whose members are directly elected by the teaching profession. Proposals to reduce the ten colleges to six met with stiff resistance, although the closure of two was announced in 1980. Whereas in England and Wales some teacher training is carried out in universities, where graduates may take a one-year course, in Scotland it is entirely the province of the colleges, which tend to be larger and perhaps more resilient than their English counterparts. In Scotland, the colleges of education have retained their separate identities but are tending to survive by diversification, and by 1978 five of them had already begun to offer courses other than teacher training; in Northern Ireland, also, there were still three colleges of education in 1980.

Colleges and institutes of higher education

Most of the English and Welsh colleges have merged with other colleges of education or have joined colleges of further education or polytechnics and, in a few instances, universities. Some of the mergers between colleges of education and colleges of further education have taken the title College of Higher Education, or Institute of Higher Education. Like the Scottish colleges, they have tended to look for a new identity by diversification of courses, and have shown great initiative and adaptability, expanding from teacher education to management or business education, and opening up a variety of special areas such as youth work, health-related studies and trade union studies. They have also produced various new kinds of combined and specialized degrees in association with the CNAA. The fundamentally pragmatic approach has resulted in considerable differences between the colleges. Some are fairly small residential institutions taking mainly full-time students, while others have a high proportion of part-time students. Many opened their doors to mature students and although the number of these was reduced in the early 1980s, it may increase again as the number of children in schools changes. On the whole the new colleges have been very experimental and responsive to regional pressures and demands for different methods of study, and they have added considerably to the range of choice. In early 1978 a check suggested that more than eighty different subjects could be studied in the colleges of higher education. On the other hand, as relatively small institutions compared with polytechnics and universities, they seem likely to need a good deal of help and encouragement from both local and central government. An argument in their support is that the closer assimilation with the rest of 'further' and 'higher' and 'adult' education in multipurpose institutions will improve teacher training by enabling students to decide their careers not at the beginning but after one or two years on courses.

Colleges of further education and technology

In the period since the Second World War there has been what has rightly been described as 'the explosion of further education'.[15] Before the war provision was poorly organized and usually part time, for young people only. 'The truth is that our technical education is for the most part offered at the end of the day, when students are tired; and more often than not housed in premises that are ill-adapted and ill-equipped for the purpose'.[16] The years which followed saw not only a vast increase in the amount of provision, but quite kaleidoscopic changes in its form and structure. Ideas were implemented not just for local colleges, but for area and regional colleges, (most of the latter becoming Colleges of Advanced Technology and later technological universities). Money and material shortages in the early years after 1946 caused local education authorities at first to adapt existing buildings, but as resources become easier there was a spate of often lavish new building for both old-established and new colleges. Similarly there were great changes in the number and type of teachers employed in the colleges; before 1939 most of the work was carried out by part-time teachers and in 1946 there were only 4,700 full-time teachers in the whole of further education in Britain. By the mid-1970s there were over 60,000. White Papers and Reports from central government have followed each other in rapid succession and, though some were more effective than others, in general local authorities set to work with some zeal to create a comprehensive provision of work-related education in their own areas.

As a result often the most imposing building, and certainly the most visible feature of local education authority provision for the education of adults in towns, is the institution which in the past usually bore the name 'technical college'. In more recent years, however, a great variety of other titles have come into use, and the term 'major establishments' is used by the Department of Education and Science in England and Wales to embrace them all. They include 'colleges of further education', favoured by the advisory pamphlet of 1947, 'colleges of technology', 'colleges' and 'schools' of agriculture, 'colleges' and 'schools' of art, and specialist colleges such as those of building and commerce. This rather bewildering nomenclature is haphazard, indicating only a diversity of local decisions at various points in time. The same establishment may, in fact, have changed its name several times in the past three decades and in some parts of the country there is a growing tendency to use just the term 'college'. In Stockport, for example, one of the largest establishments of its kind, the 'technical college' became the 'college of further education' and then the 'college of technology', although it is usually known today as just 'the college'. On the whole, perhaps older institutions with fairly high-level courses tend to use the title 'technical college' or 'college of technology' while newer colleges or those with only low-level courses are called 'colleges of further education'. In Scotland, most are still called technical colleges. The situation is very fluid and it is not possible to ascribe general reasons for the nomenclature. The decision is a local one, and may be influenced as much by pretensions of grandeur as by real differences. Most of the older colleges, in some cases with origins going back to the Mechanics' Institutes of the nineteenth century, were relatively small before 1939 and their expansion has often touched the pride as well as the imagination of the elected councillors.

By the later 1970s the number of major establishments in England and Wales had reached 579 and in Scotland there were 14 central institutions and

63 other colleges providing daytime courses.[17] In Northern Ireland there were 27 colleges of further education. Although each college differs in many ways from every other college, some common features may be seen in the organization, the type of courses on offer and the type of students. The average college, under the direction of a principal and vice-principal, is organized on a departmental basis, the departments tending to reflect local needs but often including engineering, business studies, catering and bakery, and general studies. The number of departments, their titles and the links between them, are left to local decisions in which the principal and departmental heads play a major part although influenced by the officers of the local authority which owns the college, and by the rationalization and planning of Regional Advisory Councils for Further Education.

Most of the students in the colleges continue to be young adults, and many of them are workers with day release from their industry for just one day a week. In general, despite an increase in full-time attendance, and sandwich courses (which intersperse full-time education with full-time industrial experience), part-time students still outnumber the full-time. The level of their courses varies from elementary to advanced professional, from operative, craft or technical level to supervisory and managerial.

Some colleges have become 'tertiary colleges', taking in all the 16–18-year-old age group who have not left school at the minimum age, and in general, throughout the country, many young people have chosen to study for GCE 'A' levels in the colleges rather than the schools (bringing them the advantages and potential difficulties of the greater autonomy associated with the colleges).

However, there is an increasing number of older adults now participating in both vocational and non-vocational courses at these colleges. Many colleges provide courses in conjunction with trade unions, act as study centres for Open University courses, house WEA and other evening classes, and offer specialist assistance to adult literacy schemes. In general, they are also playing an increasingly significant role in retraining for older people.

Naturally this carries considerable implications for organization, staffing and methods as well as for the development of counselling services. A few colleges have attempted to face this challenge and some now regard themselves as the centre of the whole range of educational opportunities, whether work-related or not, available to everyone between the ages of 16 and 90. Nelson and Colne College, for example, has a full work-related programme but plans a seven-day week with a variety of non-vocational courses, non class educational activities and events such as lectures, recitals and exhibitions, joint activities with adult voluntary organizations and other attempts to meet the special needs of the adult public. Elsewhere colleges have made special arrangements for trade unions and management and have developed new courses in community or social work, and in administration or business studies. Some perhaps see themselves becoming a kind of American style 'community college'.

Agricultural education

Three of the Scottish central institutions are concerned with full-time higher education in agriculture and are financed by the Department of Agriculture and Fisheries for Scotland instead of by the Scottish Education Department. In general, education for agricultural posts, including those in estate management, forestry, horticulture, agricultural engineering etc. has tended to take place in monotechnic institutions. Originally these had a great variety of names in which 'college' and 'institute' or 'farm' and 'agriculture' seemed interchangeable but now happily they are mostly designated as 'colleges of agriculture'. In England and Wales, where overall there has been a gradual transfer of authority from the Ministry of Agriculture to the Department of Education and Science, there is a hierarchical structure of institutions. Thirty-four lower level colleges offer basic one-year full-time courses leading to national awards in general agriculture, horticulture or poultry husbandry, while some offer supplementary courses dealing with specialized branches such as fruit growing. The number of part-time day courses has also grown considerably although these still attract only a small proportion of the young people who are eligible. As increasing mechanization has lessened the need for physical strength in farming as elsewhere, so the opportunities for women have been correspondingly increased, and the colleges, originally mainly only for men, now admit women students to the full range of courses. Even so, the women are heavily outnumbered. One of the problems of day release is that it is difficult for small farmers or horticulturalists to release employees for training — in some cases they might well lose all their labour force.

Following the Pilkington Report of 1966[18] there has been a thorough review of agricultural education and of the award-bearing courses. Present developments stress improvement in the standard of entry, a rationalization of the award system, the development of more sandwich courses and specialized degree courses. For Scotland, the Scottish Technical Education Council (SCOTEC) in 1980 proposed a new structure in which there would be three qualifications: a certificate suitable for the farm worker, a diploma for the practical farmer and a higher diploma for the more scientific farmer or adviser.

Advanced courses in England and Wales are offered by seven agricultural colleges. Five of these receive a direct grant to meet deficiencies, paid by the Department of Education and Science, following the transfer of responsibility from the Ministry of Agriculture in 1964. One of these, the Royal Agricultural College at Cirencester, was founded in 1842 and pioneered this kind of education. It specializes in agricultural science and estate management and like the other colleges it is residential with its own farm. In total the five colleges have about 900 student places but plan expansion. The remaining two advanced colleges, in Lancashire and Essex, are run by local authorities and can each accommodate about 200 students for either two-year or one-year diploma courses. There are also a small number of specialist establishments such as the forester training schools, run by the Forestry Commission, the Royal Horticultural Society's training gardens at Wisley in Surrey, and the Royal Botanic Gardens at Kew and Edinburgh. The Royal College of Agricultural Engineering, established in 1960 at Silsoe in Bedfordshire, is the last survivor of ten so-called 'National Colleges' established for particular specialisms in the post-war period. The others were concerned with food technology, rubber technology, aeronautics, leather selling, heating, ventilating, refrigeration and fan engineering, horology and instrument technology and foundry work.

After the issue of the Robbins Report most have been absorbed into other institutions, especially polytechnics. The tenth, the Royal College of Art, founded in the nineteenth century, but given the status of a National College in 1949, was granted university status in 1964.

Education in the armed services

Education in H.M. Forces is the responsibility of the Ministry of Defence, working through three Directorates concerned with education in the Royal Navy, the Army and the Royal Air Force. Though each service has developed its own distinctive type of provision, all have given much encouragement to educational activity of all kinds in order to develop 'mental alertness, skill and knowledge', to equip personnel 'with the wider knowledge relevant to his military calling which he requires in order to assume increased responsibilities', and to ensure that all become 'well informed citizens'.[19]

Part of the provision is technical training related to efficiency in the performance of particular service duties, and this tends to predominate in the Royal Navy and the Royal Air Force. Changing ideas about defence, as well as new weaponry and new concepts of strategy and tactics, require this provision to be recurrent throughout a service career, and, as may be expected, the Services give it much emphasis. In peacetime in fact the life of a service-man or woman is predominantly training and within the broad picture there are a number of special schemes. Whereas, on the whole, the Navy and the RAF admit only those who have reached a fairly high educational standard, the Army, while also rejecting many applicants (for example, in 1973, 58% were rejected) does make special provision for some new recruits who are low in educational attainment. This is given in a School of Preliminary Education where ten-week courses of training are provided to bring up the standards of English and arithmetic. In 1978–9 nearly 450 attended. All the Services have promotion examinations and provide education to prepare for these. In the Army, for example, potential senior non-commissioned officers (sergeants and warrant officers) take Education Promotion Certificates (EPC) in subjects such as communication skills, military calculations, military management and 'The Army in the contemporary world' while officers may take the Progressive Qualification Scheme (PQS) at two levels, the subjects including 'International relations' and 'The soldier in society' as well as 'Leadership' and 'Man management'. In 1978–9, nearly 3,000 took the first level EPC examinations and about 1,700 took the advanced level EPC, while for each of the various papers of PQS, the figure ranged from just over one hundred to five hundred candidates. There are also courses and seminars for senior officers (Lt.-Colonel to Brigadier) often arranged in conjunction with universities. Further opportunities are available in the Staff Colleges possessed by each of the three Services.

Besides this type of work-related education, there is provision for personal, individual education. Where possible education centres and infor-mation rooms, often with a library, are established in land bases or ships. In these, classes may be housed and facilities such as textbooks, language tapes etc. provided. Courses may lead to recognized public examinations such as the GCE or City and Guilds certificates, or may be concerned with cultural or hobby interests of the type to be found in civilian evening, non-vocational centres. The Services tend to give a particular stress to citizenship and current affairs and to the learning of foreign languages. Correspondence courses are made available and there is a special Forces Correspondence Courses Scheme (FCCS). Service students may also enrol for the Open University on the same basis as civilian students. Where possible they are advised to enrol in the usual LEA course provision, and many units develop their own societies for music and drama. Considerable attention is paid to resettlement education which is viewed partly as 'a management task with an influence on morale and on both internal and external recruiting'. Besides advice and counselling, resettlement courses include some special professional and trade training, made in co-operation with the Manpower Services Commission and with organizations such as the Regular Forces Employment Association (RFEA).

Most of the work is now carried out by a special staff of full-time officers — in the Royal Army Educational Corps (RAEC), or the Royal Navy Education Service or the Royal Air Force Education Branch — although these have the assistance of other Service personnel and collaborate as fully as possible with civilian agencies such as the LEAs and the universities. With the latter in England and Wales there is a Committee for University Assistance to Adult Education in H.M. Forces (CUA), which continues some of the work organized during the Second World War, and in Scotland there is a Scottish Central Committee for Adult Education in H.M. Forces which is composed of representatives from each of the eight Scottish universities, senior officers from the three Services and an assessor from the Scottish Education Department. Much of the civilian contribution meets specialist needs for expertise outside the usual range, and is often given in a residential form. The Army's Institute of Adult Education has its own research department, and there is also an Army School of Instructional Technology (ASIT) whose role is research and the development of instructional techniques, together with advice, consultancy work and training in courses arranged at the Beaconsfield headquarters. These include such subjects as job analysis, learning systems, audio-visual aids and interview techniques. Some of the training aids and kits produced by ASIT are held in very high esteem and are widely used in industry. Within ASIT some RAEC officers are employed as Training Development Advisers (TDAs). As in so many other areas of provision the quality of what is provided in the Services depends on the calibre of the organizers and teachers, and upon the kind of response they evoke. In general the educational branches of the Services tend to be below the strength they really require — the RAEC, for example, had a total of only 600 officers in 1979 — but there is no doubt that there is more acceptance of the need for education and a greater commitment to it than in many other sectors of adult life.

Education in prisons

The Home Office has responsibility for the training of the police, probation officers and prison officers, and under its auspices a series of in-service training programmes are held throughout the country. These are designed to secure professional efficiency and are conducted usually by members of the service concerned, with some assistance from outside experts. Initial training is supplemented by refresher courses and there is encouragement, for example in the police forces, to attend courses provided by university extra-mural departments and by the LEAs. An example of special arrangements is the provision of courses in criminology, for which there has been a very large response. The police also have a Staff College.

Education within the prisons is also a responsibility of the Home Office and a Chief Education Officer was appointed in 1968. Quite early in the nineteenth century, the Victorians hoped that by education prisoners would be led to see the error of their ways and become disciplined members of society, as well as perhaps gaining a few skills which would give them a better chance of employment. These ideas, however, led to many disappointments and varying attitudes, all of which are much in evidence today. Some think that the sole task of the prison system is to control and contain criminals – 'lock up and keep quiet' – and that it should be used primarily as a punishment and deterrent. Others believe that there should be extensive programmes of education to reform prisoners and to make them 'better men and women'. The Home Office Prison Department *Policy Statement* in 1969, for example, stated that:

> the purpose of education in prisons is really the same as its purpose outside, namely to help a person to have some understanding of himself, of his fellow men, and of the world in which he lives and works; to acquire a skill, trade or profession, and to pursue it successfully; to use time in ways which are useful, acceptable and satisfying; and generally to illumine the personality.[20]

Some within the prison service, however, would perhaps prefer to see it at best as a kind of opiate or just a tool of management. In recent years a staff of full-time Prison Education Officers has been appointed in association with the local LEAs. To assist them there are a fairly small number of full-time teachers but much of the work is carried out by part-time teachers, as in the evening centres outside. Some problems of relationship with the uniformed prison officers are perhaps inevitable, especially as it sometimes appears as though prisoners are getting better support than do the officers themselves for their own promotion examinations. Tension and hostility between the educators and the warders can result from a situation in which the latter can see an erosion of their own status and authority. Moreover, there is a further tension between those educators handling vocational courses and those handling more general education.

In most prisons there are four main kinds of educational provision. First, there is vocational education. Strict vocational training for people in custody is comparatively recent, but now about half take part in prison industries where they are offered operative training in practical work. There are also evening classes in subjects such as technical drawing, motor engineering and building calculations. Negotiations have taken place with both employers and trade unions about this training and about entry to relevant occupations on release. There is some recognition of changing needs in a changing world but vocational training is still kept distinct from other educational work, and tends to be somewhat narrowly conceived. Second, there is provision of remedial education, much needed in view of estimates that perhaps 30% of prisoners have a reading age of less than twelve. Third, a small number take courses, often of a correspondence type, which lead to conventional examinations in the world outside the prison. These show high pass rates and tend to be much quoted as evidence of success. Fourth, there is provision for leisure-time hobby interests, an offering which sometimes leads to accusations that 'prison is a holiday camp', but which does help to build up confidence and self-respect, and may provide for a more satisfying use of leisure time, and lead perhaps to less antisocial behaviour. These evening classes have the same sort of subject range as that found in most LEA evening centres. Attendance at educational activities is voluntary except for some types of trade training, literacy tuition during working hours and the provision for young people under the age of 21. Help from outside comes from the WEA and from the university extra-mural departments especially for more advanced courses,[21] and some prisoners take Open University courses. Most prisons have a library with a reference section as well as a collection available for loan, normally on a weekly basis.

Problems of the work lie partly in the nature of the attendance, particular difficulties being the short-term prisoners and those who are moved from institution to institution. There are also problems of accommodation; while a few prisons have good classrooms, many have to make do with cramped, converted cells, prison chapels, borrowed kitchens or draughty, prefabricated buildings. Perhaps, above all, there are difficulties created by the prison situation. In overcrowded prisons with two or three prisoners to each cell there is a lack of privacy for study; security and censorship impose a tight control on access to books and to items such as oil paint and tools of all kinds; and the general atmosphere tends to stifle independent thought and replace it with a passive, uncritical approach.

The disadvantaged and work-related education

One of the somewhat neglected areas in work-related education for adults is that of the disabled and the disadvantaged. Their general education will be discussed in a later chapter but it seems appropriate in this chapter to draw attention to their work-related needs. In contrast to earlier views, stress is now being given both to equipping the disadvantaged so that they can be gainfully employed, and also to integrating their education as much as possible with that of other students. A voluntary organization, the British Council for Rehabilitation of the Disabled (REHAB) sets out 'to make tax consumers into taxpayers' and has pressed for full vocational training though with the warning that 'on no account should a patient be trained for work that will not be available to him on completion of a course'. There is still, however, a tendency to make a sharp distinction between 'education' and 'recreation' for the disabled and to concentrate on provision for the latter. As a result, comparatively few work-related training opportunities are available and those which do exist are piecemeal and largely inadequate. They occur mainly in the larger centres of population and problems are therefore particularly acute in rural areas. Some local authorities in the towns have attempted to provide courses through their Welfare and Social Service departments, though they may draw on teachers employed by the Education department, a situation which often leads to confusion and frustration. For the disadvantaged adult immigrants and ethnic minorities, LEAs have tended to be preoccupied with providing English language classes, and for other groups, too, more attention has been given to basic education than to direct vocational training. Such provision as does exist is mostly of a segregated kind, and only a few colleges, such as Brixton College of Further Education, have endeavoured to respond to the strong pleas for integration. Some adjustments obviously have to be made — blind students, for example, may require adaptations of tools and machines, and deaf students need modified teaching methods — but the main problem would appear to be the need for a change in the attitude of the public in general and of employers in particular. If there is enough good will and determination, and if job opportunities for the disabled and disadvantaged could be opened up, the organizational problems could quickly be resolved. Adjustments to factors such as accommodation and the timing of courses have been made without much difficulty in the few places that have become active in this field. There are many unmet demands, however, and it would seem that, on the whole, we have only scratched at the surface.

The state and advisory councils

As indicated above, the major part of work-related education is provided in locally-administered institutions over which central government exerts a varying degree of control and direction. The state also contributes by the provision of special reports and regular publications, and is often aided in its work by the establishment of unpaid Advisory Councils and committees. Some of these are shortlived while others last for many years, even decades. Thus for the United Kingdom as a whole there are bodies such as the Standing Advisory Committee on Grants to Students, the UK Council on Education for Management and the Research Councils for Science, and for Social Science, Medicine and Agriculture. In England and Wales there was an important National Advisory Council on Education for Industry and Commerce (NACEIC) which lasted for thirty years from 1947 to 1977 and had wide terms of reference with a membership including representatives of local authorities, university institutions, industry and commerce, and teaching staffs. In keeping under continuous review a very wide area of further education it produced a large number of reports on subjects which ranged from public relations to special areas such as agricultural education. Other councils of particular note have been the Advisory Councils on the Supply and Training of Teachers (NACTST and ACSTT which also lasted for thirty years from 1949 to 1979) and on Art Education (NACAE established in 1959), and reference will be made in a later chapter to some of the more recently established Councils for 'continuing education' and 'community education'. Sometimes special units are set up such as the Further Education Curriculum Review and Development Unit and a National Consultative Group for Training and Further Education, the latter jointly established by the Department of Education and Science and the Manpower Services Commission. Central government may, in fact, at any time establish a special committee of enquiry to look at a particular aspect of education and this network of committees provides a framework for review and guidance and for the promotion of co-operation. On the whole they appear to command attention at the highest level of educational policy making, although much depends perhaps on relationships with the political party in power, and the possible conflicts between recommendations and declared political policy. At certain times, political party decisions to reduce the amount of central government activity may much curtail their work.

Many branches of government besides those carrying the title of education are, in fact, involved in work-related education. The Department of Health and Social Security is much concerned with the education of nurses and social workers, and with health education generally, while detailed work in this field is carried out by separate bodies such as the Central Council for the Education and Training of Social Workers (CCETSW) or the Health Education Council. The latter 'promotes and encourages' the provision of relevant courses of study. In Scotland the Scottish Health Education Unit is supported by central government and the Scottish Council for Health Education by the local authorities and the Health Boards. Both provide a national framework for the growth of community health education activities. The Ministry of Transport is responsible for the training of air pilots, ships' officers, railway staffs and driving instructors, while the Ministry of Agriculture has looked after agricultural education although some of this is being handed over to the control of the Department of Education and Science. Also, following the report of the Haslegrave Committee in 1973, four special Councils were set up with particular reference to technical and business education.

In general, there has been controversy over the proportion of work-related education to be provided directly by agencies of government, central or local or, instead, by independent bodies. It can surely be argued that both can make essential contributions and that they are complementary and often interlocking providers. Naturally, government is well placed to provide major resources and to gather information as well as to exercise influence and to give leadership. It is also uniquely able to provide the planning and organization for large-scale and complex activities. Voluntary agencies, on the other hand, can often do more than government at grass roots level to stimulate action and pioneer change. For instance, at the present time these agencies are endeavouring to help in the aftercare of prisoners, although they are underfinanced and provision is limited. Certainly, government and voluntary agencies between them provide the basis for an adequate system of recurrent work-related education, and without heavy expenditure this could be adjusted to meet our current needs — particularly those of the poorly-served older age group.

Examinations and awards

Matching the great variety of work-related provision, there has developed a complicated network of examinations and awards so that the explorer of the 'jungle' is likely to be totally bewildered by the plethora of qualifications and the multitude of strange initials. Most have been created on an *ad hoc* basis in answer to particular needs, and just as there are changes in the knowledge and skills required in the various occupations, so there is constant development and modification of awards available. In the post-war period the number of awards has risen considerably at both 'advanced' and 'non-advanced' levels, to use the terminology adopted by the Department of Education and Science. According to the DES, advanced courses are at degree level, whereas awards in 'non-advanced further education' (NAFE) are those up to the standard of GCE 'A' level or its equivalent.

Degrees

At advanced level, universities are empowered by their individual Royal Charters to award degrees and they determine their own syllabuses, setting and marking their own examination papers and other forms of evaluation. Originally the University of London was founded (in 1836) as an examining body and the 'London External' degree provided the route to a degree for many thousands of students who were unable to attend a university. In 1979, for example, over 25,000 external students were registered of whom just over half were overseas. As from September 1977, however, the University of London has ceased to register as new external students those attending full time in polytechnics and other institutions in the public sector of higher and further education, and those who are normally resident overseas. It now directs the external system to those whose occupation or commitments make it impossible to attend regular courses of instruction, or who wish to prepare by primarily home-based study for a relatively specialized degree in a field appropriate to such private study. Many arts subjects are deemed appropriate as well as music, laws, economics and divinity but the offer in general has been much reduced.

Today the wider role is largely taken over by the Council for National Academic Awards (CNAA) which was founded in 1964 by Royal Charter with the authority 'to award degrees and other academic distinctions to students who satisfactorily complete courses approved by the Council in further education institutions other than universities'.[22] These include the polytechnics, the Scottish central institutions and many of the 'major establishments' and colleges of higher education, as well as the Services Staff Colleges. The CNAA has taken care to make sure that its degrees are comparable to those in the universities and it validates courses only after a rigorous examination of the college proposals, the quality of the staff, the general facilities available and the whole educational environment. It offers B.A., B.Sc. and B.Ed. courses, a Diploma in Higher Education and higher degrees, and these awards have bcome generally acceptable throughout the country to industry, the professional institutions and academic bodies. Courses may be full-time, part-time or sandwich, and although there is normally some insistence on minimum entry requirements, mature candidates are judged on their individual merits. On the whole, CNAA courses, especially part-time, have a high proportion of adults over the age of 21; statistics in 1977 from the DES suggested that at that time 95% of people studying part-time for CNAA courses were over 21. Since its establishment, the CNAA has acquired a good deal of power — a course which it refuses to validate, for example, has no real future in a college — and it has come under attack particularly from the polytechnics, some of which would like to award their own degrees in the same way as the universities.

Open College Awards

A further route to a degree has now been opened up in the north-west of England whereby mature students without formal qualifications may take a course of six study units, which on completion is regarded as equivalent to two GCE 'A' levels and hence an entry to appropriate degree courses in the University of Lancaster and in Preston Polytechnic and various other CNAA institutions in the region. These 'Open College' courses were pioneered by Nelson and Colne College, in north-east Lancashire, on the grounds that normal GCE 'A' levels were not appropriate for mature adults, and by 1980 the offer of these courses had spread to eight institutions in the north-west of England. The first two units are introductory, on study techniques and scientific method, and the other four are selected from a variety of options in the arts, sciences and social sciences. Some units provide for home study but otherwise the college part-time courses may be taken during the day or evening to suit the convenience of the student. Personal tuition plays a major part in this form of provision.

Another type of course encouraging mature student entry is the special Certificate in Foundation Studies for Mature Students offered by the New University of Ulster. This one-year course is also recognized as equivalent to two GCE 'A' level passes. Various other interpretations of the words 'Open College' have been put forward from time to time, many exploring ways of making the organization and methods of the Open University effective at sub-degree level. Both the Russell and the Venables committees expressed some support for this kind of development, but there is little evidence so far that central government finance would be available for any of the models put forward. It is also clear that the attempts by some to link the term to the provision for the 16—18-year-old group are likely to be hotly resisted by other educators.

Higher National Diplomas and Certificates

Although being gradually replaced by the new BEC and TEC awards described later in this chapter, courses at advanced level which are still available are the Higher National Diplomas and Certificates (HND and HNC), awarded after the satisfactory completion of courses in subjects concerned particularly with technology, business management and science. HND courses are usually three years in length, taken on a full-time or sandwich basis, with annual internal examinations assessed by an examiner appointed by the relevant professional institution; despite modifications they are still fairly broadly based with an element of general liberal education, and still regarded by many as the best route to membership of a professional body. HNC courses tend to cover less ground, to be based on day-release and evening attendance, and to be controlled rather more by the Regional Examining Boards; nevertheless they still provide a route to professional membership in some industries. In art education, the major advanced course is the Diploma in Art and Design (Dip. A.D.), taken full time for three years, and regarded as equivalent to a university first degree course. Some professional bodies such as the Institution of Civil Engineers set their own examinations for various levels of qualifications and many LEA colleges provide advanced courses leading to these as well as to CNAA awards and their own diplomas and certificates.

Ordinary National Diplomas and Certificates

In 'non-advanced' work the Ordinary National Diplomas and Certificates (OND and ONC) have for some time offered qualifications regarded as equivalent of GCE 'A' level. Administered by Joint Committees representing education departments, college staff and professional institutions, they provide alternative routes, ONDs being normally obtained after a two-year full-time or sandwich course, and ONCs after a two or three-year part-time day or evening course. These awards, too, are being progressively replaced by the newer TEC and BEC awards.

City and Guilds and Royal Society of Arts awards

Awards are also offered by the City and Guilds of London Institute (CGLI), an independent organization created in 1880 and now a major examining body offering examinations in over 300 subjects, particularly for craftsmen in the fields of engineering and applied sciences. The number of students has increased rapidly in recent decades rising from about 30,000 in the late 1940s to nearly 500,000 in 1980. City and Guilds courses account for about a quarter of all college enrolments and in some areas have an even larger share. The majority of students are part time, many on day release, but the awards allow for different modes of attendance and for varying periods of study. In recent years there have been variations in the use of each type of course; on the whole there has been a decline in the City and Guilds share of the day-release and evening-only modes but some rise in the percentage taking full-time and sandwich modes. This may indicate a permanent trend, although as yet the preponderance of part-time study is still clear. Although City and Guilds offers advanced awards — a few people hold its Insignia Award which is based on experience, a good record of achievement and responsibility in industry, and the satisfactory completion of a thesis — the typical student is a young apprentice taking one of the fairly low-level courses which, although varied, may be regarded as the staple diet for operatives and craftsmen. The CGLI is self-financing from the fees it charges for its services and from the subscriptions it receives from industrial companies and other organizations which give it support. Up to 1980 it provided administrative services for TEC and BEC, but a decision was then taken for total separation. City and Guilds technician courses in the whole of Britain are being withdrawn on the introduction of appropriate TEC or SCOTEC programmes and awards to replace them but all other courses, especially those for craftsmen, continue, as well as those for technicians in overseas countries.

Another example of an independent examining body is the Royal Society of Arts (RSA), founded originally in the eighteenth century. This has come to be most important in the field of commerce, offering a network of examination and certificates in almost every aspect of business life. An example is the Private Secretary's Certificate, introduced in 1965, which can then lead to the Private Secretary's Diploma, a professional qualification for secretaries at top management level. Like the CGLI, the RSA sets national examinations, for which each year there are up to 600,000 subject entries.

Professional bodies and regional examining boards

In technology, science and commerce there are more than 150 professional organizations concerned with the maintenance of standards within their particular field, with the regulation of recruitment, and with the levels and characteristics of training. About half act as examining bodies, some, such as the Radio and Television Retailers Association, conducting their own examinations, while others exercise a considerable influence on the LEA colleges offering professional courses. As already noted, the latter must normally seek approval from the professional organizations for both courses and examinations leading to membership. Many professional bodies impose stringent requirements, typical examples being the various engineering institutes such as the Institution of Electrical Engineers (IEE) and the Royal Institute of British Architects (RIBA). There are also six Regional Examining Boards in England and Wales, such as the Union of Educational Institutions (UEI) based on Birmingham, and the Northern Counties Technical Examinations Council. They offer examinations in many subjects, mainly at non-advanced level.

TEC, BEC, SCOTEC and SCOTBEC

Over the years, therefore, a wide range of awards has grown up, some provided by colleges, some by independent national organizations, some by joint committees of interested parties, some by single professional bodies and some by statutory central organizations. From time to time attempts have been made to rationalize the range of courses and awards, and to reduce, by some degree of co-ordination, the competition for students and the apparent waste of effort. As early as 1933 an agreement was concluded between the Board of Education, the CGLI and the existing Regional Examining Unions which tried to achieve this objective, but it became increasingly ineffective. A further attempt in 1955 established a Standing Committee of Technical Examining Bodies which later became the Council of Technical Examining Bodies (CTEB). This has been able to perform some useful work and in 1980 announced an agreement to establish a unified national examination system for craft and operative further education as part of the work of the CGLI.

The major attempt so far to rationalize technician training came from the 1969 report of the Haslegrave Committee[23] which led to the establishment of four special councils: The Technician Education Council (TEC) and the Business Education Council (BEC) for England and Wales and their Scottish counterparts, SCOTEC and SCOTBEC.

TEC was founded in 1973 with the appointment of the twenty-five members of Council. Later it set up various advisory panels and twenty-two 'programme committees' for particular subject areas such as printing and electrical engineering. Trying to create a unified national system of studies under the umbrella of one council in place of what the Haslegrave Committee deplored as a 'bewildering proliferation', it has introduced a single structure of awards — the certificate and higher certificate, diploma and higher diploma — based on a flexible programme or scheme of study, and a unit credit system. TEC awards can, in fact, be obtained through a variety of modes of attendance; as the council declared soon after its establishment: 'It will be possible to obtain a TEC award through full-time, sandwich, block-release or evening study, or by a combination of more than one of these modes. There will also be opportunities for students who cannot study regularly in a college to obtain an award.' The council has been anxious to involve the colleges and their staffs, and also industry, in the planning of the units and of the whole programme. Its efforts, however, have produced many protests from college staff about the extra work involved, and about the enforced reorganization of many college programmes. However, in contrast to the old system of planning by an outside agency, the colleges have been encouraged to develop initiatives and ideas of their own within a broad framework of TEC guidelines, so that there can be both flexibility and the chance of innovation. Ultimately it is anticipated that all existing schemes for technician education will be entirely replaced by those of TEC and SCOTEC, and that a simplified national system of awards, recognized by all industrial employers, will upgrade the status of the technician in society.

The Business Education Councils, set up in May 1974, have tended to follow a more traditional approach relying more on a centrally devised code curriculum and some national examinations. Three levels of qualifications, compared to the two for TEC, have been put forward: a 'General' Certificate (one year part-time) or Diploma (one year full-time or two years part-time); a 'National' Certificate (two years part-time) or Diploma (two years full-time or three years part-time); and a 'Higher National' Certificate (two years part-time) or Diploma (two years full-time or three years part-time). On the whole close links have been established with the Industrial Training Boards and with the Training Services Division of the Manpower Services Commission. In association with the Educational Authorities and the Development Board of the Highlands and Islands, SCOTBEC has set up a Directed Private Study Scheme for students living more than a reasonable travelling distance from a college of further education.

Regional Advisory Councils

How far the schemes of the business and technician education councils can be expanded and improved depends very much on the resources made available. A somewhat different approach to the problem of duplication has been to deal with it through some kind of regional planning. The industrial regions of the country were the first to be involved but since the Second World War, a full network of regional councils has been established for all parts. These bodies will be discussed more fully in a later chapter but it should be noted here that they have played a major part in attempting to bring some degree of rationalization to the provision of work-related education within their area, establishing appropriate committees, and generally planning both the amount and location of courses in some detail. By advice and by arranging contact, many local conflicts of divergent interests have been resolved.

As for the provision of work-related education in general, the provision of examinations is thus a great mixture of ventures. Old and new live side by side, and attempts at rationalization often seem to meet with severe resistance. The central government in Britain has been reluctant to follow many other European countries in passing laws which would give the provision more shape and equity. Despite all the range of courses, the major problem is that there are still gaps in the pattern. It is not merely that over 30% of the population never take an examination but that large sections never get a real chance to do so.

References

1. Ministry of Education Pamphlet no. 8 *Further Education,* 1947, HMSO, para. 21.
2. Department of Education and Science. *Continuing Education: Post-Experience Vocational Provision for Those in Employment.* A Paper for Discussion, 1980.
3. Ministry of Labour and National Service, *Training for Skill: Recruitment and Training of Young Workers in Industry,* 1958, HMSO. (The Carr Report.)
4. Central Advisory Council for Education (England), *15 to 18,* 1959, HMSO. (The Crowther Report.)
5. Department of Education and Science, *Day Release,* 1964, HMSO. (The Henniker-Heaton Report.)
6. Department of Employment, *Training for the Future,* 1972, HMSO. (The Carr Report.)
7. See THORNTON, A.H. and BAYLISS, F.J. *Adult Education and the Industrial Community,* 1965, NIAE.
8. Department of Trade and Industry. *Report of the Committee of Inquiry on Industrial Democracy,* 1977, HMSO, Cmnd 6706. (The Bullock Report.)
9. There has been comparatively little research in this area but for the most recent information see the work carried out by WILLIAMS, G. and WOODHALL, M. and published in *Independent Further Education,* 1979, Policy Studies Institute, to which the following paragraphs owe a considerable debt.
10. See WISEMAN, J. 'Proprietary school education in the United Kingdom' in OECD *Learning Opportunities for Adults, Vol. IV, Participation in Adult Education,* 1977, OECD, Paris.
11. See WOODHALL, M. 'Adult education and training; an estimate of the volume and costs', also in OECD *Learning Opportunities for Adults, Vol. IV,* 1977.
12. *Report of the Prime Minister's Committee on Higher Education* 1963, HMSO, Cmnd 2154. (The Robbins Report.)
13. Department of Education and Science, *A Plan for Polytechnics and Other Colleges: Higher Education in the Further Education System,* 1966, HMSO, Cmnd 3006.

14. Department of Education and Science, *Teacher Education and Training,* 1972, HMSO. (The James Report.)

15. This is the title of Chapter 1 in CANTOR, L. and ROBERTS I.F. *Further Education in England and Wales,* 1969. This was reissued in a revised edition in 1979 with the title *Further Education Today: a Critical Review.*

16. Ministry of Education Pamphlet no. 8 cp. cit., para 27.

17. For details in Scotland see the Scottish Education Department's *Further Education in Scotland: Directory of Day Courses.* Figures are from the 1978–9 edition.

18. *Report of the Advisory Committee on Agricultural Education.* NACEIC, 1966. (The Pilkington Report.)

19. All phrases in the various manuals and handbooks of the services.

20. Home Office Prison Department, *Education in Prisons, Policy Statement* No. 1, 1969, p. 7.

21. See FORSTER, W. *The Higher Education of Prisoners,* 1976, University of Leicester, Vaughan Papers No. 21.

22. See the Charter of the CNAA.

23. This Committee on Technician Courses and Examinations was set up by the National Advisory Council on Education for Industry and Commerce (NACEIC).

CHAPTER 5

Residential and quasi-residential education

Does it matter where adults are accommodated for their education? Over the years there has been much argument about the possible effect of the type of premises housing courses for adults and the controversy continues unresolved. Does accommodation deter or encourage people and if so what features are important? Can it be a handicap or an aid to learning? Practice shows wide differences of approach. In the nineteenth century the providers of many Mechanics Institutes — the centres of adult education at that time — thought that at any rate the outside of the building should be impressive, perhaps even a little pretentious, with Greek columns and porticos, and, as already noted, many impressive new buildings have been erected in recent decades for technical education. But otherwise much of the education of adults was, and still is, housed in borrowed rooms designed for other purposes, often in premises which no one else wants, sometimes indeed in buildings which are half derelict and condemned for other uses. Some believe that 'high thinking' and spartan living go together and they scorn the comfort and amenities of some of the new purpose-built accommodation. They reject the argument eloquently put forward in Cambridgeshire in the 1920s by Henry Morris that the design and beauty of educational buildings profoundly influence the learning process. Few of the providers of education for adults in Britain have so far developed a building programme for non work-related education which even begins to approach that of the recent *Volkshochschule* in the German Federal Republic, or the special adult education buildings of Scandinavia, or the 'palaces of culture' in Eastern Europe, many of which, like the old Mechanics Institutes, occupy key central positions.

One aspect of the argument about accommodation is that concerned with the educational values of residential provision. It has been said that the case for good residential accommodation rests upon three factors, which Donald Garside, former warden of a residential college, listed as 'detachment', 'concentration and continuity' and 'community support'.[1] Removal from the distractions and anxieties of day to day life, helps the learning process, it is said, and the contrast has often been drawn between the adult student in a quiet study bedroom or library of a residential college, and the same student trying to study part time at home, surrounded by children at play, a television or radio on at full volume, and a partner engaged upon domestic chores. Religious retreats and the dominance of collegiate life in the older universities emphasize the asserted value of an atmosphere free from the stresses of the outside world. Undisturbed by the preoccupations of work and home, the adult can concentrate full time on the educational process, and, according to the Russell Report, this 'full-time study makes sustained intellectual demands and . . . produces much more rapid intellectual growth than is possible under conditions of part-time study'.[2] With books and other resources always at hand, it is said that the student has more time for assimilation and integration, for the development of a sense of proportion and perspective. Moreover, help comes from living in a learning community where common problems are shared, and where the sense of fellowship and habits of intelligent co-operation prevail. The argument often then develops with a double stress. First, it declares that close social contact breaks down barriers and removes prejudices, much value being placed on the opportunities to mix together, socially as well as educationally, people from different occupations, social backgrounds, ethnic groups etc. Second, it stresses the importance of congenial and agreeable surroundings, an environment which is 'stimulating', 'civilized and studious' according to the brochures. At a quite early date Harold Hunter wrote of the value of 'the social experience of living in gracious surroundings while mingling with representatives of different walks of life'.[3] With gardens, pictures, music and a corporate life, 'the dye sinks deeper and takes a more lasting hold', said Sir Richard Livingstone[4] about the Danish Folk High Schools, and much has been made of the value of even a short period of residence in inducing change, stimulating new interests and leading people to a more prolonged educational effort. It is also said that new methods become much more possible, especially those which allow for experiential learning. Finally, it is argued that only in a residential situation can there develop the close personal tutorial guidance, the unhurried, friendly encounter of mind with mind in an informal setting, through which adults can reach greater maturity and personal development. The reduction of tensions allows greater learning to be achieved. 'There is nothing more important than adult education,' said Livingstone[5] 'and the residential colleges are the most effective form of it.'

The problem, however, is that so far there has been no conclusive proof of these assertions, based on research evidence. Almost everyone associated with residential provision is tempted to agree with the case put in the previous paragraph, but many would like more definite evidence of its effectiveness in educational as well as financial terms. Even so stalwart a supporter as Ross Waller declared that colleges 'cost a great deal in money and effort, and are only justified in the degree to which they are socially useful and relevant'.[6] Residential education for adults certainly appears to be relatively expensive, and in times of inflation, the costs of food, property maintenance and domestic services are major problems. Faced with rising costs, the value of a graceful environment has been questioned, as has the whole concept of full-time residence in special premises: is this now outdated, irrelevant to modern needs, and portraying an image of an exclusive society in which ordinary people cannot really share, and to which they feel considerable antipathy? It has also been argued that withdrawal can mean a dichotomy between ordinary life and study which tends to make the education received somewhat unreal. There is some evidence that lengthy removal from home and family can produce a sort of cultural distance between student and home, and the Ministry of Education in 1947 pointed out that it is 'a serious step . . . for a mature man or woman to leave employment for a year to pursue a course of study at a residential college'.[7] As it does not appear possible to envisage bringing the whole family into residence, because of the extra maintenance and facilities required, some potential students reject the opportunity and indeed may feel that just as much learning can be achieved at a local non-residential establishment.

However subjective and unproven the arguments may be, it is nevertheless clear that there has been a widespread growth of residential provision for adults throughout the world, both in the richer countries of Europe and America and in some of the poorer nations of Africa and Asia. Britain, indeed, has tended to lag behind. Scandinavia, for example, with a population less than a third that of Britain, has nearly four hundred residential Folk High Schools; pro rata Scandinavians have almost twice as many *colleges* as the British have *places* for long-term post-school residential education. Similar contrasts can be made with the *Heimvolkshochschule* in Western Germany. In Britain the existing residential provision has come into being in an empirical, haphazard way, with no integrated planning, so that the overall picture today is very patchy. Its origins are extremely mixed. Part of the background lies in the summer schools which the University Extension movement developed from 1888 onwards. These summer schools were taken up with enthusiasm by students of the Workers' Educational Association after its foundation in 1903, and together with ideas drawn from residential undergraduate reading parties, were a main influence on some of the short-term colleges such as Holly Royde (1944) and Wedgwood Memorial College (1945). Some of the long term colleges — Woodbrooke, Fircroft and Avoncroft — took part of their inspiration, however, from the guest houses set up by the Adult School Movement and the Society of Friends from 1897 onwards, and part from the Danish Folk High Schools which had developed in the nineteenth century in accordance with the ideas of Bishop Grundtvig and leaders such as Christen Kold. Impressed by these Folk High Schools, Sir Richard Livingstone made a strong plea in 1941 for the massive growth of a similar provision in Britain, and his famous little book had an important influence on individuals such as Dorian Williams who founded Pendley Manor College, Behrend who pressed for the establishment of Burton Manor College, and the leaders of the Women's Institute movement who created Denman College. The Danish influence, however, has been weaker than in other parts of the world such as the USA and some parts of Africa, and in general, Britain has nothing which strictly compares with the Folk High School. Some of the later British development in fact owes more to wartime educational schemes in H.M. Forces, where experimental residential training courses, sometimes just a weekend in length, became numerous, and where towards the end of the Second World War, Army Formation Colleges were established to help rehabilitation by short residential courses. Residential education for adults has depended for location on the availability of premises, and for the most part it has been the result of chance circumstances and the ideas of a few individuals for whom the colleges were acts of faith.

Long-term colleges

There are nine active long-term colleges in which courses of a year of more in duration are provided for mature students. In order of foundation, they are:

1899 Ruskin
1903 Woodbrooke
1909 Fircroft
1918 Co-operative College
1920 Hillcroft
1921 Plater (formerly the Catholic Workers College)
1927 Coleg Harlech
1937 Newbattle Abbey
1978 Northern College.

(Two earlier long-term colleges have since become inoperative: the Labour College which was founded in 1909 and closed in 1929, and Avoncroft which opened in 1925 and became a short-term college in 1939.)

Each college is unique and few generalizations are valid. The earliest college, Ruskin, was founded in Oxford by two Americans[8] and the aim was declared to be:

> To produce sensible citizens, to give workers in this country a proper and educated grasp of those forces which have tended to make Society what it is, so that they may bring minds thoroughly trained in the evidence of the past to bear upon the great questions of social reform that now confront all sections of society.[9]

The college would enable workers to share in the riches of a liberal higher education, and was to be the central part of a network of 'Ruskin Halls' throughout the country. A student was not expected to 'rise out of his class' but to return to his community and so 'raise through influence or precept, the whole class to which he belongs'. In fact, in the years which followed these statements, many students changed their jobs and did not return to their communities. Some have served the Labour movement as local councillors, Members of Parliament and trade union officials while others have become social workers and teachers of adults. Ex-students include a former Vice-Chancellor of Manchester University, a General Secretary of the TUC, a Minister of Fuel and Power, a Kenyan Minister of Economic Development, a Professor of Industrial Relations and a Malawi Ambassador to West Germany.[10]

Ruskin College today is governed by a Council consisting largely of trade union representatives and it provides a choice of courses designed 'in subject material and method to be suitable for adult students'. In general there are two-year courses leading to College Diplomas in labour studies, development studies, history, literature and social studies. Although independent of the university, the College has made special arrangements to enable students to take the Oxford University Special Diploma in social studies. A further indication of vocational purposes is seen in the College Special Diploma in applied social studies which is recognized by the CCETSW as a full qualification for social workers. There are also one-year programmes of study and at fairly frequent intervals there are four-week advanced courses in trade union studies initiated with the help of the TUC. Since 1919 women have been admitted and there is now usually a total of between 180 and 200 students in residence, including a limited number from overseas. Most of the students are financed by scholarships and grants from trade unions, from the state or local authorities, from charitable trusts, or from the College itself. As with most of the long-term colleges, no formal educational qualifications are required for admission.

Fircroft College owed much in the beginning to a group of leaders in the Adult School Movement who were admirers of the Danish Folk High Schools. One of this group, George Cadbury, eventually gave his house in Birmingham to be the main building of the college and to this have been added additional buildings for student accommodation, an assembly hall etc. The declared purpose was much the same as that of the early Ruskin College: to enable workers to develop their personal capacities so that they could play a more responsible part in their community, both at work and at home. Founded with this object, with a stress on liberal as distinct from technical studies, the college concentrated on one-year courses, and tended to keep the total number of students relatively low, only expanding reluctantly, under pressure, from thirty to fifty students in the 1960s. Despite the declared objects, many students have used the college for mainly vocational purposes, going on to universities or colleges of education, and changing their jobs usually to work in the social services field. In 1975 there was a dispute between the principal and the students over the manner in which the college was governed and over the use of its funds. This led to much criticism of the trustees and the board of governors, to trade union 'blacking'of the college after the dismissal of tutors, and to the closure of the college for a period of five years.

Fircroft was for men only, but since 1980 has been open to both sexes. The only other single sex residential long-term college is Hillcroft, in Surbiton, which was founded with the aid of a generous benefactor, Thomas Wall, as a 'Residential College for Working Women' over the age of 21. It set out to equip students for a 'fuller and better life', 'to help them broaden their outlook, enrich and develop their personal life and . . . to discover their own capacities for creative work in the community', but in recent years it has tended more and more to concentrate on study designed to help women with new future employment. Most students now move on to new jobs as teachers, librarians, social welfare workers, housing managers or similar occupations.

Another college which set out to meet the needs of working men and women is Plater College in Oxford. Sometimes described as the 'Catholic Ruskin', its concern has been with man as an individual in modern society, and with fitting students for 'responsible positions' in their community. It centres on the Catholic faith and the creation of lay social apostolates, but it takes students from any Christian denomination. It offers one and two-year courses in social sciences with special reference to the social implications of Christianity, and most of the eighty students now take an Oxford University Special Diploma either in social studies or in public and social administration.

One long-term college has been founded in Wales and one in Scotland, but none in Northern Ireland. Founded under the stimulus of Dr Thomas Jones, Coleg Harlech, in Gwynedd, is open to men and women over the age of 21 from all parts of the United Kingdom and overseas. It offers one-year, non-examinable courses in liberal and social studies, but more recently there has developed a two-year course leading to the University of Wales Diploma in general studies, an award generally accepted for university entry. As in the other colleges, some students return to their former work but most go on to further study and a change of job. Even so, the avowed purpose remains that outlined by the late Henry Gethin Lewis, the donor of the original college building: 'to enlarge the vision of its students, to develop their latent capabilities for leadership, and to stimulate their mental and spiritual growth'.[11] Coleg Harlech has become a centre for Welsh culture, the headquarters of Welsh recorded music, and with its well-equipped modern theatre, an arts centre with a varied programme. It also serves as a home for conferences, runs its own summer schools and accommodates educational activities organized by the Workers Educational Association and other bodies. In Scotland there is Newbattle Abbey College where, as at Coleg Harlech, there is a one-year course for 'personal enrichment', although most of the seventy students it accommodates take a two-year Diploma course, in this case in liberal studies which has a variety of options such as history, government and politics, English literature, philosophy, sociology, logic and social and economic policy. The Diploma is being recognized for university entry and the social studies option constitutes a basic social worker's qualification.

The most recent of the long-term colleges is the Northern College which opened with fifty students, and the intention to increase the number to 120 as soon as possible. Very much a response to one of the recommendations made in the Russell Report,[12] the college is housed in Wentworth Castle, and was founded by a consortium of local authorities. These constitute the Council of Management together with the WEA, neighbouring university extra-mural departments, Sheffield City Polytechnic and the TUC Regional Education Committee. Two kinds of courses are offered. First, there are longer courses which lead either to a certificate after one year's study, or to a diploma after two years. These include three options: trade union and industrial studies; local and community studies; gateway and liberal studies — but all students have the same preparatory core course in the first term. Second, the college offers shorter courses of between four and ten weeks in duration for 'men and women who are looking for ways to improve the contribution they can make in the residential or industrial communities where they live or work'. The college has a good library and has developed a research and documentation facility linked especially to questions of a social, economic or trade union nature in South Yorkshire. It has had strong support from the National Union of Mineworkers.

Two colleges stand a little apart from the rest. Woodbrooke, in Bourneville, is a Quaker foundation offering studies in modern religious thought, literature, biblical interpretation, international and social affairs and the beliefs and practices of the Society of Friends. Accommodating sixty-five, it seeks to prepare men and women for 'responsible living' and to provide an opportunity for deepening spiritual life. The other long-term college with very distinctive features is the Co-operative College which was founded in Manchester, and moved to Stanford Hall, near Loughborough, in 1946. Owned and run by the Co-operative movement, it is in many ways the most magnificent of the long-term colleges, surrounded by 300 acres of parkland and possessing a well-equipped theatre, sports fields and swimming pool. It is the apex of Co-operative provision, offering education to all sections of the movement, although most of its work is distinctly vocational and designed for employees in the retail stores. Thus there are the Diplomas as already described, especially in the areas of Co-operative development, administration and management. The hundred or so students, mostly in their twenties and thirties, include some officials from the Co-operative movements in the developing countries for whom special courses are arranged. Besides the long-term career development courses for managers, directors and secretaries, there are short courses of members' education, designed to improve the quality of co-operative democracy and consumer affairs, and some 'short intensive courses' on subjects such as various specialized aspects of retail management.

In all their diversity, these colleges offer fewer than 700 places and advertise little for fear of being overwhelmed by a demand they could not hope to satisfy. In 1969, for example, it was estimated that the potential demand was a 'pool' of 170,000 with an annual addition of probably 7,000 potential new recruits,[13] a situation which gives weight to the view that there is a considerable reservoir of untapped educational ability. Each college is an independent institution governed by a Board which may well represent many divergent interests, and each has developed in its own unique way. Most of them began with inadequate accommodation, but by a process of conversion and acquisition have developed ways of satisfying their needs for larger and better libraries, adequate common rooms, individual study—bedrooms and sports facilities. After the development plans of the 1960s, most increased the size of their annual intake. Even so, they usually have to reject about two-thirds of all applicants using a selection process which each college devises independently. None require formal entry qualifications but most look for evidence of classes attended or voluntary activities undertaken, and some ask for an essay, as well as an interview and written support from an evening class tutor. Once accepted by a college, a student becomes eligible for grants from central government and in some cases from local authorities, and in addition there are a number of bursaries from trade unions or other agencies and also support from charitable trusts.

In this 'alternative route for the adult late developers', as the Russell Report described the colleges, the value of a place in college depends very much on the character and experience of the students. Some find it difficult to acquire the habits of self-control needed in independent study, despite the aid of seminars and private tuition. Some enter with problems of self-expression, although many active in trade unions and other organizations may be very practised in public speaking. There is a lot of flexibility within many of the courses, as well as a great variety of informal activities and some may find this type of freedom a bewildering problem. On the other hand, as indicated earlier, there has been a growth of examination-based Diplomas and other awards which may restrict freedom of choice, while at the same time providing a stepping stone to a change of occupation. This tendency to provide more and more work-related study has been seen as a threat to the earlier objectives of a liberal education and a challenge to the underlying philosophy of the colleges. They are sometimes accused of seeking to impose the value systems of the upper middle class or of becoming mere appendages of the universities, or of being grossly out of date in their approach and methods. There is also some danger that students may be overstretched or face personal problems which may result in broken marriages or alienation from old associates. It has been said that a person who fails to survive the college course may well become a kind of stateless person, unable to proceed to a new job, yet finding great difficulty in getting back to his old one. Most students, however, do survive and make the change to new jobs, proceeding perhaps first to a university or other college or institution. In view of the difficulties of leaving home and family, there would seem to be some need to experiment rather more with combinations of residential education and local courses. As it is there is plenty of evidence of an impressive record of achievement, of the many ex-students who have gone on to make important contributions to society. Those attending are now linked in the Mature Students Union (MSU) founded in 1974 by students in the colleges to promote the particular interests of all mature students. By 1979 the Union had affiliations from over a hundred organizations.

Short-term colleges

It is easier, of course, for people to get away for shorter periods, and since 1944 there have developed many colleges offering courses as short as one or two weeks, or just a weekend, with an occasional course of two or three months in duration. By the end of the 1970s there were about fifty of these colleges in England and Wales, but none in Scotland or Northern Ireland. These are even more varied than the long-term colleges. Many owe their location to the availability of large country houses which, because of such factors as rising costs of upkeep, the difficulty of getting servants and increased death duties have proved to be no longer viable for private use. England was perhaps particularly lucky in having a good number of these manor houses and halls which just after the Second World War could be bought at a low price and converted for use in the education of adults. Some suffered from dry rot and structural weaknesses and in the early days they were somewhat austere, but by the early 1970s most of the new owners had tackled these problems, added lecture and common rooms, put in central heating and interior sprung mattresses, and built up sizeable collections of audio-visual equipment. As students showed a more and more marked preference for single study—bedrooms, most colleges attempted to make provision for these either by building new blocks or undertaking sometimes quite massive conversions of existing buildings, outhouses and stables. Some, however, were defeated, in part at least, by the very large rooms in old manor houses. The struggle for a bar in some instances took longer to resolve but in most colleges this is now accepted despite the disapproval of the more puritanical governors who believe that alcohol and education do not mix. All the colleges now seem to put much emphasis on their amenities; 'The utmost comfort in accommodation, excellent food,' says Burton Manor; 'We pride ourselves on our cuisine,' says a brochure of the Lancashire College, and the general theme is perhaps summed up in an advertising phrase from Holly Royde: 'Welcoming, friendly, sociable.' Although in size they vary from those taking two dozen people to those housing at least eighty, they clearly seek to offer all that a very good hotel can offer, a feature which makes them considerably different from much of the other educational accommodation available to adults. Perhaps the most magnificently appointed is Denman College, where

74

the owners, the National Federation of Women's Institutes, called upon their County Federations to provide the furnishings.

A few of the colleges are privately owned either by individuals or by voluntary organizations, a handful belong to universities, but most now are in the possession of local education authorities, sometimes in combination with each other or with voluntary agencies. At one period in the 1960s it seemed as though there was a fashion that encouraged every self-respecting local authority to have a short-term residential college. Perhaps in the financially more difficult days of the late 1970s, they came to wish that they had not taken on so costly a venture, but despite the rising fuel, food and labour costs, most authorities seem to take considerable pride in their colleges. Their views on financial questions are reflected in the very variable fees they charge for courses and in the number of bursaries they offer to assist students. They are also seen in the attitude to new buildings, the Lancashire authority being the first to create a purpose-built college which opened in Chorley in 1975. The earliest of these short-term colleges is Holly Royde owned by the University of Manchester and administered by the University Extra-Mural Department. Opened in 1944 and although now with considerable additions, the centre of Holly Royde is still a nineteenth-century merchant's house set in five acres of land well within the city boundaries. It drew a great deal on the inspiration of Ross Waller, the Director of Extra-Mural Studies, who in 1938 founded the Lamb Guildhouse with a group of people who believed in the value of weekend residential education for adults. This association put all its assets into Holly Royde when the college opened even though its use in the early years was mainly for Services education.

Most wardens, or 'principals' as they may be entitled, tend to stress the importance of liberal education as the paramount feature of their colleges. At an early date, however, it proved relatively easy to fill the colleges with non-vocational liberal courses at weekends, but very difficult to do so during the week. At the same time, it became clear that to be economically viable at all the colleges had to be full all the time, seven days a week and for as many weeks as possible each year. The empirical, unplanned answer which emerged was to hold work-related courses from Monday to Friday and to build up a series of regular closed or sponsored courses, arranged by a great variety of organizations for their own members or employees. Examples are courses for supervisors in Marks and Spencers, employees of the UK Atomic Energy Authority, Inland Revenue Staff, those working in the Health or Social Service departments of local authorities and for teachers, magistrates, midwives, the police, caretakers, librarians and social workers of all kinds. Usually the structure and methods of these courses are arranged jointly with the warden. Some are induction courses requiring little previous knowledge but others are advanced courses designed for specialists in industry or the professions and demanding a high level of vocational knowledge and experience. The liberal, non-vocational courses, when held, are open to everyone, 'irrespective of age, experience, education or background' as the advertising brochure for Burton Manor put it in 1978. The same publication went on to say: 'We try to offer something for everyone . . . courses in the arts, crafts, music, languages, antiques, bridge, radio and television, history, beauty care, folk and ballroom dancing – and much more.' The balance of subject area varies from college to college but all have a very wide range, as a glance at the index of the half-yearly *Calendar of Residential Courses* clearly shows.[14] The subjects offered in each college are a reflection of the interests of the staff, of any specific purposes which the college may have been created to serve and of the nature and problems of the region around it. As may be expected, the weekend courses attract a very varied selection of students who come with many different motives: some obviously want to learn more about a subject, while others look more to the enjoyment of meeting people with similar interests, and exchanging ideas, views and experiences. Many indeed appear not to have been previously associated with other forms of education for adults. An indication of the total numbers involved each year was given in the Russell Report as 48,500 in courses of less than three days and about 18,000 in courses of four to six days, but there are considerable variations year by year. The costs of the courses are also very variable. Some colleges have charges not very different from those of a good hotel; some are well below; some are heavily subsidized from the rates while others may notionally be expected to meet at least all the non-academic costs from student fees. Whereas students on the work-related courses are likely to have all costs reimbursed, students on other courses may have to pay the full fee themselves. Even so, at the present time, very few fees seem to approach the full economic cost.

One method of keeping the cost down has been to employ only a minimum of full-time staff. In some colleges there is only a warden and one or two secretarial workers; others add a vice-warden, and perhaps one or two full-time tutors or lecturers, but most of the tuition is carried out by part-time teachers appointed for specific courses. Although often a local or national expert, the 'guest teacher' who comes in for a single session or a half day may find it difficult to integrate with the rest of the course despite the efforts of most course directors. Students are not now expected, as in the early days of Ruskin College, to prepare their own food but they may well be expected to make their own beds and to help the skeleton domestic staff keep the place tidy. The wardens, especially those of the first generation, come from very many different walks of life. Among them have been a pre-war advertising manager, a wartime army commander-in-chief, a former production engineer and a retired inspector of factories. In the early life of most colleges separate living quarters were not available, which tended to mean that the warden was on call and accessible throughout the twenty-four hours of each day. Even with separate living accommodation it is difficult for wardens to get away from student needs and, indeed, as many of them have an almost proprietorial and paternal concern for the college, they do not always wish to do so. Their paramount concern is to stimulate the social and leisure life of the community and as 'mine host' or even the new 'lord of the manor' they press forward with special drama performances, music recitals and arts festivals as well as the high pressure development of courses. The wardens meet together in the Association of Principals of Short-Term Residential Colleges, just as most of the heads of the long-term colleges meet in the Residential Colleges Committee.

Summer schools

Besides the increase in the number of short-term colleges in the decades after the Second World War, there was also a proliferation of summer schools, usually in hired premises. Those of the University Extension movement in the 1880s and 1890s were an inspiration for the development of residential education in general and the universities and the Workers Educational Association, jointly or separately are still the largest providers. Most of their summer schools are held in university or college buildings and follow a programme in which the students meet in relatively small tutorial groups for part of each day, have periods available for private study, field expeditions or recreation, and come together as a whole school for occasional general lectures, social activities and other activities such as music recitals designed to enrich the experience. Courses tend to be one week in duration and before the summer school takes place the teachers may suggest appropriate course reading and written work, and may sometimes hold a collective meeting of intending course members. A few summer schools are open only to those who have been following a course of study such as, for example, a University of London Extension course leading to a Diploma. The theme, however, is generally enrichment rather than examinations, and the summer school is often viewed as part holiday as well as part study. This is particularly true of summer schools held overseas but organized by the universities, the WEA or other organizations. Examples are the Manchester course in Salzburg at the time of the music festival, an Edinburgh study of the palaces of Russia and a Glasgow study tour of the Isle of Man. In Scotland, special summer school courses are linked to the Edinburgh Festival and there is perhaps a tendency to give more stress to the history, geography, geology and language of Scotland. Another major provider has been the British Council which has organized summer schools for overseas doctors, librarians, social workers and especially for foreign teachers of English. Individual trade unions, as well as owning colleges, have also developed regular summer schools reputed to be more hard-working than most. Local education authorities have been more concerned with short-term residential colleges than with summer schools, but one important exception has been the Glamorgan Summer School in Barry, South Wales, which held its sixty-sixth meeting in 1979. This provides a wide range of fortnight-long courses particularly in arts and crafts, and in drama and music, but including some languages and sports such as swimming and sailing. A special feature is refresher training for teachers of non-vocational adult classes. The school has an international flavour, being open to those from overseas as well as from the whole of Britain. Accommodation is provided in the polytechnic and in colleges, schools and hostels in the locality, and there is a vigorous social programme.

Residential education for adults in the form of summer, Easter or winter schools or 'weekend' schools now has a great variety of sponsors as may be seen by the following examples. The churches provide not only religious retreats but summer camps and short courses throughout the year. Industry and the trade unions have also seized the opportunities of relatively cheap accommodation provided by many holiday hotels during the off-peak season. Provision is also made by a great variety of voluntary agencies, examples being the International Folk Dance Society, the Historical Association, the Rural Music Schools Association, the Central Council for Physical Education and the Highland Association *(An Comunn Gaidhealach)*. In some of these the only central focus is the main meeting place, with classes perhaps scattered in a variety of premises and members sleeping in tents, lodging houses or hotels, an arrangement which may perhaps be described as 'quasi-residential'. This is a long way from the closed community of an isolated residential college but carries, nevertheless, something of the detachment, concentration of effort and community support to which Garside referred. Some, of course, have moved on to the provision of more permanent residential accommodation, which they own and run as conference or study centres without a permanent staff other than a caretaker and perhaps part-time domestic workers. Each course then brings its own director of studies.

Field studies

A distinctive type of provision is made by the Field Studies Council, which was created in 1943. This manages Field Study Centres in a number of locations in England and Wales. Most of the courses are one week in length and there are some weekend courses, all designed to provide opportunities for the study of various aspects of the outdoor environment, the subjects ranging from geology, geography and biology to local history and landscape painting. Each centre has a Warden—Director of Studies, usually a graduate and well versed in local knowledge, and he or she is supported by expert tutors as well as by administrative and domestic staff. Most of the courses welcome beginners and there are special family courses with reduced prices for children under the age of 13. There are also some specialist courses for teachers with a strong emphasis on field techniques and teaching methods, and some courses particularly suitable for the disabled. Stressing the promotion of a better understanding of the environment, the centres also provide working facilities and expert guidance for school parties, college students and individual naturalists and artists whether or not they attend the organized courses. A recognized charity, the Council depends on membership subscriptions and on fees charged for the courses and the other services they provide. In Scotland, the Scottish Field Studies Association seeks to offer similar opportunities and gets some contribution from the Scottish Education Department and local authorities. It maintains one residential field centre at Kindrogan in Perthshire where there is accommodation for up to sixty students in a large country house and there are excellent facilities for the study of many types of habitat. The Association also runs courses in other parts of Scotland, notably at Lamlash on the Isle of Arran and at Millport on the Isle of Cumbrae. A later development has been the rise of residential study centres in the National Parks, the first four being in Snowdonia, the Brecon Beacons, the Peak District and the Yorkshire Dales. Courses are usually short, a weekend or four days being common, and the subjects of study include geology, industrial archaeology, botany, painting, caving (where possible, as at Whernside Manor in the Dales), farming and forestry.

Study holidays

'Study holidays' and 'study tours' are now popular phrases. As early as 1899 the CHA , then the Co-operative Holidays Association and now the Country-wide Holidays Association, was developing guest houses which combined recreational and social aims with the provision of 'facilities to busy men and women for continuing their education throughout life'.[15] Stemming from a church rambling club in Colne, Lancashire, the arrangement of daily excursions outdoors has continued, although the earlier stress on the provision of direct teaching by invited lecturers has tended to be much reduced. It could be said that personal development rather than cognitive learning has become much more important and that 'learning by doing', by having an experience in common with others on an equal footing, is today more valuable. This would certainly be echoed by a later organization, the Holiday Fellowship, also founded by T.L. Leonard, which in its title picks out the companionship, the 'fellowship', the 'learning to live together', which has been a central feature of much of British liberal education for adults. Other developments of study tours and holidays include cruises particularly in the Mediterranean with guest lecturers on board. There appears to be a growing commercial interest in the idea of selling residential 'holiday courses' for profit, in itself an indication of growing public support. This carries some risk of exploitation, but is a development not to be ignored in a world in which holiday camps, such as those of Butlins and Pontins, have a considerable impact on the outlook and attitudes of many people who do not attend the more formal educational classes.

Conferences

Within the wide spectrum of residential education for adults we should also include the residential conferences which have been growing in number in recent decades and are concerned with almost any aspect of life in the community. With their series of talks and discussions, together with the array of audio-visual aids which are often a vital part of the proceedings, it is difficult to distinguish them from the short courses in the residential colleges. Part of the problem of accommodation for the education of adults seems to be met by the offer of spare rooms in universities and other institutions during vacations, and by hotels which in some cases have come to depend for survival on 'conferencing'. This development is underlined by the growing number of advertisements by hotel proprietors, including British Rail, which draw attention to the availability on their premises of 'quiet, well-lighted, conference rooms'.

Other residential provision

As early as 1949 there were proposals in the Church of England for residential colleges but most development has taken the form of residential Diocesan Centres which are used by special groups. A notable development in church provision has been the work of Luton Industrial College, established in 1957 by the Methodist Church as a lay training centre designed to assist its mission to technology, industry and commerce. This is a well-equipped college with fifty-one study—bedrooms, two lecture halls, library, refectories and college chapel. The Church of Scotland runs full-time one-year residential courses at St Colm's College, Edinburgh, and St Ninian's Training Centre, Crieff, for people who wish to study and examine their Christian faith at a level that shorter local courses are unable to reach. These do not, however, qualify people for any particular sphere of Christian service. In Sheffield, the Urban Theology Unit has a one-year course for graduates who wish to relate their theoretical knowledge of sociology or religious studies to a practical situation and also arranges short residential courses of from three days to two weeks in length on a variety of subjects including theology, community studies, international affairs, participation techniques and politics. Political parties have also developed an interest in residential opportunities. Besides the Liberal Party Summer School, perhaps the most noteworthy example is at Ashridge where the Conservative Party's 'Bonar Law College of Citizenship' ran short courses from 1928–39. In 1946 it reopened as a short-term residential college and now, as 'Ashridge Management College', it offers a series of management development courses for all levels of manager, as well as some specialist courses in subjects such as industrial relations and marketing.

The future of residential education

Various questions have to be asked concerning the future of residential education in Britain. Do we need more colleges of either a long-term or a short-term nature? Partly it would seem that the answer depends upon an assessment of the balance between the advantages and possible disadvantages of this form of education, and partly upon the willingness of people to avail themselves of the opportunities so offered. Some of the problems of the long-term colleges have been discussed earlier and perhaps it is now the short-term college which receives most of the criticism in Britain. Besides the difficult question of cost, there are assertions that the courses are shallow and too short to allow for systematic study, that they lack coherence, and that despite the euphoria sometimes engendered, they fail to achieve any enduring worthwhile educational result. Against this, there is some subjective, though substantial, evidence that residence makes a significant impact on the development of interests and awareness, and that even a short absence from home and work 'can effect quite remarkable learning and attitude changes'.[16] There are no short cuts to learning and perhaps an enjoyable weekend makes it seem too easy, but, as noted earlier, a relaxed atmosphere helps to reduce emotional barriers to learning. This kind of relaxed, face-to-face, understanding atmosphere is what the colleges are supremely able to create and, with a full-time educational staff, they can claim to be more conducive to learning than most hotels or other hired premises.

The willingness of people to come depends basically on their expectations and their individual assessment of the value of the experience. If sent by employers on a work-related course, their reports may well influence future use or non-use of the provision. If the course is not work-related, the response may be conditioned by the length of the average holiday and by the reaction of the rest of the family as well as by the cost. Earlier in the century the generally low pay and lack of holidays made attendance at non work-related courses difficult if not impossible for most of the population. With greater affluence and with lengthening holidays and non-work time, the demand for residential education might increase and it is possible to envisage regular study leave in a residential setting becoming more of a norm. An increase in the provision for the whole family might help development. Some experiments have already been made in a few 'family summer schools' and special 'family courses' in colleges, and it is of course a feature of the holiday camps, but Britain has given far less attention to family education than, for example, France with its residential courses provided by the *Confédération Nationale de la Famille Rurale,* the *Ecole des Parents* and the *Union Féminine Civique et Sociale.*

Other questions relate more to physical conditions. Is there, for example, an optimum size for a college or any other kind of residential provision? In view of the possible alienating effects of luxurious premises and their rising costs, should consideration once again be given to the provision of rather more spartan conditions for residential education? Or have the British now become too accustomed to a higher degree of comfort and amenities? Would it be enough just to add residential wings to technical colleges, colleges of higher education and similar existing institutions, some of which have already inherited some residences from the old colleges of education? Or should future development be only in purpose-built or specially adapted separate accommodation?

Would the value of short-term residence be improved by devising consecutive series of courses, perhaps in the form of linked but spaced weekends or midweek periods — a rather different kind of 'sandwich' course? If the short-term residential courses are only 'a hostel along the way, a temporary stopping off place'[17] should not there be greater attempts to integrate them with surrounding non-residential work? Perhaps in this way, they could become a great stimulus to all local educational endeavours and to the general involvement of the population. In view of the wider Scandinavian response to their Folk High Schools, by what methods can the majority of the British public be led at least to taste the existing possibilities? Or should residential education in Britain be reserved for those in some position of leadership on the grounds that it is too expensive a tool for general use?

In many ways it would appear that fully-planned, intensive learning experiences which only briefly interrupt the normal job and family commitments, can with great advantage follow or be interwoven with other forms of study. In the United States a rigorous in depth 'conference course' model has been developed for those taking external degrees, and in Britain the Summer Schools of the Open University provide a further example. On the other hand, some would suggest that there is an important place for a special separate, if short, residential course to meet particular individual needs unrelated to other course of study. How much autonomy should colleges, and their wardens, have in making their own estimates of what is required and in controlling their own affairs? Finance no doubt determines the answer in part and there is the general question about the amount of subsidy, if any, which should be made; some advocate a heavy subsidy while others believe that charges should be increased at least to keep pace with rising costs and rising expectations. If the latter course of action is followed, will it accentuate the existing tendency to have a mainly middle-class clientele?

It would seem that so far no clear answer to these questions has been given in Britain and that people have been content to let the development drift, therefore running the risk of collapse under the strains of uneven demand, overworked staff and *ad hoc* expediency. The greatest danger in the early 1980s however, would seem to be the threat of closure on simple financial grounds. LEAs looking for economies in their educational budgets find it difficult to resist the temptation to remove a provision which seems inevitably expensive, and inflation has put a severe strain on those owned by private individuals or charities. Not much saving can be made on the already skeleton staff and there are limits to cuts in ancillary staff or educational material. High 'economic' fees would also destroy the purposes for which many were established. The colleges are, however, a national asset which, if destroyed, would be hard to replace.

References

1. GARSIDE, D. 'Short-term residential colleges: their origins and value' *Studies in Adult Education,* I/1, April 1969, p. 27.

2. Russell Report, para 250.

3. HUNTER, H. 'Residential adult education I – a new field reviewed' *Times Educational Supplement,* 1 July 1949, p. 445.

4. Livingstone, R. *The Future in Education,* pp. 50–51. This was a famous seminal little book published in 1941 by CUP, reprinted three times in 1941, twice in 1942, and thereafter in 1943, 1944, 1945 and 1949.

5. Ibid.

6. WALLER, R.D. in *Holly Royde, 1944–65: Thoughts on the Occasion of its Twenty-First Anniversary,* 1965, Holly Royde College.

7. Ministry of Education Pamphlet no. 8. *Further Education* 1947, HMSO, para 149.

8. Walter Vrooman and Charles Beard. Both had come to study at Oxford University and both had contacts with radical movements. See YORKE, P. *Ruskin College,* 1899–1909 (1977).

9. *Ruskin Hall News and Students Magazine,* Vol. I, No. 1, Dec. 1899.

10. Sir William Mansfield Cooper, George Woodcock, Sir Richard Marsh, Tom Mboya, Tom Lupton, T.S. Mangwuzu.

11. See the *Prospectus.*

12. Russell Report, para 255.2, 'Consideration should be given to the establishment of one further college in the northern half of England.'

13. See HOULTON, R. 'A cause for concern' in *Residential Adult Education – Values, Policies and Problems,* 1978, Society of Industrial Tutors.

14. Published by the National Institute for Adult Education (England and Wales) this quickly became almost a 'best seller' reflecting the amount of interest in this type of provision. The Scottish Institute of Adult Education published *Stay and Study in Scotland,* the last issue of which appeared in 1979.

15. SADLER, M.E. *Continuation Schools in England and Elsewhere,* 1908, Manchester University Press, p. 96.

16. Unpublished document by D. GARSIDE, 1974.

17. *Times Educational Supplement,* 7 Sept. 1962, p. 239.

CHAPTER 6

Self-education: home study, distance learning and broadcasting

What seems perhaps to be a complete contrast to the group in a residential college is the isolated individual learning at home in spare moments, interspersed with other activities. Very much surrounded by the affairs of the world, with studies interrupted rather than concentrated and continuous, and lacking the support of fellow learners except possibly that of a spouse or family, the solitary learner is in a quite different environment for education. Yet this individual self-help is without doubt the method by which most adults search for information, advice, ideas or understanding. Exact statistics are, of course, not available, although a Canadian research team led by Allen Tough[1] estimated that in 1977 almost three-quarters of adult learning efforts were initiated and planned by the isolated individual. This 'self-directed' learning may, of course, include choosing to enrol in a class or group, but it is clear that much of it is individualized learning, carried out alone. Very large numbers of people at all economic and social levels, who do not join any form of organized formal education, manage their own learning and development in this way, and it is undoubtedly of greater importance than is usually recognized. Many of these individual learners seem to seek personal help from a very wide range of people besides teachers and some would argue that in this way almost everyone becomes a teacher as well as a learner. It can be argued, however, as Tough and his associates suggest, that if people are to develop their full capacity to manage their own learning, they need much more help than they get at present. Moreover, the ability to educate oneself should be the major objective of formal, organized education, and there should be training in the 'tools of study' from an early age. Paul Lengrand, writing about lifelong education[2] declared that one of the two main current responsibilities of education was 'to equip each individual to become in the highest and truest degree both the object and the instrument of his own development through the many forms of self education'.

Books and magazines

Those with the necessary 'know-how' often have private book collections which they can consult, and they have been much helped since the 1930s by the issue of the relatively cheap paperbacks from Penguin Books or from the increasing number of their competitors. Originally sold for as little as six old pence each, these paperbacks still make possible the build-up of a considerable private collection of both reprints and new editions. Their link with the education of adults was consciously in the mind of Allen Lane, the founder of Penguins, and this was seen particularly, for example, in the appointment of W.E. Williams, then Secretary of the British Institute of Adult Education, as one of the advisory editors for the 'Pelicans', the series of authoritative paperback books on a wide range of intellectual interests. These have become a library of modern knowledge at a modest cost, and perhaps have been rather more successful than the bound cheap editions started earlier, such as those of Everyman and the World's Classics. Doubts have been expressed, nevertheless, about the intelligibility of some of the more designedly educational non-fiction paperbacks and certainly only a minority, though a sizeable one, is led to buy them. Far more, however, buy informative periodicals appropriate to their interests. Besides the women's magazines with their vast circulation, there are specialist weekly or monthly publications concerned with trades and professions, religion, sport, various types of 'do-it-yourself' and hobbies such as gardening or photography; in all, over 2,000 regular magazines are available, each containing information, often practical in nature, overt advice and implied values. The person with enough know-how can also buy various series of informative books such as the *Teach Yourself* series. It may be the craftsman wanting specific details, a holiday traveller wanting to learn a little of the language of the country to be visited, the newly married wanting information on household electricity . . . almost every type of information need is catered for, though naturally with varying degrees of success.

The press

In a later chapter specific consideration will be given to the contribution of libraries, art galleries and museums to the education of adults, and it is sufficient here to draw attention to their importance for those who know how to use the facilities for their own self-education. Similarly, the potential educational effects of the press may be briefly noted. The circulation of the national morning and Sunday papers, now nearly a score in number, shows variations year by year but on average is about 15 million. It is estimated that probably between 10% and 15% of the total is obtained by the so-called 'quality' newspapers such as the *Observer, The Times* or the *Guardian,* often regarded as having influence more on the leaders than on the mass of the community. On the educational value of the 'popular' press such as the *Daily Mirror,* the *Sun* or the *Daily Express,* there can be much debate, but it seems unwise to disregard the impact even of such items as the sports pages, the nude pictures, and the comic strips with their not infrequent blend of reality and fantasy. Do they just result in the 'production of adultized children and infantile adults'?[3] Are they a force moulding the attitudes and understanding, the values, ideas and behaviour patterns of many members of the British public? The papers most fully read are, however, the local newspapers. Usually more sizeable than the average national daily, these tend to be more serious in the amount of news and in presentation, and they provide a ready source for those seeking information, comment and ideas about the local scene. There are now over 1,200 with weekly editions as well as about a hundred appearing in the evenings or mornings. Some newspaper men have said that they are not in any sense educators, and draw a sharp distinction between education and supplying information but this is a point of view which many educators do not find tenable. More important perhaps are the questions whether there is any intention to educate in the minds of editors and proprietors, how far the papers are regarded as agents of propaganda, and whether education, however construed, is a conscious motive for readership.

Cinema

Earlier in the century these questions would have been asked about the cinema, then often regarded as a very powerful medium for spreading knowledge and ideas. With the arrival of television, however, the number of cinemas has been sharply reduced and those which remain are thinly attended, the main clientele being young people, and the type of film more concerned with horror or sex or both. Most individuals thus rarely turn deliberately to the commercial cinema for education. On the other hand, they may decide to join a film society, of which there are now nearly five hundred in Britain. These provide opportunities to see films not exhibited in the commercial cinemas, such as old classics and 'art' films mainly from abroad, and to help people to study films and become more discriminating. The activities of these societies are aided by the British Federation of Film Societies which was founded in 1945, and developed as an advisory body, publishing a magazine called *Film* and maintaining a library. It is now linked to the British Film Institute, founded in 1933. With a declared purpose of fostering the study and appreciation of the art of the film, including its use in television, this organization is very much engaged in educational work, publishing periodicals such as *Sight and Sound,* providing lectures, organizing conferences and giving general assistance to students and others. It is also the official national archive depository for television as well as film recordings.

Private Tuition

Some individuals wanting educational aid turn to private teachers. The full statistics are unknown but it seems clear from circumstantial evidence that there is a substantial amount of private coaching in sports such as golf, in languages, music and many other subjects. This tends to be still a feature more of middle class education than of other sectors of the population, but private tuition for the playing of darts or billiards is not unknown in working class circles. Mostly, perhaps, it is the singer or instrument player, the business man wanting concentrated language learning or improvement in the games he plays, or the swimmer, or beginner ballroom dancer. On the whole it is a commodity to be bought except where the tuition is between friends, one more knowledgeable than the other. Following the reductions in local authority provision in the period since 1979, it would appear that there has been a boom in private 'consultancy' as well as in fee-paying classes designed to make profits for the provider.

Postal tuition

In many subjects areas, the individual is much more likely to seek help from postal tuition and in recent years there has been a rapid increase in self-improvement courses. Many of these are concerned with fitness and health, linked often to home exercises, or to better diet habits, but the subject range is in fact very wide. Perhaps the most famous is Dale Carnegie's *How to Win Friends and Influence People,* a course which world-wide has been bought by over six million people. Others are concerned with, for example, improving reading speeds, or developing the ability to dance, cook, arrange flowers and make speeches. Some provide not only instructions but also gadgets, tapes or records, the latter being a special feature of language courses. Linguaphone, for example, offers courses in thirty-four different languages, and there are plenty of advertisements stating that 'You can learn French, German, Spanish ... (or any other language) in 30 hours' or in a similarly short time; earlier in the century, the time was often 'three months'. Very many of these commercial courses rest on an assumed human desire for esteem or status; some are so expensive that it would seem much cheaper to get books from the public library; some seem to work very well while others give little satisfaction. In general, in providing a course in terms of a set of instructions, information and printed stimuli, but no tutor, they rely a great deal on self-discipline and on the strength of will brought by the individual. Success depends upon determination and perseverance, a factor in all learning, which is often ignored by the purveyors of these courses which tend to lead people to think that results can be obtained without much effort.

Correspondence courses and colleges

Though still not quite free from this criticism, the major correspondence colleges try to meet it by a full use of tutors. Essentially their correspondence courses consist of batches of study material sent by post to the student who then completes the required reading and exercises, and returns the latter to the college for attention by an appointed personal tutor. The exercises are marked and the student receives comments, advice and general guidance. Thus providing an 'organised provision for instruction and education through the post',[4] the colleges grew separately from the main provision of education, and for a long time they suffered from disapproval and official neglect. The first provision seems to have been in 1840 when Pitman started teaching shorthand by post, but the main organized development came in the 1880s and 1890s when many of the colleges such as Wolsey Hall, Foulkes Lynch and Chambers were founded. Many began by an individual undertaking private coaching. In the past few decades there has been a quite dramatic growth, despite the increase in other forms of provision, and this has been accompanied by moves to achieve complete respectability. A major step forward in this desire was the establishment of a Council for the Accreditation of Correspondence Colleges in August 1969, following the report of the Gurr Committee, which was set up by the leaders in the field. This seeks to prevent unscrupulous practice by colleges. Despite the attacks by educators accustomed to traditional face-to-face teaching, and the sharp practices of a very small number of providers, correspondence education has become, in fact one of the major sectors of work-related education.

Development, however, has not been confined to the profit-making commercial colleges working mainly in the vocational field. Three of the long-term colleges at one time provided correspondence courses, although of these only the Co-operative College on behalf of the Co-operative Union, still does so. The National Adult School Movement also provided postal courses from 1917 to the 1950s, and some individual trade unions, such as the National Association of Local Government Officers (NALGO) make provision. In 1964 the Trades Union Congress took over the schemes hitherto organized by Ruskin College and by the National Council of Labour Colleges. The Methodist Study Centre, established in 1927, offers correspondence courses for lay preachers, Sunday School teachers and club leaders as a means of obtaining the London University Certificate of Proficiency in Religious Knowledge. It also provides courses to help students who are intending to enter the Ministry or the order of deaconesses. As already noted, the Army in particular uses the Forces Correspondence Course Scheme which at one time had up to 40,000 enrolments per year, and although this figure is now much reduced, the scheme is still of some importance.

Similarly, correspondence education plays a vital part in the work of the College of the Sea, established by Mansbridge in 1938 as part of the Sea-farers' Education Service which he had earlier created in 1919 to assist the education of merchant seamen. Backed by some financial support from the Department of Education and Science, the shipping industry and various trust funds, the college provides some courses linked to professional training – for example a GCE mathematics course taken by a ship's officer *en route,* perhaps, to a degree in nautical science – but most are for general education, especially in languages. The college pioneered the use of language tapes and programmed learning methods, and at an early date built up a counselling service to 'encourage and enable any seafarer to develop his capabilities to the full'. As the Director has said;[5] 'The College put the student in touch with a personal tutor . . . the tutor recommended books, suggested written work and guided the studies; the College of the Sea lent the books and acted as organizer.' The number using the service has varied from 1,500 to 3,500 per annum. Concerned to improve the quality of the whole of life at sea, the Seafarers' Educational Service is also prepared to advise the seafarer on any subject, 'educational' or not. The provision of ship's libraries has been regarded as a first essential and with them has developed guided reading and tuition from mainly honorary tutors on shore. More recently there have been some attempts to arrange for teachers to go out with the larger merchant ships such as the bulk carriers. The first of these was an artist who formed classes and gave general lectures, as well as private tuition, during the voyages.

The range of subjects available in correspondence courses in Britain is now prodigious. The rise of professional associations, especially in commerce and administration, and their demand for qualifying examinations, led to the expansion of the provision earlier in the century and today almost one-third of enrolments are in the business or commercial field in subjects such as banking, secretarial work, accountancy and law. There is also a high demand for courses leading to GCE examinations or to university external degrees or other academic qualifications. To these may be added courses for policemen or nurses, those working in local government and members of the public wanting general or recreational education who are willing to pay the relatively high cost. Unsubsidized, the fees until recently have been a good deal higher than those for equivalent courses in local authority centres, but many of the major colleges provide some refund of fees if courses are discontinued. Most of the correspondence colleges specialize in particular subject areas and each has developed its own method of operation to deal with the essential tasks of preparing the courses, despatching the lessons to students, receiving student written work, arranging contacts with tutors and providing an advisory service.

In view of the relatively high cost and other problems for the student, it may seem surprising that quite so many choose this road. Most have vocational motives and a very strong incentive is provided by the desire to get a better job or to be adequately qualified in the one already held. The method also seems to be peculiarly suitable to the personal circumstances of some students, especially married women with young children, people who are very mobile and those who live in remote areas. It has been said that the average correspondence student is a 'restless person frequently changing his domicile and his job'[6] and it is clear that one of the great attractions of the method is that it allows people to study at their own pace, and to plan the time and place of their studies in their own way. Perhaps this explains why it is undertaken by so many who live not in remote places but close to educational institutions, and why, for example, there were over 700,000 correspondence students in 1969 in the well-populated Netherlands. Studies in the USA as well as in Britain suggest that fairly large numbers prefer to study at home.[7] Probably at any one time at least 500,000 students are enrolled in correspondence courses in Britain; of these there are more men than women and a moderately high proportion of younger people in their 20s — perhaps a reflection of the search for vocational qualifications on a part-time basis.

There are, of course, problems in using a correspondence course and no other method. The home environment may be unsuitable for adult learning in view of the possible absence of peace and quiet, and of difficulties created by child care and illness. There may also be problems connected with a person's work, for example overloading, or changes in working conditions, or a general lack of support from employers. The strain of the demands of job, domestic responsibilities and social life may lead to withdrawal from the course. Above all there are structural difficulties, partly the absence of face-to-face contact with tutor or fellow students, partly the impossibility of adjusting one course to meet the heterogeneous needs of students very mixed in age, schooling, social class and employment, and partly the inevitable time gap between student work and checks on progress. A delay of even a week or two can cause a fall in motivation and this can be intensified if there are problems of erratic postal deliveries. Some students, too, lack the confidence in themselves that would enable them to use the method with success. Not all postal course tutors have the time or the inclination to show sufficient interest to deal with this. Most, however, are experienced in class teaching, most are graduates and, though some are retired, most are aged between 30 and 60.[8] In general they undertake the work on a part-time basis, motivated apparently more by their preference for working in their own time and at their own convenience than by the fairly meagre extra income so obtained.

Looking to the future, it seems clear that the correspondence course student needs more support, partly in the form of financial aid. The 1962 Education Act gave power to the LEAs to make discretionary awards but their response has been extremely varied and some have not used the power at all. Partly the student need may be for more guidance over personal problems, methods of work and other factors which underlie learning difficulties. Help seems to be needed especially in the early stages of a course, the point at which there are often most drop-outs, but support is required throughout the course to maintain determination and self-discipline. The accredited colleges give attention to these aspects affecting the quality of their courses and try to avoid the stress on rote learning and memorization without comprehension, which is always a danger if there is no direct face-to-face contact with teachers. Live contact with teachers and other students is sometimes possible in the occasional weekend or other meeting, and more use might be made of telephone conversations as demonstrated, for example, by Athabaska University in Edmonton, Canada, in its specialist approach to distance education. Correspondence education has now become much more respectable and has shown that it can have an important impact both on the individual and on the community in which he or she lives, but perhaps its real future lies in co-ordination with other methods. In Eastern Europe compulsory attendance at sessions with the postal study teacher has been arranged for some courses but elsewhere there is more division of opinion. The impact of technological developments from Telstar onwards seems to facilitate more co-ordination and there would appear to be value in combining correspondence courses with part-time class study, and with intermittent periods of full-time, perhaps residential, study. In this way, the role of the postal course would be 'not to supplant, but to complement, support, extend'. One example of this kind of use might be the in-service training of teachers in all parts of the country as well as those in remote areas such as the North of Scotland, for whom some experimental modular units have already been provided.

National Extension College

One non-commercial college which has carried out a good deal of experimentation in this area is the National Extension College (NEC). This was founded in 1963 by the Advisory Centre for Education and has incorporated the old University Correspondence College which had been established as early as 1887. Operating as a Trust with unpaid Trustees, any surplus has been used to develop new courses and services. It has produced a range of correspondence courses which include some introductory courses, courses for GCE 'O' and 'A' levels, and for external degrees, and some courses for professional qualifications such as those of the chartered engineers and the Institute of Linguists, as well as for part of the requirements of the Library Association and the Law Society. Besides the courses, provision has been made for textbooks, language tapes etc. and a Student Advisory Service has been developed. In 1978, for example, there were seventy-six courses and nearly 9,000 enrolments.[9] The College has also undertaken a number of grant-aided research and development projects such as that on *Just the Job* which was designed to test the contribution which television and radio programmes, together with printed materials and individual counselling can make to helping unemployed school leavers. Also financed by the Manpower Services Commission, a Basic Skills Unit was formed in 1979 which set out to design, prepare and publish individual learning packs for use with the Youth Opportunities Programme. Other experimental home self-study packs and supportive materials have also been offered in association with radio and television series. An example is the basic numeracy course *Make it Count* jointly prepared by Yorkshire Television and the NEC in 1978, the materials including a workbook, a puzzlebook and a card game. Other examples are a tape-study pack on *Studying Poetry* and a pack for the ATV programme on Disraeli, which arose as a pilot project put foward by an informal group under the title Northern Group Learning. Further co-operation with Yorkshire Television resulted in 1980 in a new numeracy course entitled *Numbers at Work*.

The NEC has also explored the possibility of an 'Open learning' system by which a local college of further education offers augmented correspondence courses for students in its own locality. Entitled 'flexi-study', the scheme enables the student to have NEC correspondence course materials, the help of a staff tutor who deals with written work and provides tutorial support by post, telephone or face to face, and also access to all the normal facilities of a college such as laboratories, library and audio-visual resources, careers services, examination entry procedure, canteen, etc. This kind of 'total learning package' has spread fairly rapidly since the first venture in 1977 by Barnet College of Further Education. It seems to be of particular help to shift workers or others who find the normal kind of college attendance difficult if not impossible, and also to those with minority interests who are too few in number in any one are to warrant a normal class. As an example of what can be made available, the Abraham Moss Centre in Manchester offers flexi-study courses in nine GCE 'O' level and nine 'A' level subjects as well as preliminary courses in English, mathematics and study skills, further expansion being planned for the near future. The NEC has also experimented with help for the Open College Federation of the North West, to which reference has already been made, beginning with the production of two units concerned with *'Study Techniques'* and with *'Scientific Method'*.

Open University

In size, by far the greatest experiment in the use of multi-media resources for the individual student is the Open University. Established by Royal Charter in May, 1969, and opened to students in January, 1971, this independent autonomous body provides an opportunity for adults to study at home, particularly for first degrees. Its objects were stated rather more broadly in the Charter as being:

> The advancement and dissemination of learning and knowledge by teaching and research, by a diversity of means such as broadcasting and technological devices appropriate to higher education, by correspondence tuition, residential courses and seminars, and in other relevant ways, and . . . to provide education of University and professional standards for its students, and to promote the educational well-being of the community generally.[10]

Besides the use of multi-media instructional methods, the Open University is also committed to the principle of open access to higher education by having no formal entry requirements, in contrast to the long tradition in the United Kingdom of academic selection before university entry. As the Planning Committee said in its 1969 Report: 'We took it as axiomatic that no formal academic qualifications would be required for registration as a student. Anyone could try his or her hand, and *only* failure to progress adequately would be a bar to continuation of studies.' It also set up a credit system for its awards, again drawing nearer to university practice in America, Canada, Australia and elsewhere. Even so, it has not compromised on standards and has fought hard to gain recognition, now achieved, that its degrees are equivalent to those of any other British university. It has been argued, however, that this has meant the maintenance of an unfortunate traditionalism.

In practice, the Open University now has about 70,000 students, generally over the age of 21, with an average age of the mid-30s, and either in full-time employment or working at home. Most of them attend undergraduate courses, beginning with a foundation year course, in arts, social sciences, mathematics, science or technology. The essential basis of a course is specially-written correspondence material, sent out regularly to each student in a 'package' which may include equipment such as materials for science experiments, as well as assignments for completion and return for comment by a personal tutor, or marking by computer. This system of continuous assessment allows students to see what grades they are getting. To the package are linked radio and television broadcasts, specially produced by the BBC, and opportunities to meet other students and tutor—counsellors in local study centres, of which there are now nearly 300, usually housed in LEA premises, open in the evenings and equipped with broadcasting receivers. First-year students must attend a one-week Summer School and this is a requirement also of some of the later courses. Candidates are restricted to a maximum of two full credit courses in one year, and six credits are required for the B.A. degree and eight for the B.A. Honours degree. Candidates are advised that they should be willing to spend at least twelve or fifteen hours per week on their studies, a sizeable commitment. A number of preparatory courses have been developed in various parts of the country for the intending Open University student both to prepare a person for study and to help him or her decide if the proposed action is right in terms of aptitude as well as of time available.

The Open University also offers a programme of postgraduate studies leading to the degrees of B.Phil., M.Phil., and Ph.D. The normal minimum entrance requirement is a good degree from a British university, although 'applications will be considered from those without this requirement who can show that their alternative qualifications, professional experience or previous research are a suitable preparation for postgraduate research'.[11] Students are expected to work on a part-time basis, studying and using research facilities in their home area, and supervision is provided both by the University's own academic staff and by suitable external supervisors from higher education institutions near to the students' homes. Provision is also made for a small number of internal students at the headquarters built by the University at Milton Keynes. This is now a sizeable central base where detailed planning of courses is carried out in the six Faculties of Arts, Educational Studies, Mathematics, Science, Social Sciences, and Technology.

91

A third strand in the Open University provision is that of Associate Student courses. These are non-degree courses, often of about ten months in duration, which are designed for those who wish to gain knowledge in a new area or to update their existing knowledge. At the end of a course, students can obtain a letter recognizing attendance or, if they also complete the assignments and examinations required, they can receive a Course Certificate. Shorter courses of only eight to twelve weeks are also being presented which provide basic knowledge in a wide variety of subjects. These began with child care, and have included preparation for retirement. In a rapidly-changing world, these Associate Student courses seem a vital service and a Committee on Continuing Education established in 1975 under the chairmanship of Sir Peter Venables, recommended considerable developments in this work.[12] At the present time those who fail to meet the needs of a degree course have few real alternatives to which to turn and the growth of these associate student courses might well open the doors for a much wider variety of students. The last phrase of the objects laid down in the Charter — 'the educational well-being of the community' — might then become more of a reality.

As might be expected, there are some problems in the present provision by the Open University. The basic philosophy suggests that everyone is entitled to access to as much education as he or she desires, but open access is not achieved if people do not know about the facilities or misinterpret them. It would seem that there are still problems of publicity to be solved. Similarly the cost of a credit course seems too high for some sections of the population and LEAs rarely pay the tuition fees except for those at the Summer Schools. Even so, about twice as many apply as can be admitted each year while total resources remain restricted, and there has developed both a waiting period for entry and some introduction of quotas designed to achieve a greater spread of occupations and a more even regional distribution. The lower income and educationally deprived groups, however, are still underrepresented, although the Open University can claim rather more success in attracting these sectors of the population than can the more conventional universities. People make their own estimates of the value of the courses and of their own capabilities and, as with all distance learning, there are problems of finding a suitable place at home in which to study and listen to and view the broadcast programmes, and the further problem of travel to and from study centres.

To help students by direct counselling at a more local level, the Open University has thirteen regional offices, ten in England and one each in Wales, Scotland and Northern Ireland. In these the full-time staff, which consists of a regional director, deputies and senior counsellors, is available for consultation and advice, and they recruit part-time tutor—counsellors for work largely in the study centres. With such personal contact it has been thought that many of the difficulties which lead to student withdrawal can be overcome. Not all students, however, use the study centres, and there have been suggestions that money could be saved by a cut-back in face-to-face counselling, however detrimental this would seem to be. Finance is a constant problem, and arguments about the cost-effectiveness of the whole institution have not been accepted as conclusive despite the research evidence produced by the Open University which suggests that its operation is cheaper than that of the traditional universities. As a result, there are suggestions from time to time that, despite the open door principle, student numbers ought to be pegged to a maximum fixed number, such as 40,000, and even that teaching materials might be much reduced, especially for the higher levels. No doubt these suggestions will be resisted with the aid of the Open University Students' Association (OUSA) which by 1979 had over 70,000 members and 200 branches. Other pressures include the problems of available radio and television time, the Open University programmes tending to be pushed more and more into inconvenient hours at each end of the day. This situation might be eased by a fourth television channel or by the use of video cassettes.

Various questions remain to be asked. As the Open University gets older will it cease to be innovative and become just 'a middle class correspondence college, offering nothing radically different from any other conventional institution of higher education', as was once suggested?[13] Will it more and more be used as a way of transmitting information to passive consumers, instead of 'setting minds alight' and developing a real personal understanding? Certainly some of the students, conditioned to believe that the absorption of information is all that matters, tend to regard it in this way as they strive to pass their assignments. The Open University has shown that many thousands of people are fully capable of degree level education, though casualties of an élitist child education system; but should it seek to serve a wider group of the population by the development of lower-level post-experience courses? As it is, are the courses pitched too high for the majority of workers who may wish to change or update their career skills? Should the Open University, with other bodies, try to establish a national credits system to allow for both comparability and easier transference between courses to help an increasingly mobile population? Already it has some links with the CNAA — an agreement, for example, allowing for some student transfers — and it can be argued that it now has the necessary prestige to give a lead. Whatever else the Open University, as an institution offering distance learning, has achieved academic acceptability, and recognition, for example, by the professional bodies. Though it does not provide the experience of three years' full-time life on a conventional university campus, it does perhaps more readily meet the needs of mature people with jobs and family commitments. In doing so it has made a very significant contribution.

Broadcasting

Television is provided by the British Broadcasting Corporation on two channels (BBC 1 and BBC 2), and by Independent Television through, at present, fifteen programme contractors operating regionally under licence from the Independent Broadcasting Authority (IBA). At the moment of writing, one independent commercial channel is operating in each area but a second one is actively planned. Almost all households have at least one television set and well over half have colour television. On average, adults view television for about twenty hours per week.[14] Four national radio programmes are broadcast by the BBC, and there are at present twenty BBC local radio stations and about the same number commercially provided. Plans exist for the development of up to ninety more local independent commercial stations and up to another fifty-five BBC local stations. Surveys suggest that on average each household has two or three radio sets and that each of these is in use for about nine hours per week. It also seems that about 90% of all radio 'listening' is done as an accompaniment to some other activity such as reading, shaving, bathing, washing up or driving a car.

This extensive provision gives broadcasting enormous impact and power for good or ill, especially as not infrequently a television programme has an audience of more than 20 million. It comes to people in their own homes or cars, and inevitably has an effect on people's thoughts, attitudes and behaviour patterns. At an early date, its potential for education was recognized and a former Director-General, Sir William Haley, declared that 'broadcasting, despite all its diversity, must be regarded primarily as an educational medium'. The Charter of the BBC from the beginning has declared that the function is 'information, education and entertainment', an order of priorities somewhat changed in the ITV Charter which declares in favour of 'entertainment, instruction and information'. Just what the implications of these words should be, however, has been the subject of endless discussion, in which attempts have been made to distinguish between 'educative' and 'educational', as well as between 'educational' and 'instructional', the latter usually being taken to imply training for a skill, or no more than a very limited study. However, much depends upon people's motives and attitudes; if they wish, they can seek for education from a 'non-educational' programme, and conversely broadcasting authorities can seek to educate in programmes not so labelled, a process sometimes termed 'education by stealth'.

At present, many programmes without an educational label clearly have a potentially educative effect. Interests can be greatly extended and new ideas awakened, and there is a good deal of evidence for this in subjects such as art and archaeology, ballet and music, drama and novels. The broadcasting, from the early days onwards, of music of all kinds to those who hitherto had little or no opportunity to attend concerts seems to have changed both the approach and the behaviour of the general public. Similarly, television has enabled millions to see plays of all kinds, by Shakespeare, Shaw and Tschekov as well as by modern dramatists. It seems also to have brought the classic novel to popular attention; perhaps the most famous example was Galsworthy's *Forsyte Saga* which, televised in a series of episodes, drew many millions of regular viewers. It has provided imaginative experiences, as well as knowledge, in programmes such as Sir Kenneth Clark's series on *Civilization,* Bronowski's *The Ascent of Man* and Attenborough's *Life on Earth,* all of which attracted relatively huge television audiences. There is also the contribution of the various news bulletins: evidence suggests that people acquire much of their political knowledge from news broadcasts, talks and debates. Documentaries may stimulate an imaginative understanding, or at least some awareness of other people and their alternative life styles both in their own country and overseas. 'Educative' broadcasting may include panel discussions, satirical programmes, quiz programmes, holiday programmes, sports commentaries and religious programmes. Often it is said that broadcasting 'conveys the cultural heritage' in terms of codes of behaviour, attitudes, and values. Jean Rowntree quite early suggested that broadcasting was concerned with 'the making of an informed society, a community of individuals with a working knowledge of the physical world they live in, some idea of its political situation and the power to enjoy their cultural tradition'.[15] As so few seem to show an understanding of scientific principles or a sense of historical perspective even after many decades of broadcasting, success in these objectives seems somewhat limited and perhaps these objectives should be questioned.

A fear of its possible success, however, often seems reflected in the views of those who assert that broadcasting distorts the cultural heritage, manipulates the public and processes people to accept certain attitudes and values. The BBC is often regarded by some as the voice of the Establishment. Richard Hoggart believed that broadcasting in general, and perhaps commercial broadcasting in particular, pressed the public to a 'cultural classlessness', encouraged by the tyranny of the ratings and the financial pressures of advertisers.

Other challenges have suggested that much of broadcasting conveys a cheap, superficial and trivial view of life. 'Pop and prattle' was Christopher Chataway's comment on Radio 1, and the 'soap operas' such as *Dallas* and the long-running *The Archers,* are often attacked. Similarly it has been said that viewing and listening create passivity and dependence, a loss of initiative and an illusion of understanding knowledge too easily acquired. There is, however, some evidence that many of the news and current affairs programmes are not very intelligible to many people so that the Jimmy Young show, with its information and interviews supplementing the music, may be performing a real service; and it is clear that some broadcasts provide a considerable stimulus to activity, whether this is cookery and gardening, or social work enterprise and community action. Whatever the comment and criticism, a good case can be made out for Brian Groombridge's view that 'television through its geneal output . . . is now the chief agency of adult education in this country, and a principal educational influence on the entire population'.[16] Moreover, the radio is a force in its own right, not subservient to television, and local radio may develop an importance similar to that of the local newspaper. BBC publications also have considerable sales and *The Listener* reaches a sizeable minority of the population with sales of over 100,000 copies each week. Originating in a 1928 recommendation of a joint committee of the BBC and the British Institute of Adult Education, this was designed to be a regular weekly educational journal putting into print not only many of the broadcast talks but also reviews and special articles.

As the years go by, there is a tendency for educators of adults to dwell on the power of broadcasting to reach those who would not otherwise come into contact with organized educational provision. Perhaps inevitably this has given impetus to the view that broadcasting should assume a direct teaching role and many attempts have been, and are being, made on both radio and television. A few statistics illustrate this: in 1976 about 6 hours of radio and about 10 hours of television per week were concerned with the direct education of adults, as well as the 33 hours of television and 26 hours of radio broadcast per week throughout the academic year for the Open University and the 16 hours of radio and 13 hours of television transmitted to children's schools per week in term time. This was a sizeable programme, exceeded at that time only by Japan. In the programmes for adults are included particularly language courses in all the major European languages, but extended to other languages such as Welsh, Gaelic and Arabic. Normally these are supported by records or cassettes and by books and other literature. There is a wide range of other subjects including courses in various crafts such as pottery, dressmaking and cookery, current affairs, sports such as badminton and canoeing, dancing, art and design, literature, trade union studies, car maintenance, photography, education (for both parents and teachers), nursing, general health, salesmanship, engineering, literacy and numeracy. A list of the current programmes put out by the BBC is given in the sheets 'Look, Listen, Learn', usually inserted in the *Radio Times* twice a year. In support of these direct teaching broadcasts it is said that the courses have the best teachers available and the backing of a range of audio-visual aids unmatched in the usual college evening or day-time course. It is also asserted, as with correspondence courses, that broadcast courses have a particular value for women at home with young children, and obviously cookery and dressmaking programmes, for example, are designed with this audience specifically in mind. Although out of the comparatively large viewing or listening audience only a minority are likely to complete conscientiously the required exercises or reading, the size of this minority is often greater than the total number of evening class students in the subject throughout the whole country. Some language courses, for example, have had over two million viewers and have brought a sale of tens of thousands of records and booklets. Not all subjects are so easily adapted to broadcasting, however, and some aspects of the arts and sport are believed to require personal contact and individual guidance.

Despite the evidence that some people have undoubtedly 'taught themselves' with the aid only of broadcasting, the authorities on the whole have encouraged a partnership between broadcasting and other agencies. Before the emergence of the Open University, there were experimental programmes linking television with correspondence tuition, group study and practical work, notably one in 1965–6 on *The Social Workers*[17] and one in 1966–7 on *Teaching Physics to Adults.*[18] In the 1970s there were radio programmes on 'Living decisions in family and community' and 'What right have you got?' which led to an optional assessment at GCE 'O' level. Students of the course on rights were encouraged to join groups and undertake practical investigations of situations involving the rights and responsibilities of citizens. Local radio has established links with university extra-mural departments and the Workers' Educational Association, and also with the Councils of Social Service and organizations such as the St John Ambulance Brigade. An early example was a six-programme course on 'Living today' put out as a joint venture of BBC Radio Merseyside and the West Lancashire and Cheshire District of the WEA. It seems likely that such collaboration will develop further, though the problem of creating a really effective liaison throughout the whole of Britain remains unsolved even in the well-established area of schools broadcasting. It may be noted that the broadcasts to children's schools have an estimated eavesdropping adult audience of at least half a million. Both the BBC and IBA have full-time Education Officers, and appropriate committees, and there are also specialist education producers.

Despite the successes in operating alone, especially in providing information about all kinds of subjects, and experiences particularly in music and the arts, it seems likely that the main educational contribution of broadcasting will be that of a partner in the learning process, one of several agencies helping the adult. Collaboration was seen as the way forward both by the Russell Committee and by the Venables Committee.[19] Broadcasters face problems of the use of air time to meet conflicting interests. No matter how many stations come into existence and how much local radio may develop a major role, there will remain the problem of achieving a balance between minority and majority wishes and between national community needs and those of the individual. Community cable television has been suggested as another way of reducing the problem but there are practical issues yet to be solved and all the first five cable experiments in Britain were allowed to disappear. Broadcasters, too, have yet to overcome the weaknesses of 'passive' studentship created by the absence of direct contact with a teacher. Can the development of more participatory broadcasting help? Moves have been made to bring some of the viewing or listening audience either into the studio or on to the phone, but by its nature this method can affect only a minority, and it is difficult to make it constructive. At an earlier date, 'wireless' listening groups, on lines later followed by Farm Radio Forum in Canada and its equivalent in India, tried to provide direct active contact through the post but it was abandoned soon after the Second World War as being unproductive in an age when people listened as individuals rather than as groups.

A question which needs to be asked is whether in the future there will be any need to *broadcast* educational programmes at all, at any rate in normal viewing or listening hours. Greater use of video cassettes would enable the home student to screen a study programme when he wished and to record it automatically, rather than to attend at the fixed broadcasting time as is at present normal. A commercial firm is, in fact, already producing ten-lesson courses on video tape for use in learning French and English. The development of the 'television game' indicates the use of a television set for purposes other than the reception of transmitted broadcasts, and accessibility to computerized stores of information via the screen of a television set has already arrived in the Prestel viewdata service of the Post Office which links the store with the telephone and a modified television set, and in the various teletext schemes such as ITA's 'Oracle' and the BBC's 'Ceefax' which in turn could be linked to similar services in Europe and America. At present these developments are costly and hence available only to the few, but it is likely that in the future, most students are likely to obtain factual information from sources of this kind, probably preferring it to other means. Just as the whole education system in Britain has greatly changed since broadcasting began, so the educational role of broadcasting can be expected to change radically in the course of the next few decades. Presumably it will continue to be a great stimulus to interest and to be in a broad sense educative, but it seems likely that it may cease to attempt the direct educational teaching task. A broader question is its effect on the citizen and on parliamentary democracy. 'The question facing television,' Brian Groombridge has said, 'is, will it continue to alienate us from the world and from the possibility of effective action, by transforming an environment we are powerless to affect, either into an object out there about which we are continuously but patchily informed, or into a spectacle to divert, titillate and uselessly appal us? Or will it help us create a society in which effective action is possible?'[20] Perhaps we need to press for an Educational Broadcasting Council, to monitor the process, to have executive powers to deal with possibly competing interests and to try to ensure that change is beneficial to both the individual and the community. It may well be that with the rapidity of technological change, the self-educator may use broadcasting in ways which at present are apprehended only dimly, if at all.

References

1. TOUGH, A. *Major Learning Efforts: Recent Research and Future Directions,* 1977, Ontario Institute for Studies in Education. The exact figure is given as 73%.

2. In *An Introduction to Lifelong Education,* 2nd edition, 1975, Croom Helm and UNESCO, p. 50.

3. MACDONALD, D. *Mass Culture: the Popular Arts in America,* 1957.

4. Definition given by W.J.A. HARRIS in 'Education by post', *Adult Education,* 39/5, Jan, 1967, pp. 269–273, 277.

5. HOPE, R. 'Adult Education at Sea', *Adult Education,* 42/3, pp. 143–147 and 150.

6. HARRIS, W.J.A. Op. cit.

7. For Britain see the evidence in GLATTER, R. and WEDELL, E.G. *Study by Correspondence* (1971) and for the USA, see JOHNSTONE, J.W.C. and RIVERA, R., *Volunteers for Learning* (1965).

8. See HARRIS, W.J.A. *The Distance Tutor,* 1975, Manchester Monographs, no. 3. This was the first research study of teachers in correspondence education.

9. See National Extension College, *Annual Report* for 1979.

10. Charter of the Open University, para 3.

11. OU Postgraduate Prospectus. In the 1980 version, para 3–2.

12. Open University *Report of the Committee on Continuing Education,* (The Venables Report), Dec. 1976, O.U.

13. 'The Open University: revolution, evolution or stagnation?' *Times Educational Supplement,* 25 Jan 1974, Part 1, Stevens, Auriol, 'Priorities at the centre', p. 21.

14. See, for example, *Social Trends,* 1979 edition, published by the Central Statistical Office.

15. ROWNTREE, Jean. 'New issues in educational broadcasting', Chapter VII, in *Trends in English Adult Education,* ed. RAYBOULD, S.G. 1959, Heinemann.

16. GROOMBRIDGE, B. *Television and the People,* 1972, Penguin Education Special. p. 20.

17. See HANCOCK, A. and ROBINSON, J. *Television and Social Work,* 1966, NIAE.

18. See WEDELL, E.G. and PERRATON, H.N. *Teaching at a Distance,* 1968. This described an experiment linking ABC Television and the National Extension College.

19. See Russell Report, paras 256–62 and Venables Report, especially paras 88–98.

20. GROOMBRIDGE, B. op. cit. p. 24.

CHAPTER 7

Leisure-related studies

Education for Leisure by the LEAs

Despite the amount of self-education, most people in Britain think of the education of adults as going to a class in which there is a teacher present, and the largest recorded numbers of students are those in attendance at evening classes. Well over two million people each year go out on winter evenings to join such groups and most do so for reasons which are not primarily related to their paid employment or to examinations and qualifications. Those who believe that the only 'real' education is that which leads to self-advancement through vocational awards, however, tend to deprecate evening classes of this kind as being a sort of luxury, the pursuit of 'hobbies', 'mere recreation'. As noted earlier, a Puritan outlook has exalted work-related education to such an extent that it is perhaps not surprising that leisure-related education has been held by some to be unworthy of serious concern. The Education Acts themselves have tended to draw distinctions between 'education' and 'leisure-time occupation'[1] even when suggesting that both should be provided, and many in power in local authorities have questioned the validity of spending public money on the promotion of activities or facilities designed to improve the quality of 'leisure'. Others, in contrast, argue that there is a vital need for education to help adults use their increasing leisure in a constructive or creative way, and to develop all aspects of personality and human relationships. Sir Fred Clarke attacked 'the sharp and disastrous duality of work and leisure which is one of the most significant symptoms of the modern *malaise*', and stressed 'the potential unity of the individual life an the subtle interpenetration of all its activities and interests'.[2] In an industrialized community, which tends to remove opportunities for self-expression and self-realization, it is said that leisure-related education becomes a paramount need, essential to the preservation of sanity, human dignity, and perhaps civilization itself. 'In future, education for living is the only education which will count.'

There are, of course, problems of definition and problems of attitudes. 'Part-time' and 'full-time' can be viewed as having only a relative distinction, although a full-time course is very different from evening classes where the norm for part-time study has tended to become a two-hour class meeting once a week. 'Leisure' can be viewed in many different ways. Is it just a period of rest, 'non-work', 're-creation' or a positive period in which freedom of choice and opportunities for alternative activities occur? Is unemployment

– or retirement – the same as leisure? Obviously different interpretations are likely between the person who draws great satisfaction from a paid employment which gives opportunities for social contact and varied experiences, and one whose work is monotonous, repetitive and personally meaningless. It seems clear that in the second half of the twentieth century attitudes to work and leisure have become more fluid. Much educational thinking and argument, however, is still based on a dichotomy between 'work' and 'leisure' and between 'education for work' and 'education for leisure'. Besides the indication of this in the Education Acts, it can be seen very clearly in the 1947 Ministry of Education Pamphlet No. 8 in which the main chapter headings are 'Preparation for work' and 'Learning for leisure'. Though the latter is said to be necessary for a 'full and satisfying life'[3] it is clearly regarded as a separate entity, though without a very precise meaning. The provision is to be made for anyone 'able and willing to profit', but how this is to be determined is not made clear. Perhaps the time has come to try to end the dichotomy and to give up talking about education for leisure as separate and distinct; the type of education with which this chapter is concerned may be thought to be more related to leisure interests as at present defined but it certainly has an impact on all other aspects of life. The terms of reference for the Scottish Alexander Committee seem to show the sort of modification that may be needed: it was to consider 'voluntary leisure courses for adults which are educational but not specifically vocational'.[4]

To date, however, most local authority councillors and officials tend to regard their other educational duties as more important, and to feel only a minor commitment to education which is not work-related. When the financial climate becomes difficult, supposedly leisure-related education tends to be regarded as expendable, the first 'inessential' to be discarded, and perhaps a 'frivolous frill' on which money can be easily saved. The Education Acts from 1944 onwards make it clear that the LEAs have a duty to secure the provision of 'adequate' facilities, but so far the definition of 'adequate' has not been tested in the law courts. The statutory ambiguity has led to wide differences of interpretation, at one extreme being those who declare that it means the provision of all types of facility, while at the other there are those who believe that it can allow for almost no provision at all. A few authorities seem to have acted on the latter view in the late 1970s and early 1980s, but it remains true that as far as the broad picture of the whole of Britain is concerned the LEAs have without doubt become the major providers of leisure-related education, teaching over eighty per cent of the students in organized classes, employing most of the teachers and owning most of the buildings and equipment it uses. Even if there are more savage cuts still to come, it is unlikely that this general picture will radically change in the near future, although it may cease to be valid for a few more areas.

Different interpretations by so many different LEAs, some with firm policies others working from an equally influential *ad hoc* opportunism, make it impossible to provide a clear description applicable to all areas at all times. What follows, therefore, is an indication of possibilities and characteristics to be found somewhere in Britain; these may be grouped loosely under the three broad headings of evening centres, separate adult education centres, and multipurpose institutions. There are almost infinite local variations within these categories and there are not infrequent modifications within a single

Authority as political changes take place or different personalities come to positions of power.

Evening centres or institutes

With historical origins going back far into the nineteenth century, the evening institutes have been described as 'convenient lodging houses for awkward educational problems'. An early date they supplemented inadequate elementary child education and were often regarded in socio-political terms as places which helped to improve the morals, obedience and general pursuits of the poor. Against a background of child labour, long hours of work and severe living conditions, the early 'night schools', as they tended to be called, helped both young people and adults who had never been to school or who had had only the most limited education. Most were at first provided by churches and philanthropic bodies, and they grew up in isolation. After the 1870 Act, evening schools grant-aided by the central government became possible as extensions of the children's day school, and it is not surprising, therefore, that the typical evening centre of today is usually housed in a children's day school. Each LEA opens up those schools it thinks fit, and the number varies from year to year according to local policy decisions. Some Authorities prefer to concentrate all activities in only a few buildings, perhaps supposedly to save heating costs, while others think dispersion over a large number of centres provides each citizen with opportunities relatively close to home, a matter of financial importance to less well off individuals in times of rising transport costs. The total annual number of evening centres in Britain in the last twenty years has thus varied from over 10,000 to under 6,000. Financial cuts may reduce the number to a much lower figure. Although some areas have no evening centres at all and there are differences between towns of the same size, the broad picture is one of schools, usually secondary, open on three nights a week during school terms in the winter period from September to about April. In some places, particularly in rural areas, church and village halls may be hired to provide meeting places. Some attention has been paid to the need to provide adult chairs, but there are still considerable difficulties over the storage of equipment for adult classes, and in some schools over the uses of laboratories and practical or art rooms. The teacher of the adult class may still be confronted by 'Do not touch' notices, blackboards covered with writing marked 'Do not remove' and by a caretaker who, at the end of a long day, wishes to close the school as early as possible. Some centres have a handful of students, others a thousand or so, especially in the large urban comprehensive schools, and the name 'institute' with its somewhat unfriendly image, is more often replaced by a more inviting title, 'centre' perhaps being the most common.

The type of student is now radically different from that before 1939. In place of the tired youngsters who were trying to make good the deficiencies of early schooling, women came into the evening centres in large numbers during and just after the Second World War, and now tend to outnumber the men by three to one. In the main, the ages most represented are those from 30 to 55 but there are also old age pensioners over the age of 80 as well as young people who have just left school at the age of 16. Most, if not all, vocational studies have been removed to the colleges of further education, and with them have gone most of the 16-20 age group. Some students are *habitués,* regular attenders each year at evening classes, while others may attend only one course in the whole of their lives. It would seem likely that although only about 6% of the adult population are in classes at any one time, and perhaps only 4% in Scotland,[5] probably about 40% of the population have participated at some time during their lives.

The subjects of study show a wide spread of interests. In view of the predominance of women it is not surprising that courses related to the home and family have been the most popular; these include dressmaking and needle-craft of all kinds, crafts related to home improvement such as painting and decorating, cookery from basic to cordon bleu, furniture repairing, car maintenance, gardening and household electricity. All courses are open to both men and women but there is a similar major female response to 'physical education' in all its forms; including keep fit, games and sports, a wide variety of dancing, including folk, modern and old time, yoga, and activities such as rock climbing and orienteering. Other popular subjects are languages, predominantly French, German, Spanish and Italian but ranging to Russian, various Asian languages and a dozen others, including Welsh and Arabic. There is also a large variety of music, art and drama courses, which include group instrumental music making and choral singing, painting, sculpture and decorative crafts such as pottery painting and flower arrangement, and acting and play production. Provision is made for lip reading and basic education classes and tuition, and there are special classes for the physically handicapped, while in the field of the liberal studies, history, economics, and social sciences, and literature are regular features, together with combined 'community study' courses. There is also a demand for first aid and health education. Where vocational courses remain, they tend to be concerned with office skills, such as shorthand and typewriting, although there are a few dealing with basic qualifications in, for example, the electrical or building industries. A medium-sized town may well offer 150-200 different subjects in its evening centres. Most tend to be in practical crafts, physical education, creative subjects and languages, but the more academic, liberal study subjects may also be included. Traditionally the latter are the sphere of university extra-mural departments and the WEA, as will be seen later in this chapter, and many local education authorities, perhaps particularly in Wales and some parts of Scotland, see their 'duty to secure provision' as being fulfilled by support for these bodies.

Most of the staffing in the evening centres still tends to be part time. The principal may be the headmaster of the day school, or another local school teacher earning a useful, though not very lucrative, supplement to his or her full-time salary. Almost all the classes are taught by part-time teachers, and only in certain areas have moves been made to provide training to help them. Just as there is a considerable turnover of students, perhaps one-third being newcomers each year, so the teachers have a considerable number of drop-outs and replacements. Some show undoubted ability and impressive skills[6] but in general the overall staffing is grossly inadequate. In only a few evening centres has there been a real attempt to get student participation in management, and most students, indeed, seem conditioned not to expect it. Facilities in general vary a great deal. Many new children's schools have been

102

built since the Second World War and these have good equipment, if the adults are allowed to use it. Many adults, however, go to classes in old schools where even the heating and lighting leaves much to be desired. Perhaps some of the older students expect little else.

Adult education centres

As well as the possible problems and conflicts of interest which may be created by the use of children's schools, 'evening only' provision is obviously difficult for adults on shift work, and for anyone whose work or life style makes it impossible to reach a centre at that time. It also makes it more difficult to justify the appointment of full-time heads and teachers for the adult provision. To provide a more adequate service therefore, some LEAs have turned to the establishment of separate full-time centres, open throughout the day as well as the evening. This is a policy which has received support from the Association for Adult and Continuing Education as well as from the Educational Centres Association and from the researches of Mee and Wiltshire.[7] Separate centres are housed, however, in a variety of premises, often in old large houses or redundant schools, including some which have been condemned for use by children, but also in almost any kind of spare building that becomes available, including old hotels and an old mill (in Sowerby Bridge, Yorkshire). 'Premises for adult education come by accident, seldom by design,' said the Hutchinsons. 'Like the cast off clothes of a long family . . . such buildings descend the order of educational priorities.'[8] Some old buildings have been much renovated, and with additional buildings have developed not only full adult facilities in each classroom, but also common rooms and canteens to enrich the corporate life. One example is the Whitefield Centre, housed in an old school but made attractive by fittings and furnishings. It offers the same range of subjects as an evening centre, but provides them in the day time as well as in the evening, and has developed extra social activities, clubs, field trips and summer school ventures. With a full-time head and some full-time staff, it has been able since its foundation to develop a 'lively, stimulating and friendly atmosphere' and to serve more fully the needs of adults in the area around it.

A few LEAs have gone further and have created purposebuilt centres for leisure-related education just as they have built special colleges for vocational education. Possibly the most outstanding example of early development is the 'City Lit.' in London which was first established in 1919 and finally given a new, specially designed, building which was opened in 1939. This provides about a thousand classes, but it is also a place where students can follow their own interests in clubs and societies. As a 'literary institute', one of a network of institutes provided by the Inner London Education Authority (ILEA) it has a particular concern with intellectual and cultural activities, and its major subject divisions are humanities and science, drama and speech, art, music and foreign languages. The enrolment in any one year is usually 15,000-20,000, but it manages to provide fairly full opportunities for student consultation and counselling. It also has a special Adult Education Training Unit which provides training courses for both teachers and administrators concerned with the education of adults. This Centre for Adult Studies has a library of some 24,000 books together with collections of gramophone records, slides and maps, and it runs its own bookshop. There are also social facilities in the form of a canteen, coffee lounge and bar and a City Lit. Association whose affairs are in the hands of the self-governing Students Council. In recent years the City Lit. has acquired an extra building near by and has developed some residential courses in seaside and country centres away from London, and some occasional study tours abroad. 'We hope,' says the brochure, 'that the City Lit. is more than large buildings full of classes', but rather 'a meeting place for people of different backgrounds, ages and nationalities who have come together to develop common interests.'

Having sent a delegation to look at the provision in Germany and other parts of Europe, Manchester rehoused its College of Adult Education in a purpose-built building in 1974. Like the City Lit, this has a common room and lounge, a restaurant and a library, and through a House Committee of elected college members, it promotes social activities. It has a multipurpose theatre, an insulated suite of music rooms, a sports hall and science laboratories. Its range of subjects is similar to that of the City Lit, and it has developed special GCE courses designed primarily for adult women wishing to prepare themselves for entry to teaching and other professions. There are a few other similar purpose-built centres, such as the 'Birtles' in Wythenshawe, set in the middle of the shopping precinct with a display shop window, but the total number in Britain seems pitifully small when compared to the provision in other European countries, especially in new towns such as Marl in Western Germany. Supporters of the separate centre argue that it provides a much-needed identity for leisure-related education for adults, a place which adults find more agreeable than rooms surrounded by ebullient apprentices or the remnants of present-day sixth-form culture. They also argue that such a 'collegiate centre' could be the focus of provision in the area, a 'head office' for outlying places, a 'power house from which impetus and enthusiasm flows'.[9] Several LEAs have, in fact, devised an area structure, in which evening centres are grouped round a central unit all being placed in the care of either an area organiser or an area principal, the latter title perhaps indicating a greater stress on teaching work. Typical examples are those in Surrey, Warwickshire or West Yorkshire. In Scotland the Alexander Committee noted that 'regrettably there are very few such centres' and recommended that centres for community use should be developed as soon as possible; the committee however put much stress on joining together leisure-related education for adults and the youth and community services and 'community education centres' thus tend to include all three elements. Some feel that there is a danger that, like many of the 'community centres' in England, they might lose their educational content. 'We are not concerned with Social Centres,' said Wiltshire some time ago, 'nor do we need to smuggle education in through the back door of social activities.'[10]

Village colleges

Though the financial arguments are by no means conclusive, some critics feel that separate accommodation for leisure-time education for adults, even if desirable, would be too costly in the foreseeable future in Britain. As a supposedly more economical alternative, they stress the virtue of dual use or multipurpose buildings in which facilities for adult leisure-related education are combined with those for other sectors. Early examples of this are the Cambridgeshire Village Colleges which were pioneered in the 1920s under the inspiration of Henry Morris, then Secretary for Education in Cambridgeshire. The first opened at Sawston in 1930, three more were added before war broke out in 1939, and since then the whole of rural Cambridgeshire has been covered by a dozen or so colleges. In these a post-primary school is linked with educational accommodation for adults and usually with premises for youth activities, public health services and a public library, together with outdoor recreative facilities. Each college has been planned to serve a surrounding cluster of villages, which in this flat county are fairly evenly spaced, and attention has been paid to the provision of adequate public transport arrangements. Morris was much concerned with attempts to revive the village communal spirit and tradition and to counter the drift to the town, and he wanted the colleges to be an accepted part of the daily environment: 'As a community centre for the neighbourhood, the village college would provide for the whole man, and abolish the duality of education and ordinary life.'[11] In the colleges, therefore, can be found a great variety of classes and club activities, youth club events, and social events such as dinners, dances and wedding receptions. Morris wanted to create a beautiful setting for the corporate life, and made use of outstanding architects such as Gropius and Maxwell Fry, in an attempt to achieve works of art as well as 'worthy public buildings'.

Community colleges and schools

After some delay, Morris's ideas were imitated and modified to meet local situations in many parts of the country, especially in Leicestershire, Cumbria, Devon and Gwent. One of the problems has been to adjust an idea originally put forward for a flat rural area, to the needs of hill areas or urban estates or the bleak centres of some cities, and the forthcoming answers have been very varied. In hilly areas as in Wales, the valleys are the communities to be served; in other places, the focus may be on the whole of a small town, or a neighbourhood suburb of a city. The broad picture is one in which more or less extensive facilities for several groups of the population are brought together on one site or campus, to which the name 'community college', or 'community school' or 'community campus' is then attached, although without much degree of precision.[12] The simplest form is the attachment of adult and youth wings to a secondary school. Les Quennevais Community School in Jersey began in this way when it was established in 1964 as a secondary modern school planned with extra physical facilities for adults, and developing into a unit used by the whole community. Such an arrangement allows for a fuller use of school accommodation both throughout the day and evening, and also during weekends and school holidays. To achieve this, however, a 'community school' has to be made attractive and welcoming to adult users, deliberately setting out to be of service to everyone and to counteract adverse public attitudes based on schoolday memories of the isolation of the school, and the motto 'Parents wait at the gate'. The amount of the accommodation, too, has to be adequate if there are not to be severe limitations on the effectiveness of adult participation especially in the daytime, but also in the evening if school children are encouraged to develop their own extra activities outside school hours.

Careful planning has been a characteristic of the Leicestershire Community Colleges which drew their inspiration from Cambridgeshire and have acquired a similar fame. The first college came into being in 1954, and thirty developed within the county area in the next twenty years or so, perhaps the most noted being Countesthorpe College which opened in 1970 with a unique circular plan. Most of the colleges are in small town communities of between 7,000 and 20,000 people, thus contrasting a good deal with the Cambridgeshire colleges, but equally setting out to be a focal point for a multitude of community activities, educational, cultural, physical and social. Stress is laid on education as a lifelong process and on community involvement. In an attempt to plan for integrated development, the head of the school is also warden of the Community College, and the full-time adult and youth tutors are expected to have some teaching commitments within the school. Likewise the school teachers are expected to undertake duties in the adult sector. Activities range from formal classes to creative expression in music or art, from vigorous physical groups to free discussion over cups of coffee, from opportunities for conferences and club activities of all kinds to quiet reading in comfortable surroundings. The objective has been to give as much autonomy as possible and each college has an elected Council and Committee of Management with control over financial matters subject to the general supervision of the Authority, a matter which can give rise to strained relations. Subject to general County policy, the declared aim, however, has been to let each local community run its own college.[13] Financial cuts, however, seem likely to destroy about half the colleges during the early 1980s.

Even larger complexes exist in a few cities. Sheffield, for example, developed a plan for fifteen to twenty 'community campuses' in which an adult education centre would be joined to a comprehensive school together with youth clubs, sports centres and libraries. The first of these, Rowlinson, opened in 1968 on a thirty-acre site with a thirteen-form entry comprehensive school as its base. Besides full facilities for the usual wide range of adult leisure-related classes, it has a large, well-equipped sports centre with swimming pool, a cafeteria and full provision for outdoor and indoor pursuits. The Sutton Centre in Nottinghamshire is situated at the back of the town market place and houses a community school, leisure centre, youth services coffee bar and discotheque, and a day centre for the physically and mentally handicapped, as well as a youth employment bureau, adult classes of the WEA and the university extra-mural department, a teachers' centre, school health clinic and a chaplaincy. The largest community campus in Britain is the Abraham Moss Centre in North Manchester which occupies a thirty-two-acre site. This includes a college of further education as well as a large comprehensive school, a non-vocational adult education centre, a theatre, sports hall, swimming pool, sauna baths, squash courts, youth centre, crèche, old people's social centre and library, all buildings being interconnected. Such provision raises questions about size as well as about the involvement of the community. Are ordinary people likely to be intimidated or turned away by the vastness of such a complex, through which they can find their way only with the aid of a guide? Is a large comprehensive school the right sort of base on which to build a 'community college'? By present day standards the first village colleges were small and some have suggested that the right base would be a primary school. Is the large comprehensive school, which may be attended by many children who travel some distance by bus, too remote from the real community? Are the needs of people really met by these 'hypermarkets of corporate life', so described by Colin Ball, a former head of community education in one of Leicestershire's Community Colleges? He added 'Morris seemed to favour the corner shop.'[14]

By 1976 twenty-five LEAs had a declared policy to establish 'community colleges' and over 200 schools already existed which called themselves 'community schools'. Inevitably it seems that there can be considerable tension between the adult and children's sections of a multipurpose establishment. The ways of a traditionally disciplined school are likely to be at variance with the informal, apparently undisciplined, creative learning atmosphere of modern adult provision. Though it is said that the combination may improve the behaviour of all concerned, teachers as well as children and adult students, the difference of ethos is not helped by administrative factors such as conditions of service, in which the professional school and adult sector staff have different pay scales and different treatment by the Department of Education and Science. The school headteacher may be supportive or antagonistic, willing to co-operate, or a jealous guardian of 'his' or 'her' school. Some have argued that the solution is to appoint an adult educator to be in charge of the whole establishment but this might only increase the tension. It also seems true that, at present, adult users tend to view the head and the teachers as being primarily concerned with the children, and that obviously there is need for much sensitivity among the full-time staff.

Colleges of Further Education

A further type of combined provision is to bring all forms of education for adults under one roof but to exclude those below school leaving age. In most instances this means that all the evening centre type of leisure-related provision takes place in a college of further education as well as the work-related classes. In a few instances it may be concentrated in a special wing or annexe or, as in the case of Rochdale, in a separate college building physically linked to the college of art and the technical college. In many colleges, arrangements for leisure-related education are carried out by a separate department which may be labelled the Adult Studies Department, the Department of Adult Education or the Department of General (or Liberal) Studies. Colleges may be said to have a potential advantage over schools in their traditions of departmental independence, but this can mean undue separatism and no real links with those providing vocational education. There are still problems of different age levels and ethos; young people tend to predominate in work-related classes and many appear to behave in ways unacceptable to older adults. Not infrequently, fears are also expressed that the work-related sector might 'drive out' the leisure-related studies. Similar problems, however, exist in the non work-related community education centres of Scotland which bring together adult and youth provision. Despite the avowed policy of integration, the link is often not easy. Possibly this kind of stress may be less developed in the polytechnics, most of which are now including non-vocational courses for adults within their programme as well as occasional seminars and conferences.

A few colleges of further education, however, seem to have achieved some success in dealing with these issues, and to have moved a long way towards a concept of the institution as the central agency for all types of post-school education and cultural activities in the area around, both providing classes and servicing the needs of voluntary organizations and individuals. Perhaps the outstanding example of this comprehensive view is Nelson and Colne College, a medium-sized establishment in north-east Lancashire, which declares its intention as being to meet all the 'educational, cultural and recreational needs' of the community in which it is situated. Besides the usual 'further education college' range of full-time and part-time courses for young people wanting to meet the occupational requirements of commerce and industry, it also offers general education for students of all ages, up to GCE 'O' and 'A' levels, and a very wide range of non-examination leisure-related classes. In addition it has developed a service for Open University students and pioneered the scheme of 'Open College' courses for special entry to Lancaster University, to which reference has already been made. It also became one of the first 'tertiary' colleges in which all full-time students in the area over the age of sixteen come to the college instead of attending sixth-forms in schools. Vital though the full-time students of all ages are in terms of staffing and finance, much importance is attached to the establishment of more casual, informal opportunities for learning. These include exhibitions, displays and demonstrations, initiatives such as the development of a Hallé Concert Club, and a talking newspaper for the blind, various special events such as public meetings and concerts and a large number of joint operations with bodies such as the North-West Arts Association, the Community Relations Council, the Civic Trust, social service organizations and local industry. The college seeks to put its resources, including its sports hall, at the disposal of the community at all times in the week, and it has developed as an information centre and a place for advice and counselling.

General problems of LEA provision

Such a solution is unlikely to be the universal answer. There are many kinds of 'community' and people tend not to live in 'real' neighbourhoods where there is a sense of communal identity. The old communities in many urban areas have been upheaved and destroyed, amid inner city renewal projects and the suburban sprawl, while in the new townships any sense of local community seems slow to grow. Many people belong to several unconnected groups — at work, in sports, in social, religious or political interests etc. — and feel no sense of neighbourhood. In an age of car ownership, moreover, they tend to move further afield. It is argued that the concept of the 'community' college or school is thus faulty in the late twentieth century, a relic of ideas which are now outdated, and that some new basis for the education of adults should be developed. Undoubtedly in a changing world the answers to this kind of problem may also change, and it is clear that the organizational pattern ought to be a response to local circumstances dependent on factors such as the density and distribution of the population in the area, and the existence of local facilities including those of communication. What is suitable to one area may not meet the needs of people in another type of location, an obvious contrast being that of a densely-populated, urban and industrial concentration such as Birmingham and the thinly-populated rural areas of the Highlands of Scotland.

Often, however, the type of organization depends upon local attitudes and personalities. The composition of local education committees and the social philosophies of local councillors may well be the determining factor, as may be the predilections of the chief education officer. Negative attitudes on the part of college or school principals and senior staff can quickly create conditions unfavourable to the organization of an imaginative provision for adults, and the latter can become mere 'hangers-on', receiving the left-over resources when other needs have been met. The success of multi-user provision depends very much on the attitudes and convictions of the staff and so far it would appear that only relatively few accept the multipurpose role as community educators. The rest remain in separate worlds as either schoolteachers or youth workers or adult educators. Within the ranks of the educators of adults, there may also be deep divisions between those teaching work-related subjects and those promoting leisure-related education. If educational plant is to be used by all, how are minority interests to be protected? If separate establishments are to be developed, how is the autonomy of the users to be kept free from isolation and eccentricity?

Adequacy of provision also raises questions of internal structuring, whatever the general organization. As the technological revolution increases its impact on the pattern of work and leisure, the demand for morning and afternoon courses seems likely to increase, and perhaps adult educators should envisage provision open all day for seven days a week, if they are to meet the needs of all members of the community. This ideal has been put forward by David Moore, the Principal of Nelson and Colne College, and it carries implications, in terms of staffing, emphasizing the need for full-time teachers and organizers in the adult sector, and for attention to be given to ways of ensuring full caretaking and maintenance services. Similarly, there seems no reason why the provision of education for adults should be restricted to the traditional winter half of the year, or keep to school or college terms, or begin at the traditional starting dates. Already centres such as the City Lit. have developed a 'four-term year', and there have been pleas that an Easter starting date would be helpful to those attending the 'winter' courses; it would at least help them to do some preliminary planning and reading. With the growth of computerized learning services, there is a case for making these and laboratories, with attendant technicians, open to adults whenever they choose to use them. 'Coin operated adult education', as advocated by Andrew Fairbairn, the Chief Education Officer for Leicestershire, may become a standard need in the future. At present it can be argued that some adults need facilities in which they can practise skills, or workshops in which they can make articles in wood or metal which require equipment not usually available at home, or perhaps just a place in which a learning exchange can take place. The formal teacher-and-class provision may remain dominant, but perhaps more self-directed education should be envisaged within the college framework. Wanting to know more about a subject, whether work-related or not, the adult of the future may wish, as a matter of course, to have available resources for use when he or she chooses. These resources may be buildings, equipment or technicians, teachers or counsellors. In this situation 'enrolment', if it occurred at all, would be very different from the present, somewhat cumbersome, procedure, and perhaps the time has already arrived for a thorough reform of existing LEA regulations. Adults, it is said, could and should assume more responsibility for the management of their educational affairs, instead of submitting to the sort of processing they accept in so many establishments today. Though there have been some developments of groups without a teacher meeting in local education authority premises, in ways similar to those of the study circles of Scandinavia, too little attention seems to have been paid generally to the requirements of this kind of group. The general plea is for more LEA sensitivity to change and more flexibility.

LEA fees

A major issue is that of the fees to be charged to adult students. Should the whole leisure-related education service be 'free', paid for out of taxes by the central and local government in the same way as children's education in the Authority schools, or should adults pay the full 'economic' cost; or should they make some contribution, the rest being met by subsidy? Until comparatively recently, most LEAs charged a more or less nominal fee, deliberately kept low so that no one should be excluded from classes on financial grounds. From the 1970s onwards, however, there has been a tendency to increase student fees considerably and under pressure from central government policy, some LEAs have asserted the need for fees large enough to cover all costs, however difficult it is to calculate the full amount. As indicated, the result has been extraordinary variations from one LEA area to another: in some places in 1979, for example, an adult might pay 10p per hour, while in others it would be £1.00 per hour in a leisure-related class, the mean being 30p per hour.[15] These discrepancies appear to have no relationship to educational needs, and to be quite arbitrary; the decisions depend entirely upon the views of those in power and upon their estimates of the value of education for adults and of its political importance. It is clear, however, that the size of the fee influences the type of clientele. As fees are increased, so the proportion lowers of those with below average income and with the least amount of childhood education.[16] The overall number of students tends to fall for a time, but is then replaced by those with higher incomes if the centre has amenities and is reasonably accessible; in some areas such as council housing estates and some rural areas, the whole provision may be destroyed. Rural areas are also likely to suffer from high rises in transport costs and from the termination of some bus and rail services. The general effect of fee rises seems to be to enable the educationally rich to get richer, while the educationally poor get poorer, a form of discrimination which most educators of adults find unacceptable. In the course of their history some centres are said to have moved from providing remedial education for the underprivileged to being a resource centre for the more affluent.

Besides the broad question of the whole rationale of fees for adult classes — should any at all be charged, and if so on what basis? — there are a number of sub-issues. Some LEAs, uneasy about increases, have tried to keep the fee per course down by reducing the length, for example, from twenty-four to twenty meetings, or by shortening each class meeting, for example, from 2 hours to 1½ hours, but this merely reduces the amount of tuition and the quality of the work, as does an increase in the number of students in a class, another device which has been used. Attempts have also been made to reduce the overall cost to the LEA of the provision by discriminatory fees between subjects — charging more for those considered educationally less worth while — but such distinctions seem invidious and arbitrary. Who is to produce a valid hierarchy of subjects or to measure their educational effect? Similarly, there have been questions about discrimination in favour of age or special need, a system more frequently used. On what basis are fees to be reduced for the retired person, the young adult, the handicapped, the illiterate, or the immigrant? Or for the person who attends more than one class? Over the years, many LEAs have devised schedules which allow for cheap or free attendance by old age pensioners and the unemployed, and many have a system of reduced payments for a second class. A few, indeed, instituted a 'study card' or 'leisure card' which for the same fee allowed a person to attend as many classes and cultural activities as he or she wished. Most of these arrangements are now under review.

Divergent policies have created problems for those adults who wish to attend classes or use facilities in a neighbouring LEA area. Organizations such as the Association for Adult and Continuing Education campaign for freedom of access regardless of LEA boundaries — for 'free trade' — but some Authorities refuse to agree to inter-authority recoupment payments and erect solid barriers on their boundaries. In view of such problems and the general cost of collecting fees and administering discriminatory scales, some have questioned the economic worthwhileness of any kind of fee, unless it is clearly profit making and the sort of amount charged by commercial agencies. If the latter course were adopted, there would, of course, be no possibility of an LEA meeting the needs of the socially and culturally deprived, or of the lower income groups in general. The whole fee question, in fact, depends upon the view taken of education for adults and in particular of the leisure-related section. If it is thought that the latter is of minimal importance, peripheral and a sort of recreation without serious intent, then public subsidy is believed to be undesirable and irrelevant. If, however, it is regarded as being of central and growing importance for everyone because of the needs of a changing world, then it is argued that all parts of the service should be free from fees of any kind. If the community accepts 'free' public libraries, parks and gardens, and a wide range of subsidies for sport, the arts and other 'leisure' activities, then why not free education for adults wishing to widen knowledge, skills, interests, ideas and attitudes? Indeed it is often argued that this is more important than present secondary or higher education, from which some finance might be transferred, that adults are more highly motivated, coming because they want to learn, and that the service of education for adults makes a very substantial contribution to the quality of life in the whole community.

LEA-assisted provision

LEAs may interpret their duties under the Education Acts as requiring them to assist the provision made by other agencies. Partly this can be in the form of direct financial aid, either for capital expenditure or for running costs, and this may include, for example, the salary of a voluntary association centre warden or principal, or a proportion of the teaching costs. Partly the aid may be free or cheap accommodation, some LEAs operating a sort of sliding scale, in which the more educational value is credited the less the charge to the provider, and from 1945 until recently, the central government has tended to urge LEAs to provide free accommodation for adult classes provided by other agencies. Some LEAs have also granted the free use of equipment and have helped with publicity; thus in the handbooks issued by Authorities such as Derby, Warwickshire and Manchester, besides the lists of classes and other activities directly provided, there are details of those provided by voluntary agencies. Again there is no uniformity between Authorities and much depends upon the relationships which have been established and upon the attitudes of those in control. As will be discussed in a later chapter, there have been attempts to secure fruitful collaboration through local development councils on lines similar to those suggested by the Russell Report, but in other areas suspicion and antagonisms have led the LEA to decide that it will undertake most of the provision itself, or, if it decides not to provide, then to give no help to others.

Traditionally the LEAs have been willing to give most assistance to the Responsible Bodies, the extra-mural departments of the universities and the WEA, but a few other examples will show what is possible if LEAs so wish. Morley College, which began in 1880 as part of the Old Vic in Waterloo, London, is now grant-aided by the ILEA for much of its work and received from that Authority £275,000 out of the £375,000 required for the building extensions of the early 1970s. This made possible many special features of its contribution as a literary institute, providing good air conditioning, sound-proofing, lifts, common rooms, and a language laboratory as well as general resources. In Leeds, the Swarthmore Education Centre was founded by the Quakers in 1909, and is governed by a Council, half of whom are current students, elected by the membership. Though constitutionally independent, it has had generous grants from the Leeds LEA for its work, part of which consists of a multitude of classes, some run in co-operation with the LEA but others with the WEA and Leeds University extra-mural department. One of the oldest existing education centres for adults, the Working Men's College in London, also receives an annual grant from the ILEA. Founded in 1854 by the Christian Socialists so that 'the working man should have the opportunity of acquiring wisdom through education', the college maintains a full pro-gramme of classes, for women as well as men, mostly of a leisure-related type, and it has both common rooms and playing fields.

Independent voluntary agencies, of course, run the risk that the LEA will cut off their aid and so endanger the work they do, particularly if the cut is a sudden one. One of their major strengths is that they can call upon the contribution of unpaid voluntary workers, but this is not always a safe-guard to their existence, especially in times of inflation. It can well be argued that they are of particular value in a democracy and that they have a flexibility which enables them more easily and more rapidly to meet the educational needs of adults which otherwise are not likely to receive attention. 'The welfare of a country,' said Sir Frank Mears, 'like that of a plant, depends on the healthy condition of the small rootlets at the extremities of the main rootstems.' In these ways, as well as for the possible economies they can make, the voluntary agencies would seem to have a clear case for LEA support even if the Authority itself makes the major contribution of more standard requirements.

Educational Centres Association

In the first few decades of the twentieth century in England and Wales, the chief exponent of the importance of independent accommodation to the success of education for adults was the Educational Settlements Association (ESA). Founded in 1920, this brought together the non-residential centres which had been founded from 1909 onwards, the first two being St Mary's, York, and Swarthmore, Leeds. They also included Beechcroft, a most significant development which was founded in 1914 by Horace Fleming, one of the genuine catalysts in this field. The value of suitable separate accommodation had been recognized by the Christian Church throughout the ages and by nineteenth century developments such as the Working Men's Colleges and the Mechanics' Institutes, but the stress given to it by the ESA, renamed the Educational Centres Association (ECA) in 1946, for leisure-related education has been a development of considerable importance. Education is seen by the ECA as a social as well as an intellectual process, and the provision of a 'hearth and home' as essential to sound, healthy, individual and social growth. In accommodation designed or adapted for adults only, classes, courses and less formal activities can be grouped around a common room, canteen and library, and students will then gain more from contact with each other, acquiring habits, standards and behavioural patterns as well as knowledge, interests and skills.

The ECA has also stressed the principle of partnership between students, teachers and the head of a centre, and has spread the idea of a self-governing educational community. The management of resources as well as the planning of programmes and the conduct of classes should all be subject to this 'member participation' and corporate responsibility. This philosophy grew out of the early work of the settlements which tried not only to bring higher education to adults in deprived urban areas but to give members self-respect by having a voice in their own affairs. 'Non-partisan in politics and religion,'[17] the Association wants members to have 'a real opportunity to take part in . . . management and programming . . . and [to] develop a strong social and corporate life from the educational activities.'[18]

After a period of difficulty in the early 1950s, the ECA has achieved a position of strength as a national voluntary body, and now has in membership well over a hundred centres, the majority of which belong to the local education authorities, including the City Lit and many village colleges. In these centres there is usually a mixture of university extra-mural and WEA classes as well as a larger group of LEA classes, and the total number of students which the ECA can claim to represent is, in fact, well over 300,000.

There are also an increasing number of self-programming groups. Throughout, the ECA has provided information and advice to member centres, and has been a channel for the exchange of ideas through conferences and seminars, organized both nationally and regionally. Usually, for example, there are two major national conferences each year. In the earlier years, the Association issued a regular journal, under the symbolic title of *Common Room,* later revived for a time as *Phoenix,* but it now publishes only occasional papers. Concerned very much with the development of classes, it was recognized as a 'responsible body' for the receipt of direct central government finance from 1924 to 1961 when it gave up the position, feeling that with just a general grant in aid it could pay more attention to broader educational activities as well as classes. Despite its success in England and Wales, however, it has had little direct influence on Scotland and Northern Ireland, perhaps because of the different traditions, and early local authority dominance in the former and more centralized direction in the latter.

The central philosophy of the ECA has gained increasing acceptance but growth has brought some problems. The average centre today is very different from the small community of like-minded people in the early settlements and the 'hearth and home' idea has to be construed in terms of a much larger, mixed membership with very varied social and educational needs. Such a centre requires a fully professional warden or principal, and this has been declared essential by the association even though it can provide a challenge to the idea of voluntary student control. Students may be tempted to leave the running of the centre entirely to the paid head ('That's what he's paid for') and the warden may be tempted to accept. Some centres are still small with only two or three hundred members but most have several thousand, and a few more than 10,000, the average being about 2,500 to 3,000. The difficulty is increased by the fact that the older voluntary centres have found it almost impossible to maintain themselves without LEA support, and by the persistence in some LEA centres of the 'night school' concept of warden control and non-participation by students. The organization of the ECA itself has been stretched by the considerable growth in membership, and only in 1979, after the retirement of the stalwart part-time secretary, Ray Lamb, who nobly held the association together in difficult periods, has a full-time secretary been appointed. There have also been moves to develop a new regional structure in order to strengthen the role of the association at local level.

Despite all its success, some have suggested that the central principles of the ECA are outdated and invalid in the last years of the twentieth century. Do most adults want to participate in the organization of their education or just use the services which others devise and offer? Is the separate adult centre for leisure, non-work related, education the right answer in a changing world or are there satisfactory alternatives more likely to meet future needs? Is it perhaps only suitable for certain areas and certain groups of the population? Has it inbuilt disadvantages? Harold Wiltshire has pointed out the gain in status and prestige obtained by a central and dignified building for adult education, but has also noted the danger that it might become socially exclusive. Though questions continue to be asked about the 'centre idea', however, the ECA thrives and few have as yet seriously challenged the declaration by the Association, repeated soon after its change of title in 1946, that 'the primary function of any local citizen centre should be the progressive development of the individual as a member of a free society, through mental training, the encouragement of self effort and the exercise of personal responsibility'[19] The idea persists of a 'strong social and corporate life deriving from educational activities'.[20] The problem is how to achieve it.

Universities

Many of the staff in European universities question why universities should be concerned in any way with the education of adults other than the undergraduates who come for the most part directly from school. They feel that the 'diffusion of knowledge' is better left to other organizations and that, as the Rector of the University of Strasbourg said in 1956 at a UNESCO Regional Seminar, 'to include such a task among the duties of a university professor would be . . . to play down to the common man, which would be of no use or benefit to anyone'.[21] The work of a university, it is said, is that of an institution for advanced education, concerned with research and with teaching at appropriate levels to students 'known to be intelligent and adequately prepared'. Extra-mural work is thus held to be not of 'genuinely university quality', not part of the 'real' university, and internal teachers undertaking it are said to be distracted from their proper and more important functions.[22] Alternatively, others attack it on the grounds that the methods of university teaching are unsuitable for other than undergraduate students. Nevertheless, most British universities do contribute extramurally to the education of adults in some way or another, and 'university extension' in Britain is usually dated from 1873, the year in which Cambridge University took a corporate and official responsibility for the provision of courses for the general public 'outside the walls'. Just what that contribution should be is, however, subject to much argument. Some think of it in limited terms. In 1974, for example, a Joint Working Party of the Committee of Vice-Chancellors and Principals and the Universities Council for Adult Education, having declared that universities should accept a commitment to provide opportunities for 'learning throughout life', added that in so doing:

> They should concentrate on those things that they are particularly well equipped to do . . . work which demands a level of teaching and learning characteristic of universities, which truly engages the minds of their teaching staff, and which gives opportunities for study of a quality (if not necessarily the same subject matter) associated with degree awards.[23]

Others have stressed a wider university extra-mural role, perhaps even a 'duty' to influence the community at large in its outlook and understanding, to give leadership and to help ordinary people by a more democratic approach as well as by a stress on fundamental issues, underlying principles and objective analysis. They believe that universities should spare no effort to assist non-graduate citizens to develop a more trained insight, a grasp of critical standards and a mental discipline.

Before the Second World War, the feeling of social obligation to the 'underprivileged', and concern with the training of democratic citizens, provided a strong driving force moving universities to action. It also moved some university teachers to undertake long journeys to industrial cities where they gave public lectures and courses, which in turn proved to be the foundation stones of some new universities. Some of these feelings and particular enthusiasms still cause many university teachers to give individual support to local societies and activities but the official university contribution appears to be less motivated and to be directed more and more to those who have had more than the minimum of early education. The motives for participation remain very mixed. Some, for example, argue that local support is necessary for survival and that it is in the interest of universities to come out of isolation and monastic detachment and to establish good public relations through adult educational work. Some believe that university education should be more available to a larger section of the population and this has been a recurrent theme, expressed by mid-nineteenth century liberal-minded university teachers in Oxford and Cambridge as well as by those pressing for the creation of new universities in the mid-twentieth century. Scottish universities and their internal courses have for centuries been much more accessible to ordinary people than those in England, which is perhaps a major reason for the failure of 'university extension' courses readily to develop there in the late nineteenth century and for the relatively slow development of Scottish extra-mural work in general.

Variant ideas about the nature of the contribution of the universities to the education of adults have led to a complexity of answers to questions about structure and content. If universities have a 'duty' to undertake extra-mural work, how best are they to discharge it? What organizational structures are necessary? How should the work be staffed and financed? What kinds of subjects are appropriate? For whom should provision be made – for everyone or merely for certain selected sections of the population? To this kind of question each university has made a unique response, depending partly on its history and geographical setting, partly on the size and type of the neighbouring population and partly on the ideas of a few individuals.

In the first fifty years of university institutional participation after 1873, the usual kind of structure in England and Wales was a committee established by the university Senate and variously known as a 'delegacy', 'syndicate', or 'extension board'. This was serviced by an administrator who might be a full-time Secretary, or perhaps a member of the Registrar's department carrying out the work part time as a special duty. After the development of joint activities with the Workers' Educational Association, this arrangement was supplemented and in some cases superseded by a University Tutorial Classes Joint Committee, the first of which was set up in Oxford in 1907. This Joint Committee established an early pattern of an 'equal partnership', often of seven university and seven WEA representatives, but in the period after the 1944 Education Act most brought into membership the neighbouring LEAs and also representatives from bodies such as the public libraries and the Tutors' Association. Growing up on an *ad hoc* basis, this machinery has continued in many universities, although with increasing modification, as one of the methods of consultation between universities and other agencies. In Scotland, the system has had a different development, and Extra-Mural Education Committees have been created with bases in the universities of Glasgow, Aberdeen, Edinburgh and Dundee, the earliest being that of Glasgow set up in 1924. Independent of the university but serviced by the special extra-mural department, these committees with their representatives from the education authorities and the WEA as well as from the university, are therefore similar in structure to the English joint committees. They differ, however, in function in that they are the agencies for grant aid from the Scottish Education Department for administration and organization. In Scotland, as in the rest of Britain, however, a critical overhaul of the machinery, already in progress, may produce considerable modifications before the end of the century. In one or two places in England already, new, perhaps more streamlined, consultative organs have replaced the old joint committees and there have been moves to bring the organization more within the internal structure. Thus in Manchester, the old joint committee was abolished in 1973, to be replaced by a smaller Extra-Mural Consultative Council, and in Sheffield the extra-mural department became in 1976 a Division of Continuing Education within the Faculty of Educational Studies.

A major reorganization of the machinery followed the 1919 Report submitted to the government.[24] This strongly recommended the 'establishment at each university of a department of extra-mural adult education, with an academic head'. The first of these was established in Nottingham in 1920 and most of the universities founded before 1963 followed this example, although some such as Leeds (1946) and Sheffield (1947) deferred doing so until after the Second World War. These special departments have a variety of titles; in the earlier examples the older universities tended to use 'extra-mural' and the university colleges of the time such as Nottingham, Bristol, Hull and Leicester used 'adult education', while in more recent years titles such as 'institutes' or 'departments' of 'extension studies' or 'external studies' or 'continuing education' have been introduced. On the whole Scotland has kept to 'extra-mural' although, as in some English universities, the title in the 1970s has been extended to be Department of Extra-Mural and Adult Education, in an attempt to indicate a widening function. Gradually there has been a division of the country into areas of influence, most extra-mural areas tending at first to correspond with those of WEA Districts but to have little relation to local government boundaries. At the time of writing there are twenty-three extra-mural departments with related areas in England, four in Wales, six in Scotland and two in Northern Ireland, but the situation may change rapidly, especially as the geographical areas contain within them the newer universities created in the late 1960s and 1970s.

Within this broad structural pattern, extra-mural departments differ in size and complexity. All, however, have a Director, perhaps mainly an administrator with an extrepreneurial role, but increasingly given professorial status and salary and with it automatic membership of the University Senate. He is likely to have a deputy, or deputies, and administrative assistants as well as clerical staff, and he may choose to organize the department as a unity or with sectional divisions related to the type of provision, each under its own head. He will also have a staff of lecturers and tutors, some concerned with the teaching and development of a particular academic subject such as philosophy, literature, science or history, and others rather more with the organization of the work in a given part of the university region. The latter are usually known as Resident Staff Tutors, expected to reside in as well as look after a particular part of the extra-mural area, but their precise duties depend upon departmental policy. Their influence as key figures has tended to decline in some regions as organizers have been appointed by the LEA and the WEA. In all there are over 500 full-time appointments in the United Kingdom as compared to fewer than fifty before 1939; up to the late 1940s appointments were by the joint committees, under Article XI of the old regulations which permitted only two per university before 1938. They now have parity of status and salary with internal university teachers but because of differences in their work some feel that they have not achieved parity of esteem. Their increasing association with the internal department concerned with their teaching subject may help to reduce this feeling. Besides teaching extra-mural classes in the region — three or four nights per week is common — many have daytime commitments and have developed counselling and liaison work, identifying needs and seeking out resources to meet them. Sometimes this leads to criticism on the lines once expressed by Sir Eric Ashby who drew attention to the dangers of adult education being ' "laid on" by the universities in a spirit of efficient paternalism'.[25] Sometimes there are questions about the way in which the newer professionals view their work; most of the early staff tutors had a strong sense of mission and a high degree of commitment to adult education as a means of promoting social justice, and while for some this persists, the staff tutor of today knows that his promotion is more likely to depend upon research and publications. Supporting the full-time staff tutor are about 9,000 or so part-time tutors, about half from internal university departments and the rest graduates in other occupations. Extra-mural departments differ in their use of part-time staff, some wanting to use mainly members of the university while others, such as London, draw upon large numbers from outside. They also differ in their attitude to the ratio of part-time to full-time staff; some prefer most of the work to be carried out by full-time staff on the grounds that the work requires professional expertise while others believe that fluctuations in subject demand require the use of mainly part-time tutors.

In Scotland no full-time university appointments of extra-mural staff-tutors were made until after 1946 and the staff of the Scottish extra-mural departments is relatively small, except for Glasgow and Strathclyde. There is more reliance on the use of part-time tutors, despite the qualified support given by the Alexander Report to the need for more adequate full-time staffing.[26] Heriot-Watt University, lying within the area of Edinburgh extra-mural department, had no full-time staff in 1976—7, and its work outside the walls was looked after by an Adult Education Committee. In Northern Ireland, the two universities appear to be in a much stronger position. Established in 1928, the Belfast Department of Extra-Mural Studies had nine full-time lecturers and a director in 1979, while that of the New University of Ulster, established in 1972, had twelve full-time lecturers, three professors and a research fellow in its Institute of Continuing Education based in Londonderry.

Extra-mural departments throughout the United Kingdom are associated together in the Universities Council for Adult Education (UCAE), which was established in 1947 to continue the work of the Universities Extra-Mural Consultative Committee which had been set up in 1926. In, Scotland the UCAE (Scotland) was established in 1977 as part of the national body but designed to give the Scottish universities special opportunities to discuss matters related particularly to their work, and to given them also a corporate voice in discussions with other Scottish bodies. The UCAE has one representative from each constituent university or university college, normally the 'officer responsible for extra-mural work' and it acts as a vehicle for consultation, the collection of information and the formulation of 'appropriate policies'.[27] It convenes a Standing Conference on University Adult Education, usually once a year, to which are invited other representatives from the universities. It may also arrange other meetings, appoint working parties and make reports. As it does so, it tends to give a sharper focus to the problems of extra-mural work. It has also a Standing Joint Committee with the WEA.

The case for the establishment of separate extra-mural departments in universities has come under increasing scrutiny, despite declarations of support from the various committees of enquiry. The Russell Committee, for example, summed up its reasons by declaring that:

> The traditional department of extra-mural studies or of adult education, has clear and well-tried advantages: an accumulation of expertise, wide-ranging contacts in the local region, ready machinery (in the persons of its full-time staff) for consultation both in the university and outside, an identity within the university through which the claims of the work can be voiced, an identity towards the outside world and especially towards the rest of the education service that promotes the free flow of ideas, and a capability for research in the whole field of adult education.[28]

Others have felt that it tends to separatism, to isolation from the 'normal' university provision and to increasing an unfortunate tendency for universities to shrug off their full responsibility to the outside public. The Russell Report also noted that the foundation of new universities and the development of other institutions of higher education such as polytechnics created a new context, in which ways ought to be found of using the teaching resources of all the institutions of higher education. Some of the newer universities have not established extra-mural departments but have tried to find other ways of involving the whole university in the education of adults, and of integrating its 'extra-mural work' more closely with the rest of its activities. The provision of services for the adult community in the region by the whole university is seen as the prime concern of the Centre for Continuing Education at the University of Sussex and the basic aim too, of the New University of Ulster. Elsewhere studies have shown that many internal departments in the older universities already provide courses for the outside public without using the channel of their extra-mural department. A survey in Manchester in 1965 revealed that ninety departments were then so involved, especially many science and technological departments and those in the medical faculty. Some, in fact, have suggested that extra-mural education should be left entirely to the internal departments as an acknowledged, perhaps contractual, part of the work of all university teachers, although perhaps with the organization of such work made the particular responsibility of one person in each department. On the other hand some have talked of a Faculty of Continuing Education, a title already used in the Canadian University of Calgary.

To a considerable degree the structure of the machinery depends upon ideas about what type of provision is appropriate to a university. Traditionally extra-mural work has meant the provision of courses in liberal studies, although this term has never been very clearly defined and the spectrum has widened to include some of the sciences as well as the social sciences and the arts. Much of this provision has been linked to the 'social conscience' drive, to the promotion of social emancipation and 'good citizenship', and arguments proliferated about the kind of subject to be regarded as most appropriate. To some, anything other than the early staple diet of economics, history, politics and philosophy is a weakening of the effort. The aim whatever the subject, however, has been to develop minds and personalities, and, in close association with the WEA, methods were devised to provide opportunities for reflection and discussion, for the development of perspective and for the cultivation of intellectual freedom. The normal class of this kind meets in the evening once a week for two hours, has within it a good deal of student participation and requires student effort in reading and written work. As the Russell Report said, this provision is 'characterised by intellectual effort by the students, the guidance of a tutor with firmly based scholarship, and freedom from externally imposed syllabuses and examinations'.[29] Open to all without entry qualifications, and with no awards at the end of the courses, these classes have great flexibility and may include outside activities such as field work, visits to art galleries and museums and surveys. Joint work with the WEA led to the famous University Tutorial Class which meets for 24 weeks each year for three years and is restricted to not more than twenty-four students in a class, and to shorter courses of 20—24 meetings, entitled Sessional classes, or of 10—12 meetings called Terminal classes. Similar classes are also organized directly by the universities as Extension courses and in number these now exceed the number of those provided jointly. The proportion of the three-year classes has declined considerably in recent decades but in many areas the number of classes with more than twenty meetings is still substantial. It has been argued that short courses are too limited and superficial to be of a satisfactory university standard and that they cannot stimulate serious study, or help personal development among ordinary members of the public. In reply, it has been said that length is no guarantee of quality and that much depends on the type of students who attend. Certainly, people are often unwilling to commit themselves for long periods and it is clear that quality may well depend more on the motivation and experience of students, and on the teaching ability of the tutor, than on length. A compromise in some areas is the development of the 'linked sessional' in which people enrol for only one year but may then proceed to another course in the next year which is linked in subject matter and level.

From an early date, a system has been developed of providing most extra-mural classes with a set of books despatched in special 'book boxes' to the place of meeting, which may be a school, church hall or other accommodation anywhere in the region. Many of the older extra-mural departments have built up sizeable lending libraries for this purpose and have appointed full-time librarians to look after their maintenance and distribution. As a further aid to the development of the work a few departments, such as those in Nottingham, Leicester, Liverpool and Southampton, have taken up the ECA idea and established extra-mural teaching centres within their own control. As noted earlier there has been an appreciation of the value of residential opportunities, some departments having their own colleges such as Holly Royde in Manchester or Rewley House in Oxford and almost all arranging summer schools. There has also been a growth of courses held on the university campus — a development which though it helps the 'university atmosphere' makes nonsense of the term 'extra-mural'.

Since 1946, after four decades of concentration on joint work with the WEA, the independent university contribution has grown considerably, perhaps to a large extent in the form of *ad hoc* responses to pressing demands, or to the ideas of some members of staff. These take many forms. For instance, the universities of Liverpool and Southampton have both undertaken special work in either inner city areas or new housing estates. Another link with the older sense of obligation can be seen in the provision of 'university weeks' in the remoter areas of Scotland when a team of university teachers goes out to lecture to isolated villages in the Highlands or the Western Isles. Another rather more prolific development has been the provision of what the Russell Committee called 'role education' in which courses are designed to provide 'a relevant background of knowledge and appropriate intellectual skills for groups whose common element is their role in society'. Thus there are a multitude of courses for social workers of all kinds, for clergy, doctors and policemen, for local government officers and engineers, for farmers and for the armed services. The University of Surrey, for example, for some time has held courses for professional groups, including district nurses, tutors of midwives and members of the fire service. This type of provision, of course, is mainly work-related. Some extra-mural departments have moved without hesitation into the vocational field, following, for example, the pioneer work of Nottingham and Sheffield in the provision of courses for shop stewards and for special groups such as miners. Some, as in some of the Welsh departments, have questioned whether work-related education should be the responsibility of an extra-mural department at all. Some of the newer universities, without extra-mural departments, such as Salford and Strathclyde, have developed short courses which try to integrate the vocational and liberal elements by being as much concerned with personal development as with updating. Internal departments on the whole have had no inhibitions about work-related courses and, as already noted, many provide refresher courses at postgraduate level, as do the Business Schools and the departments and institutes of education. Extra-mural departments thus face considerable competition to their own ventures into the work-related field, and there has been a somewhat patchy growth, even though some have found it financially profitable.

There has also been a mixed response to examination work leading to awards. Involvement in part-time degree work has been slow despite the encouragement of, for example, Gordon Oakes, who when Minister of State for Education pleaded that 'the barriers between universities proper [*sic*] and their extra-mural departments could profitably be breached — why should these departments not offer part-time courses that could count towards a degree?'[30] The cause of part-time degrees seems to have been taken up mainly elsewhere, notably by the Open University and the CNAA, and it is noteworthy that the London external degree is administered by a Council for External Students and not by the Council for Extra-mural Studies. On the other hand, there has been a development of non-degree qualifications provided by several extra-mural departments to meet what appears to be an increasing demand, part of it not work-related. It would seem that a fairly large number of people wish to gain awards for their own personal satisfaction and to undertake examination courses in order to test themselves; however alien this wish for an award may be to the old liberal study, WEA-related courses, this is paralleled by the search elsewhere for non work-related qualifications in sport, for example, swimming, and in languages, public speaking, dancing and craft work. In the early period of the 1890s, most of the universities provided 'extension' certificates and diplomas but, except in London, these tended to die out while joint work with the WEA was the main focus. Since the 1950s there has been a growing revival of such courses, usually in the liberal studies field in subjects such as economics, sociology, literature or music. Often the courses extend over three or four years with the 'normal' twenty-four meetings each session and they may be attended by non-examination as well as by examination students, an arrangement which appears to produce no real difficulties. It has been argued that extra-mural departments should encourage more of this kind of serious study among mature adults as a lead forward to later participation in degree courses, rather than follow the American example and provide part-time degree courses themselves. Some are already moving towards courses which provide some training in study skills as well as opening up subject areas for later study. One such course is that provided by Manchester Extra-Mural Department in association with the WEA North-Western District; entitled 'Introduction to university studies' it is at present a course of twenty-eight meetings held during the daytime from 10 a.m. to 3.30 p.m.

Some universities have developed an interest in the study of adult education as an academic discipline, in the conduct and supervision of appropriate research, and in the provision of professional training courses for adult educators. This will be discussed more fully in the later chapter on 'Staffing and training', but some of the main organizational features may be indicated here. One query concerns the suitability of extra-mural departments for this kind of work. On the one hand it is said that the staff tutors have a particular expertise in teaching adults, but on the other that they know only one sector of the field and that good trainers must have a wide knowledge of the whole range of education for adults as well as a substantial experience within it. The case is, therefore, made out for specialists whose subject discipline is the education of adults and who need to give all their time to its study. This view has been challenged, just as earlier some extra-mural departments rejected the whole idea of training. The organization therefore varies and possibly reflects the particular circumstances in each university. Manchester University in 1949 established an internal department of adult education, separate from the department of extra-mural studies, while in Nottingham the work is carried out in a special division of the School of Education. Elsewhere it tends to be an extension of the normal work of extra-mural departments sometimes with most staff taking part, sometimes with only a few, perhaps comprising a special section as in Liverpool and Leeds. At present fourteen universities offer courses leading to advanced diplomas, and/or master's degrees and doctorates in adult education, broadly interpreted, and some offer shorter non award-bearing courses. These include the universities of Edinburgh and Glasgow and the New University of Ulster, while the University of Wales is becoming involved as the examining body for such awards in the Principality, although it seems likely that appropriate courses are more likely to take place in colleges of higher education. The active departments are associated in a Standing Conference on University Teaching and Research in the Education of Adults (SCUTREA), the main purpose of which is to further the work by exchanging information and ideas. Some departments, such as Manchester's department of adult education, have also given a lead in the in-service training of internal university teachers as well as in bringing together adult educators from the LEA and other sectors for regular seminars.

The role of universities in the education of adults is thus subject to a good deal of change and in some places to confusion. The traditional liberal studies work of the extra-mural departments continues in most of the older universities but to it is now added a great variety of other work. The machinery of provision is being modified and in the newer universities especially there are experimental structures. The questions about standards, length of courses, range of subjects and the type of students, continue to be debated without any apparent degree of agreement. Behind these problems, of course, are variations in the concept of the role of a university. Should it be concerned with the education of an élite or with the education of the masses? Should it confine its activities to its own campus, or should it pursue a role outside the walls in the whole community? Is it to be just a creator and repository of knowledge, or is it to try also to be the instrument of social change? In the modern world should continuing education become the central role of the whole university, and should a university be the cultural centre and centre for information and ideas within its region? Or should it focus on research as its major activity and press for a national or international role? Decisions on matters of this kind would help to resolve many of the existing confusions.

The Workers' Educational Association

Founded in 1903 by Albert Mansbridge, the Workers' Educational Association (WEA) is the largest voluntary organization of students in non-vocational classes in Britain, and it has achieved considerable international fame. Its strength varies from one part of the country to another, however, and even in the same locality varies from year to year. Generalizations therefore tend to be false; although on the whole it has had more success in urban than in rural areas, this does not apply to Wales where it has deep roots in the villages and small towns and a close involvement with the rural community in the more Welsh speaking areas. In both Scotland and Northern Ireland it has been weak and slow to develop, although perhaps for different reasons. For a long time it had no full-time teaching or administrative staff in Northern Ireland, the first being appointed in the early 1970s, while in Scotland the LEAs have been dominant and the WEA contribution to both liberal adult education and trade union studies has so far been very modest. As indicated earlier, its status there in terms of government grants is very different from that in England and Wales, where WEA Districts have enjoyed recognition as Responsible Bodies since 1924 and have thus been in receipt of direct financial aid from the central government. Beginning as a search to secure greater educational opportunities for ordinary people, it has survived many attacks, recurrent crises and periods of self-questioning, and it has shown considerable toughness and resilience. Two main characteristics stand out. First, throughout its existence it has carried the high principles of its founder in its belief in social justice and in the need for genuine, not biased, education. Without party political or sectarian ties,[31] though motivated a good deal by ideas of social reform, the WEA has pressed for greater equality of educational opportunity, and also for objectivity in study, despite the challenge from some quarters that this was not possible. Throughout there has been linked to it a stress on quality, on the grounds that only the best is good enough for ordinary people. This search for quality led to a close relationship with the universities in a 'partnership of labour and learning'. There seems to have been a touch of Puritanism about the early WEA, shown sometimes even in the choice of accommodation where sordid surroundings were held to toughen the moral fibre, but more particularly in the deep moral earnestness and missionary zeal which still possesses some of its members. Second, there has been much stress on self-government and independence, on local control by voluntary unpaid effort, and with it friendliness, co-operation and mutual respect — what in the nineteenth century was summed up in the word 'fellowship'. The hope is that by bringing together people of many different types and shades of opinion — 'some slow, some quick, some superficial, some deep'[32] — there will be a way forward to a better society. Not surprisingly the WEA has been described as 'the agent of democracy'. Of course, not all members live up to these traditions but even after over three-quarters of a century, enough idealism still prevails to cause many individuals enthusiastically to sacrifice much of their leisure time for what to them is a Movement rather than just a collection of students and classes.

As a Movement it has an interest in the education of everyone from birth to death as the Constitution makes very clear: the objectives of the Association are stated as being:

> to stimulate and to satisfy the demand of adults, in particular members of workers' movements, for education by the promotion of courses and other facilities, and generally to further the advancement of education to the end that all children, adolescents and adults may have full opportunities for the education needed for their complete individual and social development.[32]

Its main concern, however, has been the adult sector, and over the years it has established a structure both to promote demand and to administer the provision. The first essential part is the local group of student members, or 'branch', and at present there are about 170,000 members organized in nearly 900 branches, of which just under twenty are in Scotland and rather more than twenty in Northern Ireland. The members of each branch annually elect a number of unpaid voluntary officers and a committee, and together they plan a programme of adult education for the locality and undertake to promote and provide it. It is perhaps unfortunate that only a small proportion of class members choose to take part in this highly democratic process but the minority of student activists has a real voice in policy making. 'The amount of voluntary effort is still substantial,' said the Russell Report[34] and the proportion of students taking part is 'enormously greater than in local education authority or independent university class provision'. Branches, of course, differ in size, some having less than twenty members, others even over two thousand, and they determine their own officer and committee structure; in some a chairman and secretary/treasurer may be thought enough, while in a large city branch, the work may be divided between a multitude of officers and sub-committees. Each branch has its own unique features although perhaps an average medium-sized one can be thought of as a group of perhaps sixty to eighty members, of whom a quarter actively concern themselves with the organization of WEA activities in their town. All branches, however, are autonomous and have the power to do what they wish, subject to the important proviso that they can secure the necessary resources. A branch may wish to have a wide variety of activities as well as educational classes, but for the latter, after the branch committee has drawn up a list of requirements, often with details of suggested length, time of meeting and possibly the name of a tutor, as well as a subject, the branch secretary forwards it to the regional federation of branches, or 'District', with the request that arrangements be made for the appointment of suitable tutors.

Just as the autonomy of the branches was established by the early groups of students so the Districts have grown up without prior planning. Gradually the country has been divided into areas, at present twenty-one in number, including three in Scotland and one in Northern Ireland. Branches elect delegates, normally two in number, and these, together with representatives of societies which choose to affiliate, form the district council, meeting perhaps four times a year. At an annual general meeting, voluntary officers (chairman, treasurer, etc.) and a smaller district executive committee are elected for the more immediate control of affairs. There have been proposals to abandon the district council and have just one 'district committee' but so far this has met with opposition. The District also appoints a full-time paid administrative officer, the district secretary, for the execution of its decisions and the day to day administration of the area. As the District in England and Wales is the Responsible Body to which central government funds are sent, one of the major tasks of district secretaries is to match branch lists of requested courses with tutor resources known to them and to make appropriate arrangements. For the courses organized in co-operation with the university (Joint Committee classes) they work with the directors of the department of extra-mural studies. They will also carry out any duties laid upon them by the district executives and have the general task of helping the work by consultation, advice and contact with other organizations. The district executive committee is also responsible for the appointment of full-time tutor—organizers of whom there are now over 120 in the various Districts, and a much smaller number of 'development officers' or 'organizers'. Some of the tutor—organizers have a task similar to that of the university resident staff tutors in that they help existing WEA branches within a area of the District, promote the development of new branches and generally maintain liaison with other organizations. In recent years, however, many have been given special duties in different kinds of provision, notably that with industry and the trade unions, and have developed the new type of industrial branch. In general the District, besides being a means of exchanging ideas and information, may initiate new ventures, protect branches by negotiation, issue publications and organize District events such as one day and weekend schools, summer schools, training courses, conferences, rallies and festivals.

District and branches are linked together in a central organization, the structure of which has been subject to much amendment as the years have passed. With essential power democratically held by the branches, and 'responsible bodyship' in the hands of the districts, inevitably there have been questions about the activities and powers of the national centre. The governing body of the whole association, however, is the national conference, nowadays held biennially, to which each branch may send one representative and each district three representatives. District Secretaries also attend, as well as representatives of the tutor—organizers, the Trades Union Congress, the Co-operative Union, the Universities Council for Adult Education and other national affiliated bodies. Organizations which wish to support the movement may affiliate at the appropriate level: local branch, district or national; in all there are some 2,000 varying from trade unions to cultural societies. There is also an elected national executive committee to carry out the decisions of the conference and the general administration of the affairs of the association, anything indeed which is 'appropriate to the welfare of the whole Movement'.[35] This has representatives from the various sections of the movement as well as the honorary national officers elected at conference: the president, deputy president and treasurer. Servicing the national organization is a small band of full-time paid officers, a general secretary and usually three assistant secretaries with a few ancillary secretarial staff. The central organization negotiates with central government and other agencies at national level, and is responsible for general inspiration and assistance to branches and districts. From time to time it appoints sub-committees and working parties and provides the members of the Standing Joint Consultative Committee with the universities. Recent examples of advisory sub-committees are those for education and trade union studies and there have been working groups on matters such as management and organization. It also issues publications, including a periodical *WEA News* issued twice a year. At an earlier date these were more numerous and include study outlines, various notes on study methods and a regular journal, appropriately called *The Highway*, echoing the view of the national movement that it should make 'sustained efforts to establish a broad highway of free education with full equality of opportunity from nursery school to university'. Internationally the association is linked with the International Federation of Workers' Educational Associations (IFWEA) which has consultative status with UNESCO, organizes international seminars and maintains liaison with all member organizations. This was very much the creation of the British movement.

The WEA has a strong tradition of serious study and a critical approach together with a stress on social purpose. This led to a concentration on liberal adult education as the means by which everyone could be equipped for democratic citizenship and this type of education remains the core of class provision in the ordinary branches. As the 1939 Statement of Policy suggested, the WEA looks on education as 'not only a means of developing individual character and capacity, but as an equipment for the exercise of social rights and responsibilities'. Democracy, it said 'begins in the class as a co-operative process in relation to choice of subject, organisation and participation . . . This sense of democracy is integral to the WEA's view of adult education'.[36] Some of the liberal study classes are organized in association with the universities, as indicated above, but the WEA also provides its own classes, at a lower level than those jointly provided. These may still be of twenty to twenty-four meetings in length, but many are of the shorter 'terminal' class type. Much depends on the attitudes and ideas of the branch committee; some wish to maintain the tradition of longer courses, while others prefer to recruit as many as possible by short courses. Similar variations are seen in the choice of subjects, some branches retaining a predominance of social studies, while others plan a very diverse range. Each branch is different but the overall contribution is indicated by the following statistics for 1977–8:[37]

Total number of classes	About 9,000
Number of classes with more than 20 meetings	Nearly 3,000

Major subjects of study

Social studies	24%
History	15%
English language and literature	11%
Visual arts	10%
Biological sciences	8%

Examples of other subjects: Music (6%), Archaeology (4%), Physical sciences (3%), Psychology (1.7%), Geography (1.6%), International Affairs (1.6%), Welsh/Irish/Scottish languages, Literature and culture (1.3%), Religion, Law, Philosophy (all about 1%).

In recent years there has been some shift in the provision, away from the traditional liberal studies towards what have come to be called the 'Russell categories'. Reviewing the work of the WEA, the Russell Committee[38] suggested that besides the 'courses of liberal and academic study below the level of university work', there were three areas to which the association should give particular emphasis. These were:

1. education for the socially and culturally deprived living in urban areas;
2. work in an industrial context, especially classes held in factories or other workplaces, and programmes arranged in consultation with the TUC and with individual trade unions, including courses for shop stewards;
3. political and social education . . . work in general education directed to greater social and political awareness.

In Scotland the Alexander Committee similarly recommended that the major contribution of the WEA should be to promote educational activities appropriate to 'the educational needs of those adults who, by virtue of social, economic or educational deprivation, are less able to articulate their needs or who lack the will or confidence to make use of what is provided', and added that the association 'seems to be admirably placed to make a valuable contribution to the training of trade union officials and shop stewards'.[39] Since 1975 these types of work have been much expanded and planned targets have been reached in England and Wales. Part of the work for the disadvantaged has been in basic education, with courses in both literacy and numeracy for the community as a whole, and special courses for immigrants with language difficulties. In the North-Western District, for example, a guide to basic trade unionism has been provided for immigrant workers in a pack of materials with a complete Urdu translation designed for Asians from a pre-industrial environment. Much of the work with the disadvantaged is carried out in association with the LEAs and with the active co-operation of community and social workers. Attempts have been made to reach both the socially isolated, such as the elderly, the physically handicapped, and mothers with young children, and also those who are isolated in hospitals, mental homes or prisons. Yorkshire North District, for example, has been involved with the mental health field for some years and so too have the Western and South Wales Districts. A further aspect is the attempt to deal with the problems of inner city deprivation, a particular feature in recent years of the work in Birmingham and in Liverpool.

In the industrial context, the WEA has had close contacts with the trade union movement from its earliest beginnings and for a long period there was a special organization, the Workers' Educational Trade Union Committee (WETUC) reflecting this connection. The WEA now makes a contribution of up to 20% of the courses in the TUC Regional Education Scheme, and helps also by the collection and provision of background notes and other materials about trade unionism, industrial problems, changing economic and social structures and current problems. It has also extended its work with individual trade unions, and in some areas WEA 'Industrial branches' or 'Industrial study groups' have been created. Through these instruments, special courses for trade unionists in particular industries are arranged often on a factory base. The provision may include activities such as day and weekend conferences on political or economic affairs, courses on industrial relations for shop stewards, and courses on communication skills for all members interested.

The third 'Russell category', political and social education, has in varying ways always been part of the movement's provision, with its stress on citizenship and social purpose. Courses are arranged to help people to participate more effectively in community affairs, especially those engaged in voluntary work or local government. Developments have included courses organized in co-operation with socially-oriented organizations such as OXFAM and SHELTER, courses for school managers and governors, and classes in the field of Women's Studies. In the 1950s and 1960s the WEA listed the dangers in modern society as being the growing gulf between experts and ordinary citizens, the tendency for professional groups to act in isolation from the community at large, and an uncritical acceptance of 'mass culture', as well as widespread apathy and ignorance.[40] It feels that an independent voluntary organization is particularly well equipped to combat these, especially as it is able to deal boldly and objectively with controversial subjects in the areas of politics, economics and social studies which the LEAs are inclined to leave severely alone.

The WEA, however, faces a number of problems. Over the years, indeed, it seems almost to have been overconscious of problems, indulging in recurrent soul-searching exercises and establishing a series of working parties. One set of questions relates to the validity of the activities, methods and subject range of branch provision in the late twentieth century. Should it be the sort of general provider it has tended to become in some areas, or should it concentrate its work on provision for the 'underprivileged'? Should it concentrate on subjects with a 'social purpose'? Should it provide mainly long courses? Have 'standards' declined? In terms of purpose, is there too much stress on individual personal development and too little on the old 'social purpose'? There are also important questions concerning the structure of the association, its voluntary nature and branch democracy, and its use of full-time professionals. Much of the Russell type provision has been carried out by the professional tutor—organizers, especially that for the trade unions, and much of it is very isolated from traditional branch life. Inevitably, as the number of professionals has grown, there has been a tendency to leave a lot to them and consequently some weakening of the voluntary effort. The relationship between voluntary workers and professionals has been optimistically said to be full of 'productive tensions' but the implications have yet to be worked out. Similarly, the size of some of the larger branches is a source of worry in that too heavy a burden seems to have been placed on the voluntary officials, who, working at home, perhaps need some clerical assistance. Some of the voluntary workers know little about the association itself or its history, and as a result are unwilling to accept the full responsibilities it requires. The honorary branch secretaries are of key importance. Can they relate to a large enough cross-section of the population and so draw into membership more than those from their own age group, occupation or social position? Can they decentralize the work so that more members become active? Do they require more training for the task so that they can be more effective? In many parts of the country the active workers are often middle class and women of middle age, and reliance on 'personal contact' as the recruiting medium may be a deterrent to many sections of the population. The word 'worker' in some places may still carry the supposed stigma of a vague leftism, despite Mansbridge and Tawney's definition of 'all who work by hand or brain'. After the 'orgies of introspection',[41] as Sir Eric Ashby called them, perhaps the time has come for a new optimism and confidence; some of its conferences in the 1970s certainly revealed a more hopeful and youthful mood of regeneration.

It is, however, very difficult to generalize about the WEA and those who do so risk sterile arguments based upon partial evidence. Some branches are full of outgoing vigour and inventiveness while others are run by a clique of timid, self-interested and ineffective people. Some have many working-class members while others seem full of young executives and their wives. Some achieve all round success without much professional aid, while others are so moribund that they create feelings of despair and frustration in the ranks of the full-time professionals. Some are clear examples of effective training in democratic citizenship by the practice of sharing the work of the branch, while in others all is left to the overburdened secretary. Sometimes, as in many voluntary organizations, a centralizing tendency appears which seems to threaten the control by students which is basic to the movement, and to impose 'rule from above'. Sometimes the threat seems to come from the professional advisers and organizers, some of whom are demonstrably restless and frustrated and have even been known to strike for better pay and conditions (in 1974). Yet many of them give devoted service to the movement and as a professional cadre they stimulate voluntary workers to renewed effort. Much depends on the type of people recruited into the service of the branch and upon the type of area in which it is situated. In many places a good branch has a large programme of non-class activities, such as lectures, socials, organized visits, theatre parties, debates and rambles, and often new voluntary organizations such as music or drama groups have sprung up as a result of the general programme. But in other areas branch officials may regard such developments as frivolous and concentrate on 'serious study' and social reform. The development of industrial branches poses new questions about both the structure and the policy of the WEA. Is there, for example, a fundamental clash between them and the traditional branch, and no hope of integration? Arguments about the future of the WEA have gone on for decades, however. In the past it has provided for the education of many future local councillors and members of parliament as well as trade union leaders, an editor of the *Manchester Guardian*, and a university vice-chancellor. Whether it can have the same impact in the future depends partly on the value people place upon a voluntary, student-run service as compared to a public, LEA service staffed by professionals. It also depends on the willingness of people to contribute voluntary service, upon their adherence to the purposes and ideals developed by the association, and upon their willingness to translate these into effective action. As the 1967 policy statement said: 'The success of the WEA depends on what it does, not on what it says'.[42] It could also be said to depend upon an adequate supply of finance, without which much of its work and structure could be badly distorted.

Leisure-related classes provided by other organizations

Reference has been made in an earlier chapter to commercially-organized courses to help people with their work-related needs, and there is an increasing tendency for a similar type of provision to meet leisure-related needs. Almost any local newspaper has references and advertisements from time to time for classes taught by private teachers who earn their living in this way. Perhaps most marked are those for classes in which dancing is taught, whether this be ballroom, 'old-time', Latin-American or disco, and for those concerned with health, keep fit, slimming or yoga, but the range may include public speaking and most sports activities. On the whole most of these still follow the standard one night per week pattern, but some institutions offer flexible short courses, and enrolment may be for short four or six-week courses or for long courses lasting six months or more. Various types of modified arrangements, however, are possible, especially in some of the language schools where several nights a week instead of one may be combined with weekend courses, a class enjoying a kind of 'club holiday' at full economic fees. A sizeable development of the 'study holiday' bought in much the same way as any other kind of 'package holiday' seems likely, and the Butlin or Pontin type holiday camp where the visitor pays inclusive costs may become a summer school with regular courses. An example of this sort of enterprise is the provision of four or five professional teachers for a group of old-time dance enthusiasts going on a package holiday to Benidorm where regular classes are held during their two-week stay. Group travel with an educational purpose has been a feature since the late nineteenth century and many commercial firms began with earnest educational endeavours, including Thomas Cook, Poly Tours and Lunn's Tours.[43] In more recent years there has developed much cultural group travel with guides and good opportunities for study. This can vary from study holidays similar to the summer schools organized by the universities and the WEA in many parts of the world, to the non-residential one-day study visit.

Besides the commercial provision there are classes organized by hundreds of voluntary clubs, societies and associations. These depend on the express wishes of members, and sometimes on the whims of the voluntary committee, or the honorary secretary. The general, non-formal education provided by these voluntary organizations is considered in the next chapter but it seems appropriate to sketch here the broad outlines of provision of classes with a teacher. Some organizations use LEA or WEA teachers and their classes are part of the standard provision already noted, but some use their own members who are trained and expert in particular activities. This can be seen in various craft societies, some language groups, sports organizations concerned, for example, with mountaineering or angling, and in dance organizations such as those concerned with Scottish country dancing and folk dancing. Thus Esperanto societies draw on their own members for intensive courses, and many ethnic groups such as the Ukrainians and Pakistanis use members of their own communities to teach their first langue to adults as well as children. Organizations such as the Red Cross and the St John Ambulance Brigade teach their own first aid courses, etc., some of these being open to the general public as well as to members.

These are a few examples of a large field which is not well publicized. Some organizations take care to provide their teachers (or 'instructors' or 'advisers' as they often prefer to call them, the distinction being very unclear) with special training, an important example being the National Federation of Women's Institutes which provides regular instructor courses at its own residential Denman College. The churches have also long been active in this area, with the training of lay personnel for leadership and teaching work being particularly noticeable in the non-conformist churches. Bible study classes and classes on the place of religion in modern life are a regular feature in some churches, the teachers being drawn from the congregations, and assisted by teaching and study material centrally provided. At an early date, Mansbridge, the founder of the WEA, also promoted a Church Tutorial Classes Association in the Church of England which established classes similar to the university/ WEA Tutorial Classes, the first being held in 1917. Although this particular form of class has largely died out, other classes under the guidance of 'adult religious education committees' have taken their place. Other types of church provision are classes for Sunday School teachers, and the various types of weekend, one week or fortnight long residential courses provided in guest houses or colleges. The Church of Scotland, through its Department of Education Adult Christian Education Committee provides courses for Sunday School teachers, for Elders and Readers and for youth workers, while the Scottish Episcopal Church has an Adult Religious Education Committee which provides courses for the laity and the non-stipendiary ministry as well as full 'Training for Ministry' schemes. Local associations of the Young Men's Christian Association (YMCA) organize classes, and nationally the YMCA has provided much education for young workers in its special Youth Department, as well as maintaining close links with residential work in Wolfson College, Cambridge, in Coleg y Fro in Glamorgan (its own college) and Dunsford College in Sussex. The Welsh YMCA is a Responsible Body, organizing mainly terminal courses, including some for hospital patients. A recent development has been the 'Training for Life' (TFL) scheme for young people mainly aged 16 to 18. Starting in the north-west and funded by the Youth Opportunities Programme this combines some formal classes with a variety of projects.

The variety is enormous. A Spastics Association runs 'cookery classes for wheelchair cases', a branch of the National Housewives Register has a class in child psychology, a Marriage Guidance Council puts on a ten-week course for those about to be married, a physical education teacher offers a keep fit class in a public house, a Camera Club decides to have a formal six-week course on photographic enlargement taught by its president, a Gardens and Allotments Society brings in a local market gardener to teach a twelve-meeting course, just as Rostrum, the public speaking association, brings in an expert to be the teacher with the definitive title of 'Speaker of the Last Word'. Groups meet with their own teacher at field study centres and the Rural Music Schools Association has classes in some of its centres and itinerant teachers who provide for adults as well as schoolchildren. How much provision is made this way, and of what quality, remains unknown because there is no system of reporting or notification to a central authority. Anyone, qualified or not, is able to become a teacher of adults and organizations are free to use whoever they can get, if no public money is involved. The evidence at present comes from local surveys which have been rather too few in number.[44] They suggest that the provision of classes is more extensive than often recognized but that it may be intermittent, even in the major women's organizations where craft classes have been almost a steady commitment. The evidence also suggests that the 'standard' timetable of provision in the winter months is often disregarded, that classes may begin at any time of the year and that there are no set times for the beginning of courses. They start and end when the group and the teacher want and they may occupy a fifty-two week year rather than the standard twenty to thirty weeks. If everyone is to be considered a potential teacher as well as a learner it would seem that there are possibilities of further development in this type of provision. Certainly educators of adults ought to pay more attention to it and to help raise the quality of what is taking place.

References

1. Seen, for example, in Section 41 of the 1944 Education Act and in Section I (5) of the Education (Scotland) Act, 1945.
2. CLARKE, Sir F. *Re-interpretation*. 1948, National Foundation for Adult Education, Foundation Papers no. 3, p. 7.
3. Ministry of Education *Further Education*, 1947, HMSO, Pamphlet no. 8, para 74.
4. Scottish Education Department. *Adult Education: the Challenge of Change*, (The Alexander Report). 1975, HMSO.
5. See Alexander Report, op. cit, paras 34–36.
6. See, for example, STYLER, W. E. *Further Education – Part-time Teachers Speak*, p. 34, 1968. University of Hull Department of Adult Education.
7. See MEE, G. and WILTSHIRE, H. C. *Structure and performance in Adult Education*, 1978, Longmans, for a full discussion of the problems of sharing, and of the idiosyncracies of the provision. pp. 106–110 summarize their findings.
8. HUTCHINSON, E. and E. M. *Learning Later: Fresh Horizons in English Adult Education*. 1978, Routledge and Kegan Paul. p. 10.
9. See particularly the article by HOWARD GILBERT, 'A collegiate centre concept' in *Adult Education*, 43/6, March, 1971, pp. 347–353.

10. WILTSHIRE, H. C. 'Giving Adult Education a Home', *Adult Education*, XXXII/1, Summer 1959, pp. 14—17.

11. MORRIS, H. *The Village College, being a Memorandum on the Provision of Educational and Social Facilities for the Countryside with special reference to Cambridgeshire*, 1924, p. 22.

12. See JENNINGS, B. (Ed.) *Community Colleges in England and Wales*, 1980, NIAE.

13. For further information see FAIRBAIRN, A. N. *The Leicestershire Community Colleges and Centres*, 1979, University of Nottingham Department of Adult Education and NIAE.

14. BALL, C. 'Hypermarkets of corporate life', *Times Educational Supplement* No. 3105, 29 November 1974.

15. Figures in 1979 provided by D.J. BUCHANAN for the National Institute of Adult Education.

16. See the evidence in MEE, G. and WILTSHIRE, H.C. (1978), op. cit., chapter 10 and in their article 'Irreparable damage?' *Times Educational Supplement* 6 May 1977. For earlier evidence see CHILDS, A. *Social patterns of enrolment*, 1973 NIAE/ECA, and BUCHANAN, D. and PERCY, K. *Emergent patterns in LEA Adult Education*, 1969, NIAE.

17. Constitution, Part 1.

18. Russell Report, para 120. See also the ECA Advisory Leaflets: 'A Centre Members Association — the Why and How' and 'A Centre Members Association — Partnership in Action', both 1976.

19. Educational Settlements Association *Citizen Centres for Adult Education*, 1943, ESA Post-War Education Series 2, p. 13. Reissued by ECA 1949, p. 11.

20. Russell Report, para 120.

21. BABIN, M. J. See *The Universities and Adult Education*, report of the Regional European Seminar, Bangor, Wales, Sept. 1956. 1957, Ministry of Education, HMSO, p. 77.

22. A view discussed particularly in the 1948 Report of the University Grants Committee, and in Sir WALTER MOBERLY's book *The Crisis in the University*, 1949.

23. Report on the Future Scope and Organization of Adult and Continuing Education in Universities, 1974, CVCP and UCAE.

24. Report of the Adult Education Committee of the Ministry of Reconstruction (The 1919 Report or the Smith Report) 1919, HMSO, para 333(f).

25. ASHBY, E. *The Pathology of Adult Education*, 1955.

26. Alexander Report, 1975, HMSO, para 180, suggests that each university should have 'sufficient staff to enable it to carry out its extra-mural role effectively'.

27. See UCAE Constitution (1975) para 5.

28. Russell Report, para 217.

29. Russell Report, para 213.1. This seems, however, a somewhat idealized picture.

30. Speech to the National Institute of Adult Education conference in 1978. Printed in *Adult Education* 51/2, July 1978, pp. 73—83. The quotation is on p. 79.

31. Constitution, Section IV: 'The Association shall be non-party in politics and unsectarian in religion'.

32. MANSBRIDGE, A. *Adventure in Working Class Education*, 1920, Longmans, Green. Preface, p. xiv.

33. WEA Constitution (1975) Section II.

34. Russell Report, para 113.

35. Constitution VIII (5).

36. WEA Report of the Working Party on Structure, Organization, Finance and Staffing. 1966, p. 12.

37. Figures given in the *WEA National Report* for 1977–1979 but rounded to the nearest whole numbers.

38. Russell Report, para 232–1.

39. Alexander Report, paras. 185 and 190.

40. See WEA *Education for a changing society* (the Briggs White Paper), 1958, reissued in 1965, and also *Unfinished Business: a WEA Policy Statement*, 1967, WEA.

41. ASHBY, E. *The Pathology of Adult Education* op. cit.

42. See WEA *Unfinished Business* op. cit., 1967.

43. See WALLER, R. D. 'Adult Educational Travel', *Adult Education*, XXVIII/1 Summer 1955, pp. 47–62 and ROBERTS, H. 'Educational travel and the learning process', *International Journal of University Adult Education*, XVIII/2, July 1979, pp. 1–5.

44. Examples of local studies are: RUDDOCK, R. and WILSON, A. *After Work: Leisure and Learning in Two Towns*, 1959 (Bolton and Rochdale) and MORRIS, M. *Voluntary Organizations and Social Progress*. 1959. A more recent study has also been made of Lancaster and Morecambe.

CHAPTER 8

Voluntary organizations and
non-formal education

The offer of classes is extensive but there is probably an even larger number of activities that can be termed educational, though often they do not carry that label. In recent years the term 'non-formal' has been applied to these, following Philip Coombs who defined non-formal education as 'any organised educational activity outside the established formal system — whether operating separately or as an important feature of some broader activity — that is intended to serve identifiable learning clienteles and learning objectives'[1]. in contrast to the relatively unorganized and unsystematic 'informal' education of daily experiences through which people learn. In a sense much of the work described in the previous chapter is 'non-formal', though concerned with classes in which there is a teacher. This chapter, however, extends the range to activities usually without a teacher. Many of these are organized by self-help groups pursuing an interest or a hobby; others are part of the normal programme of voluntary organizations which have other aims as well as education. Some are very short-lived, dying as soon as their immediate purpose has been achieved, while others continue over many years, if with varying degrees of success. Although the exact number is unknown, it is clear that a multitude of voluntary societies exists almost everywhere in the country and that these provide organized opportunities for groups to meet in order to gain information, ideas and stimulus. As they appear to have a considerable impact on attitudes, opinions and behaviour patterns, many argue that overall they contribute in a major way to the education and personal development of a large section of the population. The examples which follow indicate the kind of evidence available.

Religious organizations

The oldest-established voluntary educational adult groups are the Adult Schools. Open to everyone, these meet for the discussion of a wide programme of subjects, often based upon an annual *Study Handbook* issued by the National Adult School Union, the central federal body bringing together some sixteen county unions. The syllabus varies from year to year but is intended to be topical; thus there have been titles such as 'Living in the sixties' (1965) and 'The Pursuit of peace' (1975). The first Adult School was opened in 1798 in Nottingham and for many years the schools concentrated on literacy teaching. Since the mid-nineteenth century however, the work has passed to 'the cultivation of the lighted mind', the first *Study Handbook* being issued in 1911. The Adult Schools are now defined as 'groups which seek on the basis of friendship to learn together and to enrich life through study, appreciation, social service and obedience to a religious ideal'.[2] The groups rely upon the emergence of natural leaders, the subjects for discussion being introduced by members, though occasionally a visiting speaker may be invited to help. Usually they meet weekly in rented premises, or increasingly in members' homes, and in some Friends Meeting Houses, a result of a long-standing connection with the Society of Friends in the nineteenth century. There is no professional teaching service except in 'lecture schools' which are held from time to time by the central organization, or by the regional unions, each of which has an honorary secretary. The central organization issues a number of leaflets and pamphlets, however, as well as a monthly magazine *One and All* and arranges summer schools, including some abroad organized by its International Committee. At the beginning of the century the movement had a large membership of over 100,000, meeting in nearly 1,000 'schools', but there has been a steady decline and recent figures suggest a membership of about 2,000 organized in fewer than 200 schools, or 'groups' as they are increasingly called. Entirely self-supporting, the movement has relied financially on the contributions of members, on legacies, and on charitable trusts. By these means the small central office is maintained. The future of the movement is uncertain although there have been signs of new growth in various parts of the country since the mid 1970s, perhaps the result of moves to appoint some field organizers. The leadership believe, as a 1974 leaflet said, 'that people matter, and that informal methods of educational fellowship can be particularly helpful in preserving quality and essential values in the changing patterns of modern life'. New 'home and neighbourhood groups' have given a more modern image to this very democratic organization with its declared characteristics of 'freedom, adaptability and simplicity'.[3] In the past it brought education to people such as Ernest Bevin, A.V. Alexander and many town councillors and trade union leaders, and it remains a unique combination of education and non-denominational religion. In terms of method, the 'schools' may be compared to the Swedish study circles.

Almost all the denominational churches have voluntary societies which run their programmes of talks, discussions, visits, etc., usually on an informal self-help basis. They elect honorary officers and, though drawing from time to time on the help of the full-time clergy and sometimes others outside their own church, they rely mainly on their own lay members. Examples are the Week Night Fellowships in some United Reformed Churches, the Church of England Mothers' Union and Young Wives Groups, the Union of Catholic Mothers, Men's Fellowships, House Groups, study groups and study circles in most churches throughout Britain. The Welsh in particular have a long tradition of religious societies. These groups usually meet once a week on church premises and may take great pains to prepare their annual programmes. They may direct most of their attention to religious matters, or range widely over almost any kind of subject. One annual programme included talks and discussions, led by members, on 'Jamaica', 'Building in the 1970s', 'the Common Market', 'Foot care', the 'National Trust' and 'Yoga' as well as travel films. There are also informal groups meeting in private homes as well as in church rooms, for bible study or other aspects of religion.

To support this kind of activity all the churches, centrally or regionally, provide advice, suggestions for procedure, booklets and other publications and some courses of training for local lay leaders. Sometimes the aim is to improve chairmanship, or programme planning, or to suggest new methods, or provide basic information. The amount of aid varies each year according to the resources available but some of the main characteristics are indicated in the following examples. The Church of Scotland has had a pilot scheme for part-time 'Advisors in Adult Christian Education' to assist local initiatives, while the Methodist Church, through its Division of Ministries, has encouraged lay training through consultations, publications and district activities. The Church of England has 'adult education committees' in most of its dioceses 'generally to assist the promotion of Christian adult education', and similar bodies exist from time to time in the other Christian churches. In the Catholic Church there is the Newman Association for graduates and the Grail which seeks to help house groups, in particular those for women. Among the non-Christian religions, the Central Jewish Lecture and Information Committee issues many pamphlets and other publications, as well as offering speakers for groups who want information on Judaism and the Jewish people.

Interdenominationally, the British Council of Churches, which represents all the main Christian churches in the British Isles except the Roman Catholic, also helps to facilitate co-operation in study and common action. Always short of finance, however, its contribution to the local informal groups has been relatively very small compared to that of the denominational churches. Of other interdenominational organizations, the Young Men's Christian Association (YMCA) is perhaps the most active in the promotion of informal educational groups. Reference has already been made to the more formal work with teachers and instructors, and to the position of the Welsh Executive Committee of YMCAs as a 'Responsible Body', but in the autonomous local YMCAs, groups form from time to time to discuss any subject in which they have an interest. These are stimulated by the general emphasis on education within the community life of the YMCA, and by publications and periodicals such as *YMCA World*. The YMCA, founded in 1844, is defined as:

A spiritual movement which exists for the purpose of uniting young people in the service of Jesus Christ, and in fellowship through activities designed to help them in the development and training of their powers of body, mind and spirit . . . and of enabling them to take their share in the service of God and their fellow men.

The local units are brought together in Regional Councils, linked to a National Council and thence to a World Alliance. The age of the 'young people' tends to range upwards almost to middle age, although like the 18+ Groups noted later, the main membership is below the age of 30. The amount of this type of fruitful but unrecorded discussion about social, political and other problems seems to be considerable but much depends on the enterprise shown by the leaders in each local centre, spurred on by the national centre. Nationally one of the main aims is declared to be that of developing 'activities which stimulate and challenge its members in an environment that enables them to take responsibility and find a sense of achievement'.[4]

137

Women's organizations

Women dominate much of the voluntary local work of the churches and political parties, as well as the evening classes of the WEA and the LEA, but particularly in the second half of the twentieth century their own independent organizations have shown great vitality. Throughout, non-formal as well as more formal education has been part of the programmes of the major organizations and the declared educational intent has to be interpreted in this light.

The largest of these organizations is the Women's Institute movement. There are over 9,000 Women's Institutes in England, Wales, the Channel Islands and the Isle of Man, with nearly half a million members, and there are proportionately similar numbers in the separate Northern Ireland Federation, and in the Scottish Women's Rural Institutes (SWRI) with over 1,200 institutes and about 56,000 members. All are the offspring of a movement which began in Canada in 1897, the first Women's Institute (WI) in Britain being formed in 1915 at Llanfair P.G. in Anglesey. Essentially a rural movement, a Women's Institute is declared to be 'a society open to countrywomen of all ages, interests, politics and creeds' which aims 'to bring countrywomen together to learn things which will be of help in their homes; to improve conditions in the village; to consider the needs of country people throughout the land and to develop a spirit of friendliness, co-operation and initiative, and to promote international understanding'.[5] With a structure not unlike that of the WEA, each WI is autonomous, electing its own voluntary officers and committee, but affiliated to a county or island federation and thence to a national federation. At present, for example, there are sixty-five 'county' federations in England and Wales, most of which have a full-time paid secretary and staff. Each national headquarters also has a full-time general secretary and a substantial staff and the three national federations are linked together in the Associated Country Women of the World (ACWW), a world organization of societies in well over a hundred countries whose concern is with raising the standard of living of rural women, as well as with the promotion of international goodwill, friendship and understanding. Non-party in politics and non-sectarian in religion, the Women's Institutes are nevertheless free to concern themselves, as a national resolution put it in 1971, with 'matters of political or religious significance'.

The major activity of the institutes is a monthly two-hour meeting which tends to follow a set pattern of a business meeting, an 'educational hour' which may be a talk or demonstration by a visiting speaker or discussions or short talks by members, and finally a 'social time' with activities to which all members are expected to contribute. In addition to this meeting, however, there are discussion groups, craft and drama groups, keep fit classes and any other group desired by members, all of which may exist on a self-help basis, as well as independent, co-operative markets organized in small towns and villages for the sale of home-grown and home-made products. Groups may also undertake project work, such as the collection of village lore in Scotland in the SWRI Jubilee Year of 1967, or the recording of the many changes now taking place in the local environment, or an organized check on matters affecting family welfare. The national and county federations assist and stimulate by meetings, demonstrations, conferences, training courses, exhibitions and publications. The movement has its own publishing company, WI Books Ltd, which has dealt with topics as varied as international affairs, drama, wine making and drug abuse. The SWRI have a monthly magazine, *Scottish Home and Country,* and south of the border there is a similar magazine entitled *Home and Country.* Members pay a relatively small subscription to the institute per year, and part of this goes forward to finance the county and national federations. In addition, some central government grants are received from time to time for educational work at national level. The policy for the movement as a whole is determined by the institutes at the national Annual General Meetings. That for England and Wales is held in the Albert Hall, London, and has 4,500 representatives from the institutes. The policy thus determined is carried out by National Executive Committees elected every two years by postal ballot, and these bodies may appoint national advisers; for example in Scotland a full-time qualified needlecraft adviser has the brief of travelling through the country giving instruction, assistance and advice as requested by the institutes.

With this structure, the Women's Institutes are strong and efficient organizations for the most part, and they have done much to help overcome inequalities with men and to further emancipation among women in the countryside. 'The first step towards the WI aim of better conditions in the country is education,' says the *WI Handbook*[6] and this is advanced in a number of ways. Partly it takes the form of a fairly substantial number of classes as noted in the previous chapter, but much of it is non-formal with groups coming together without a teacher. Both types of activity may lead members to take a short course at Denman College in Abingdon, near Oxford, where the National Federation of Women's Institutes (NFWI) established its own college in 1948. Each year over 4,000 members attend mainly three-day courses on subjects as varied as local government, sketching and painting, 'corn dollies for beginners', world population questions, 'an approach to history' or Jane Austen. Many of those who attend have never been away from home before and the development of confidence as well as of wider interests may be attributed to the regular meetings in the villages. Probably for each member the results of being in the WI are different; as an explanatory sheet suggested it means:

> Perhaps to the young girl a chance to act, to the bride cookery classes, to the mother a course on home management, to the older woman an opportunity for public service, but to all of them it means companionship, friendship and an interest outside the home, beyond the family circle.[7]

The same might be said of the sister movement, the Townswomen's Guilds, although these had very different origins and stemmed directly from the suffrage movement. The first guilds came into being in 1929 after women had at last gained equal voting rights with men in the Act of 1928. The National Union of Societies for Equal Citizenship then decided to go forward with the education of the 'new citizens' and finally reconstituted itself as the National Union of Townswomen's Guilds (NUTG) in 1933. Its declared objects are:

> To encourage the education of women to enable them as citizens to make their best contribution towards the common good. To serve as a common meeting ground for women irrespective of creed and party, for their wider education including social activities.[8]

The guilds follow the same structural pattern as the institutes with autonomous local units, linked to federations and thence to the National Union.
The only major differences of structure are that federations instead of being
county units are notionally a group of not more than thirty guilds, and hence
divide as the movement grows, and that they depend upon voluntary officers
and committees elected each November instead of paid officers. Nationally
there is an annual National Council Meeting with delegates from all guilds and
federations. The guilds also have their regular monthly meetings, though the
'social time' tends to be more informal, and an extensive provision of other
groups activities concerned with music, drama, crafts and 'social studies'. The
latter is sometimes said to be the 'heart of the Movement' in that it seeks to
provide the kind of direct citizenship training envisaged by the founders.
These groups also meet at regular times and many guild members may therefore attend three or four meetings a month, and more if they become active
as officers or committee members. They may also share in the rallies, exhibitions, and festivals of music and drama organized by the federations. At one
time there was a fairly rigid structure of sections concerned with particular
aspects such as drama or social studies but there is now more flexibility.
Similarly the early convention that they were established in places with more
than 4,000 inhabitants while the WI provided for those with fewer people has
been superseded by a more flexible though still amicable arrangement. In
some villages grown into towns, there may be a WI, as well as several TGs. In
the 1960s national advisers were superseded by a 'NUTG Education Officer'
but this too reflects the willingness to change according to need.

The total membership of the Townswomen's Guilds is nearly a quarter
of a million, and in total there are over 2,700 guilds including over 120 in
Scotland, grouped in over 110 federations (9 in Scotland). Scotland has a
separate Committee but not a separate Union. Guilds vary in the stress they
give to activities, and as the years have passed there has been a tendency in
some to move away from the older ideas. Concern was expressed at national
level in the late 1960s that the movement's organizational structure was not
best suited to the pattern of the lives of modern women, nor flexible enough
to change with the changing society. The Tavistock Institute of Human
Relations was therefore asked to conduct a research enquiry to examine
possible alternatives. The two consultants reported that the movement was
trying to perform three different tasks with only one form of organization;
these were defined as being:

1. To provide social and recreational activities for women
2. to provide educational facilities for women; and
3. to mobilise and present women's views on issues of local, national and
international importance.[9]

The results of the enquiry, however, seem to have caused little change at
guild level where members feel that the local structure is quite satisfactory
and adaptable enough. Most guilds continue to use indirect and non-formal
methods to carry out the educational objectives laid down in the Constitution
and adjust the times of meetings to suit local needs, evenings therefore being
more usual than in the WI where afternoons seem more suited to rural conditions. Free-ranging discussions on local topics or on resolutions put forward
to National Council meetings are common: these may be concerned with

funds for cancer research, legal matters and social and educational issues of all kinds. Various self-help groups may concern themselves with drama or music or with practical surveys, and larger parties visit factories and exhibitions. The organization of such visits is a regular feature of all the women's organizations and many factories employ special teams of guides to cope with large numbers of parties arriving at their doors.

Self-help and developing confidence may well lead to divisions and independence within a movement and it is not surprising that one or two townswomen's guilds, like some WEA branches in the past, have in fact broken away from the federations and central organization. A more nationalistic 'breakaway' from the WI movement is the all Welsh women's organization, Merched y Waur (Women of the Dawn) which held its first national meeting in 1968. This stresses the use of Welsh as a first language but retains the same social, educational and cultural objectives evident in the other women's institutes.

The stress on active participation and non-formal education is a characteristic of many other women's organizations. One example is the Business and Professional Women's Clubs, linked together on an international as well as a national structure, and having in membership women who have retired from full-time employment as well as those actively employed usually at an executive or supervisory level. Besides working for the removal of sex discrimination and for effective co-operation between business and professional women, the movement seeks to raise the standards of education and training for women. In its 400 or so clubs with about 20,000 members, it furthers these objectives by regular talks and discussions, study groups and inter-club meetings. Another example, which tends to have more working-class members, is the National Association of Women's Clubs which came into being in 1950 following the development of clubs which had arisen during the unemployment periods in the late 1920s and 1930s. In the early days the clubs were often known as Women's 'Mutual Service' or 'Social Service' Clubs and arose mainly in industrial areas, but in recent decades they have spread to all areas, particularly the new communities in the new towns in England and Wales. Each club is self-supporting, choosing its own officers, meeting place and times of meeting to suit the needs of the particular neighbourhood in which it is situated. It may meet once a week or twice a week, in the evening or afternoon. The objectives[10] are declared to be:

1. To provide facilities for social life and opportunities for informal education within the means of all women, and in particular housewives.
2. To give members opportunities to understand their responsibilities and rights as citizens and to encourage them to be of service to one another and to their neighbourhood.
3. To provide opportunities for members to develop their own gifts and talents, and to assist them to live a full and happy life.

To achieve these, the programmes include various group activities associated with home crafts, music, playreading, and discussions of consumer needs and of any problems the group wishes. The clubs, now numbering about 900, are linked together in local regional associations, each with a minimum of four clubs, and in a national association. Finance comes from member contributions, and voluntary donations, with some grant aid occasionally from LEAs and from central government for the educational work undertaken.

In all the women's organizations, there are great similarities in structure, activities and general theme. In the first two decades after the Second World War, most saw a rapid increase in membership and a general upsurge of strength. Thus in the 1950s and 1960s there were years which saw the formation of over a hundred new Women's Institutes, fifty new Townswomen's Guilds and fifty Women's Clubs. Since about 1970, however, the tide seems to have turned and there has been a plateau of membership and in some cases a decline. Have they satisfied the needs of certain sections of the population, but despite their size, are unable to extend to other sections? In terms of membership the WIs seem to have a cross-section of rural women, although the movement is perhaps dominated locally by the top hierarchy of the villages, and nationally by various members of the aristocracy and upper middle classes. In some areas, however, membership has been much affected by the development of commuter villages. Townswomen's Guilds are sometimes said to be full of middle aged, middle class women, yet many guilds belie this image and have a wide range of groups and social classes. With these organizations, as with the Women's Clubs and the Co-operative Women's Guilds, it is easy to attack stereotypes but in practice there are many variations. In so far as generalizations are possible, membership seems to have been more attractive to married women, and possibly the 'escape from the home' has been a feature contributing to their undoubted success.

At present there are well over a hundred organizations for women only and several others in which the membership is over 90% female. They vary greatly in type as well as in size, but all have programmes designed to help the education and personal development of their members. Some are linked to particular beliefs; besides the denominational church societies indicated above, there are, for example, the women's advisory committees of the Labour and Conservative parties and the Women's Liberal Association. Others are special interest groups associated with sport or hobbies or particular activities, such as the Guild of Lady Drivers, while others are linked to employment such as the Association of Women Launderers and the Women's Engineering Society. The Electrical Association for Women seeks to secure 'the wider and more efficient use of electrical appliances', and is organized on the standard basis of branches, federations and a national centre, with sub-branches called 'units', and organizers appointed to each of the area federations. It has grown rapidly since its foundation in 1924 and besides conducting vocational examinations for officials on the theory and practice of electrical housecraft and salesmanship, it offers a certificate examination for housewives and others in the use, care and maintenance of domestic electrical appliances. For most of the members, however, the activities are mainly one-day meetings with lecture demonstrations and discussion. Some of the other organizations also focus on particular themes, such as the Family Planning Association, some have slightly archaic-sounding names such as the 'Royal Scottish Society for the Self-Aid of Gentlewomen', and many of them, as well as the major organizations described earlier, are linked to the National Council of Women.

One of the oldest women's organizations is the Co-operative Women's Guild, which was established in 1883 to help women take their share in the work of the Co-operative movement. With the Scottish and Irish Women's Guilds it provides social, cultural and educational activities for members of

Co-operative Societies. In the second half of the twentieth century, the guilds have suffered periods of decline, with an ageing and declining membership, but they still make a considerable contribution with nearly 50,000 members. Many would like to see them now develop rather more as consumers' associations, with more education directed to raising the level of discrimination.[11] The former Men's Co-operative Guild, now merged with the mixed National Guild of Co-operators, has declined even more, though societies continue to organize hobby and interest groups, choirs and brass bands, outside the guilds. More attention is also now being given to consumer education through a National Consumer Project which has had a special two-year programme of national and local conferences launched in 1979. Although started under Co-operative auspices, this seeks to stimulate all groups with similar interests. Another notable organization is the National Housewives Register which was formed in 1960. This seeks to bring about 'the mental liberation of the housebound mother' through discussion of non-domestic issues and local self-help groups have been formed which hold fortnightly meetings. Sometimes the groups invite guest speakers and there have been attempts to use resource packages of material on which the group can work, on lines not unlike the 'box scheme' in Australia and British Columbia. By the mid-1970s there were over 20,000 members, three organizers, each with a small honorarium, had been appointed, and it was clear that the Register was meeting a real need.

There is a view that without more precise, planned liberal study courses the educational objectives of the women's movements will fade away. With this argument is often associated the need for more full-time staff and a stronger national centre for each organization. On the other hand, perhaps the real strength of the various movements lies in their democratic character. Is their majority educational achievement in fact personal development through meeting regularly, taking part in informal discussion, exchanging ideas, sharing mutual interests, developing powers of self-expression and creativity, being stimulated by visits, exhibitions or demonstrations, and fulfilling newly awakened ambitions? The range of activities may look somewhat disorganized but part of their success seems to lie in their responsiveness to members' interests and the way in which they draw on the service and active support of many members. Would less flexibility and a more tightly-planned approach be likely to weaken their appeal and undermine the broader education they offer?

Women's studies

Some reference has been made elsewhere to courses which are designed to help women with the problems of orientation to work and study and of re-entry to paid employment after a period of home duties and child care. Of these perhaps the 'Fresh Horizons' courses at the City Lit. are the most famous but elsewhere there are similar courses under titles such as 'New Horizons', 'New Opportunities for Women' (NOW) and 'Wider Opportunities for Women' (WOW). These usually offer a broad-based general education programme without formal entry requirements for women who wish to further their personal development and perhaps to choose new careers.

Similarly, some help is available to enable women to secure access to school and university qualifications, notably from the Open University but also from types of provision such as 'Woman School' organized since 1975 by the Adult Education Department of Hull University. This experimental programme of courses on a wide variety of subjects, including psychology, literature, music and zoology, provides a sort of entry bridge for women wishing to enter part-time degree courses. It also serves other needs, opening up contacts with a wider world for housewives and mothers, and helping them to develop abilities and plan future study activities.

The availability of such opportunities, however, is seen by many women as only a partial and inadequate way of combating the disadvantages they experience. One consequence, since the late sixties, is the growth of courses concerned with 'Women's Studies'. These question the role that women are expected to play in society and offer alternatives which are different in content and process from the traditional male-dominated provision. Both short and long-term courses, as well as weekend seminars and day schools, have been organized by universities, polytechnics, colleges of education and voluntary organizations. These take titles such as 'A woman's world' (Sussex University), 'Women, culture and sexuality' (Sheffield University), 'The economics of the family and sex discrimination' (N.E. London Polytechnic), 'Women in a changing world' (WEA), and 'The rights of women' (N. Scotland WEA). The concern with women's rights extends from the political and legal field to the position of women in trade unions and from basic education to health matters. An example is the Trade Union and Basic Education (TUBE) project which, in the inner city areas of Manchester, has developed a range of community education group activities, including courses on 'Women and health' and 'Women and money', the latter dealing with welfare rights. To assist the growth of courses and groups, the WEA established a Women's Education Advisory Committee in 1980, following the publication of a *Women's Studies Newsletter* since 1977. Since 1975, the Women's Research and Resource Centre (WRRC) has also published a *Newsletter* which includes discussion of issues and problems and gives outlines and bibliographies for various courses. Journals have also been produced such as the *Women's Studies International Quarterly, Spare Rib,* and *Feminist Review.* In the 1980s women's studies can clearly be seen as a growing point meeting women's needs perhaps more effectively than the more traditional women's courses.

Women's groups

Preceding and accompanying the development of formal women's studies courses the last decade has witnessed the growth of numerous women's groups as a grass roots response to the resurgence of feminism. These groups are committed to feminism and, as a consequence, to the development of new organizational forms that are non-hierarchical and flexible and that promote the active participation of all members. Consciousness-raising groups provide a model for many of the special interest groups in their emphasis upon informality, mutual support and genuine dialogue between equals. The aim of most groups is to promote an awareness of the position of women in society, through a critical examination of the life experiences of group members. The process at work in these groups is similar to that which Freire's work sought to promote. Many groups have generated and sustained women's centres in towns, where they function as drop-in centres, and provide a range of services and advice to women on a regular basis as well as in times of crisis.

The women's centres are often local meeting places for the many special interest groups and campaigns that have grown out of the Women's Movement. There are groups related to health and sexuality, education, the media and the arts, and for women working in many other fields. The groups provide a network of contacts and information. Some of the campaigning groups are now well known, and the National Abortion Campaign, Wages for Housework, Reclaim the Night and many others have sought to publicize specific issues in relation to demands for changes in the law. In addition, campaigns have been linked to special services provided by women for women, and the most well known of these are Women's Aid, which provides a network of refuges for battered women and their children, and the Rape Crisis Centres which operate counselling and advice services for women who have been victims of sexual violence. These organizations, like many others, have focused attention upon areas formerly ignored. They have provided women with a system of support that incorporates a wide range of learning opportunities and, equally important, these campaigns and organizations have educated the public in general.

The women in these diverse groups share a commitment to fight the oppression of women and, therefore, to social change through an autonomous women's movement, and this struggle has a profoundly educational emphasis; knowledge, information, critical awareness, sharing experiences and ideas in a non-competitive but co-operative manner are crucial to these initiatives. These notions have informed the ostensibly more formal women's studies courses, and current informal educational initiatives.

Women involved in the many groups come together at conferences and in women's festivals which provide an opportunity for many more women to participate in workshops and cultural experiences. The Women's Liberation Movement, of which these ventures are a part, has involved thousands of women, but its impact has been much wider than its numerical base. It has created a climate in which sexism may be challenged and in which the way we currently think about gender has been called into question. It may be claimed that this has created a space in which new ideas and forms may be generated, socially, politically and culturally.[12]

Clubs and community associations

Where is the line to be drawn between education and recreation? Is the instruction members of clubs receive as individuals or in groups through lectures and demonstrations to be regarded as education or not? In some clubs, such as the Cave and Mine Research Society, education seems to be implicit but is it so apparent in the many racing pigeon clubs, angling clubs, rambling clubs etc? Similar questions may be asked about the Rotary Club and its feminine equivalent the Inner Wheel, about the Round Table whose members are the younger leaders of business and the professions, and about organizations such as the Soroptimists, all of which meet primarily for social intercourse but combine with it various informal kinds of education, often in the pursuit of a specific purpose such as the promotion of mutual or international understanding. Many, such as Rotary, began soon after the First World War and hold regular weekly luncheon or dinner meetings, often with a speaker. They may also have groups giving attention to particular topical issues.

The Working Men's Clubs were founded by the Rev. Henry Solly in the middle years of the nineteenth century avowedly as an educational movement to combat the evils of drink. The Club and Institute Union (CIU) has now in membership nearly 4,000 clubs which are joined by about two million people. It has a national education committee and links with the WEA, the Co-operative Union Education Department and colleges such as Ruskin. At local level the amount of organized education is relatively small although talks and discussions, one-day schools and organized visits can be found on the programmes of many clubs, as well as the purely recreational provision of snooker tables, darts boards, perhaps a bowling green, the now financially vital bar, and a good deal of charitable activity. Many would regard as educational the training in committee procedure and the participation in management of those members who take part in the running of the clubs.[13] As with other voluntary organizations, clubs differ a great deal and it can be argued that most of them have the potential to make a more substantial educational contribution if they so wished.

A movement not educational in origin carries with it even more possibilities. This is the Community Association and Centre movement which came into being as 'local democratic action on new housing estates organizing opposition to the unsatisfactory conditions of neighbourhood life and determined to get local government authorities to do something to remedy them'.[14] This movement with its stress on community betterment has many parallels, including the work of the YMCAs and YWCAs, and the Miners' Welfare Centres which developed in the 1920s. Early moves towards 'community centres' so designated, resulted from the concern felt at the loss of the sense of community which had been shattered by large movements of the population after the 1914—18 War and by slum clearance resulting in the isolation of individuals. The promotion of community activity was one of the main objects of the National Council of Social Service (NCSS), set up in 1919, and now renamed the National Council of Voluntary Service. This body, having first pressed for the establishment of village halls, turned, with the aid of other organizations and the Carnegie Trust, to the formation of community associations on the new housing estates being built in the 1920s by the local authorities. In the industrial depression of the 1930s, community centres were also established in the older areas partly as a palliative for tragic social conditions.

After the Second World War, the NCSS established a new body, the National Federation of Community Associations (NFCA), under its auspices to look after the development of further centres, and the objective became that of enriching any kind of community by the establishment of meeting places to foster constructive social activity. Centres now exist, it is said, so that 'neighbours can come together on an equal footing to enjoy social, recreative and educational activities, either as members of groups following particular hobbies and pursuits, or on the basis of their common needs and interests as human beings living in the same locality'.[15] The groups may be branches of voluntary organizations of all kinds including many of those described earlier, such as the Red Cross, the English Folk Dance and Song Society or the Esperanto Society, or they may be purely local clubs. The activities may be social such as dances and whist drives, recreational in the form of both indoor and outdoor games, or educational in terms of music, drama, arts and crafts, talks and discussions. In accommodation, the centres are very varied, about 1,000 having their own premises, which vary from wooden huts to adapted old buildings, while others use schools, church halls, and even private houses. A few have purpose-built buildings often achieved after much voluntary effort. Their management by the community association reflects the diversity of origin and there are arguments about the place of a full-time warden or secretary even if his or her salary may be paid in full or grant-aided by the LEA. On the whole there is much reliance on voluntary leadership and member control, and the NFCA[16] requires a community association to be self-governing as well as open to all 'irrespective of politics, religion, nationality or colour' before it can be permitted to affiliate. Some are more democratic than others, however, and control has sometimes passed to a clique. Similarly social activities may swamp the educational ones. At one extreme are community associations which run very full educational programmes in their community centres, such as the vigorous one at Lymington in Hampshire which might well be called an 'educational centre'. At the other extreme are community centres where bingo, dominoes, whist and old-time dancing predominate. In between, most community associations organize enough classes and other educational activities to encourage occasional grants from the Department of Education and Science and from the LEAs. Advice comes from the statutory authorities but there has been no acceptance of an overall plan[17] and it is perhaps useful to think of community centres and educational centres as points on a continuum with education at one end and social activities at the other. As in most voluntary movements the position of a centre changes, sometimes moving to more education, sometimes to less; there is a constant process of new growth in some areas but decay and decline in others. The purpose of the NFCA is essentially to encourage development by bringing members of the community associations together to exchange ideas and experience. In its work it organizes summer schools and weekend courses, issues publications and provides special advice, especially through the three full-time advisory officers.

Provision for the community includes the needs of youth as well as older adults, and arguments have raged about the need for separate centres or for integration. As already noted, the determined effort in Scotland to bring all groups together in the community education service, urged on by the recommendations of the Alexander Report, has created problems. An interesting organization which in some ways has tried to bridge whatever gap exists is the Federation of Eighteen Plus Groups which resulted from a 1939 report of a survey by the Carnegie UK Trust entitled *Disinherited Youth.* Autonomous self-supporting groups have come into being in several parts of England, and these have carried out surveys as well as arranging programmes of talks, discussions and visits. Their objectives are to help people between the ages of 18 and 30 to 'understand and appreciate life, develop a personal

147

philosophy, acquire experience in public affairs and act in co-operation for the benefit of the community'.[18]

These examples are only a small proportion of the very many voluntary organizations in which much activity can be described as educational. The list could be much extended. Choirs in Wales concerned with the encouragement of the traditional culture may work hard over long periods and come together in local community festivals or the Welsh Eisteddfod. The Scottish Wild Life Trust with its 7,000 members and twelve active branches, linked to thirty or so local natural history societies, makes detailed studies as well as facilitating other learning activities. There are branches of the Women's League of Health and Beauty, concerned with physical education since its foundation in 1930, informal French and German 'circles' which promote the oral use of the language, international clubs, geographical and historical societies, community arts groups and so on. As conditions change, some organizations die out while new ones arise, and adaptation is vital if they are not to ossify. One of the problems of the informal approach to education is that it tends to lose its informality and spontaneity and to become too organized and structured. Good leadership seems to be of paramount importance, and to be successful in educational terms this needs to be democratic rather than autocratic. Many societies are short of resources, but perhaps above all they need informed support which has assessed their qualities. These societies, however, are for the 'joiners' and perhaps over half the population do not join any groups. Efforts have been made to engage the 'non-joiners', especially by community development workers who believe that control over social change is best achieved by educating the whole community to an awareness of needs and of the forces affecting people. Community development philosophy has stressed that people can understand what is needed if they are given a chance and that they can then seek solutions by a process of self-help. The twelve 'Community Development Projects' that were launched in various towns in the 1970s under the auspices of the Home Office as 'neighbourhood based experiments aimed at finding new ways of meeting the needs of people living in areas of high social deprivation' were thus much involved in stimulating informal education. Since then many community development and social workers have attempted to promote action through non-formal educational means and have stressed the need to secure 'unhampered participation in a meaningful setting'.[19] In an era in which there is much deprivation as well as rapid change, it seems clear that the community development approach may be the means of reaching those people on whom the older types of education for adults have patently failed to make an impact.

References

1. COOMBS, P.H. *New Paths to Learning for Rural Children and Youth,* p. 11.
2. Minute of the National Education and Social Service Committee, 1949, repeated with minor variations in most ensuing years.
3. NASU *Adult Schools, their Aims and Methods and How to Establish Them,* n.d. NASU p. 5.

4. See *The YMCA in Focus.* c.1979, YMCA. p. 11.

5. See NFWI *Constitution and Rules,* Sections II a) and b) and the WI leaflet *What a Women's Institute Is and What It Does,* (available from the NFWI).

6. NFWI *Handbook,* p. 2.

7. Statement of 8 November, 1950.

8. NUTG *Constitution and Rules,* para II.

9. MILLER, E.J. and GWYNNE, G.F. Reported in *The Townswoman,* April 1971.

10. Defined in the NAWC Constitution.

11. See GROOMBRIDGE, B. *Report on the Co-operative Auxiliaries,* 1960, Co-operative Union.

12. This section on women's groups owes much to material supplied by Dr. Sallie Westwood.

13. A useful if optimistic account was given in an article on 'Adult education in working men's clubs' by JOHN LEVITT in *Adult Education,* XXVIII/4, Spring, 1956, pp. 260–272, drawing partly upon the CIU official history, *Our Sixty Years* by B.T. HALL (1922). A more recent history is that by TREMBLETT, G: *The First Century* (1962, CIU).

14. See MARKS, H. *Community Associations and Adult Education.*

15. Ministry of Education, *Community Centres,* 1945, HMSO.

16. See NFCA Constitution.

17. The 1945 pamphlet of the Ministry of Education (op. cit.) provided a suggested blueprint but was largely ignored as being too idealistic.

18. Constitution of the Federation of 18+ Groups.

19. ILLICH, I. *Deschooling Society,* 1972, Penguin Education Special.

CHAPTER 9

Libraries, museums and art galleries.
The Arts Council and cultural societies.

'Learning to live' is still a favourite expression among many adult educators, but they differ about the meaning of 'live'. Similarly, there are many different interpretations of 'culture'. To some it is 'all the arts of living' but others define it more traditionally as music and the arts with particular reference to the productions and performances of professional artists. Opponents declare these to be the embellishments of life for an élite and assert that relevance to the life of the people as a whole has not been a prime consideration. Public taste, some say, has to be trained (or educated?) and until this has been achieved it matters little if most of the population has no personal contact with concert halls, art exhibitions, theatres, classical dance and the visual record of historical objects to be seen in museums. The argument has been growing, however, particularly since the 1960s, that the 'cultural heritage' even narrowly interpreted, should be a vital part of the personal development of all men and women, and that it should be made attractive and accessible to all. This is sometimes referred to as the 'democratization of culture', described in 1975 by Professor Boorstin of the USA as 'a vista opening concept that leads to generous and dynamic programmes'.[1] With it has developed popularization of music, drama and art through radio and television, through the issue of relatively cheap paperback books on the arts and through magazines with reproductions of the histories of art and serialized encyclopedias of the works of the great artists. The commercial entrepreneurs have also developed quite an industry in arranging visits of hundreds of thousands of ordinary people to stately homes thrown open by their impecunious owners, to art exhibitions in the capital cities, to castles and cathedrals and to various historical sites. So great has been this development that some places such as Stonehenge and the Roman Wall are in danger of damage from over patronage. Special train loads of people also descend on exhibitions in London and Edinburgh and on various arts festivals. Some expeditions are indeed organized by the extra-mural departments of the universities and some are linked to courses designed to deepen understanding. The general aim would seem to be to introduce the masses to 'culture' and to get them to appreciate it more fully.

This approach has led to improvements in the services provided by the museums and public libraries, as will be indicated below, but has met with much critical comment. The stress upon safeguarding the cultural heritage and upon getting the public to give it due appreciation has been said to be élitist and patronizing, however sincerely it may be attempted. In the 1970s the Council of Europe began to concern itself with the advance of 'cultural democracy' and placed a lot of stress on the interdependence of cultural development and education, which is thought to be vital if the needs and interests of all people are to be served. 'Culture' was to be interpreted as including 'all the agencies that make for group life, creativity and constructive action in community affairs', not just 'parks and gardens, the municipal theatre and sports stadium'.[2] Cultural development, relying mainly on non-formal methods, was thus to be more concerned with the formation of new attitudes, values, ideas and 'principles' than with the preservation of the cultural heritage, with which indeed it could come into conflict. Should the working classes be led to acceptance of an 'upper class culture' and be educated to have 'correct taste', or is there a quite different 'mass culture' which should be encouraged? If the latter is based upon life in home and factory, what educational needs arise? What exactly is meant by the 'popularization' of culture? What proportion of resources should be given to preservation and what to development? 'Culture' itself seems to be no longer fully definable and some have severely attacked the institutions which, in some way or another, are regarded as its custodians. Questions are raised about what forms of activity may be thought culturally preferable and whether cultural 'autonomy' should be given to each social class or group, in an acceptance of a 'cultural pluralism'. The background to the institutions and activities described in this chapter is thus one of much uncertainty, confusion and, in some places, distrust.

Libraries

Reliance upon access to the printed word has been a major factor in the education of adults and regarded as one of the best ways of 'opening doors'. At an early date subscription libraries were established and, despite the problems of rising costs, the idea continues today in the form of book clubs supplying usually one book per month, for example 'The Literary Guild' organized by W.H. Smith Ltd. Private collections have often provided a basis for institutional libraries and most adult colleges and centres have a library, though sometimes very small. Similarly there have developed various types of collections in many hospitals and prisons, although there is a tendency for these to be superseded by a local authority lending service. There are also specialist services such as libraries for the blind, and the provision of books for the merchant navy by the Seafarers Education Service. Reference has already been made to university extra-mural department libraries issued in 'bookboxes' to adult classes, and some moves have been made to integrate these with the major university libraries. It has been suggested on many occasions that all institutional libraries should be open to those members of the public 'outside the walls' who can show valid study reasons and some have already been partly opened in this way. Most polytechnics and colleges of higher education have, however, felt that their collections were too small even to meet the needs of their own registered students. In view of the availability of paperbacks, to which attention has already been drawn, many students are encouraged to buy publications for their own personal libraries, and, although it is clear that a large minority of adults never buys a book at

151

all, the average annual expenditure per head on books is above that for the rest of Europe.[3] The development of home study, together with the persuasion of advertisers, seems to have led to a particular increase in the purchase of encyclopedias and similar compendia, not unlike that in France where there has been a tenfold increase in the sale of such works in ten years. The number of new titles in general is high, although rises in publishing costs may reduce this in the 1980s; thirty-two thousand were issued in 1975, including fiction and non-fiction, this total being exceeded only by West Germany and the USSR.

The major provision of books, however, is in the form of loans from the public libraries in the United Kingdom which together hold over 100 million books. In 1977, for example, over 600 million borrowings took place, of which just over 40% were non-fiction. Public libraries in towns originated in the 1850 Public Libraries Act and were extended to rural areas by the 1919 Act. At first they were expressly designed for the use of the lower income groups and linked to ideas of temperance and public order but in the twentieth century they have been used more and more by the middle class and higher income sectors of the population. Only about one-third of the population are members of the public libraries, however, and these tend to be the same people who read the 'quality' newspapers and view the more serious television programmes.[4] Finance for the libraries comes mainly out of local taxation although major contributions, given by Andrew Carnegie at the beginning of the century, enabled many library buildings to be erected, and some central government subsidies are now available for about one-third of the cost of the service. The central government also financially supports the National Libraries of England, Scotland and Wales and the British Museum Library.

As it grew up on a piecemeal basis, however, there arose considerable disparities in the type and quality of library provision. At one time there were over 600 library authorities in Britain, and although this figure was reduced by rationalization in the 1950s and 1960s and still more by local government reorganization in the 1970s to fewer than 150, there is still unevenness in the resources available. The 1964 Public Libraries and Museums Act put the English and Welsh library services under the jurisdiction of the Department of Education and Science, while in Scotland it has been in the care of the Secretary of State for Scotland since the Public Libraries (Scotland) Act of 1955. The areas of education and library services now tend to have come closer together, if not to coincide, although in many areas local authorities have separate Library Committees and Education Committees. The results of reorganization can be seen in a general improvement in the quality of the buildings, whether these are light and airy new buildings or modernized old ones, in the general appearance of the books, now often displayed in their bright original jackets protected by plastic covers, and in the general freedom of readers to wander among the bookcases.

The concept of the public library as a source from which people may borrow books freely has now become traditional although some argue that libraries should have responsibility only for 'purposive reading', for serious literature for vocational, educational and cultural purposes, and not for the light, recreational publications which are nevertheless a significant part of the normal function of most libraries. To the provision of books is now added a range of other communication materials, including maps, photographs, prints, films, filmstrips, slides, musical scores and records, illustrations of all kinds and collections of cuttings. Attempts have been made to bring library material to the public by the creation of easily accessible 'service points' and in the rural areas by the provision of mobile libraries, a factor of considerable importance in parts of Wales and in the northern and western areas of Scotland. The extension of the service to all areas has been paralleled by the gradual development of a regional system for inter-library loan and of a national centre, the 'British Library', which, as the National Central Library, had its origins in the 1961 Central Lending Library for Students which Mansbridge created to serve the WEA. Through this system anyone has access to any book in the United Kingdom and indeed to books elsewhere under international arrangements. Librarians, as well as caring for the stock of books and other materials and maintaining its adequacy, are urged to make sure that all citizens know of its existence and to make it imaginatively attractive. Most librarians are eager to serve the public in this way and to respond to requests from individuals. They also welcome the opportunity to give personal guidance to students and frequently prepare book lists. In the larger towns there is often special provision to meet the needs of local commerce and industry, using modern techniques to produce a full information and documentation service. A telex, as well as micro-photography and photo-copying services, is now a more general provision.

In this way, the public libraries are a vital information service supporting the education of adults as well as having other duties such as that of meeting recreational, social needs and of being a depository for historical material. Problems arise, however, when it is suggested that the educational function should be extended. A fairly common practice in many library areas has been to provide sets of books, including multiple copies and sets of plays, to LEA or Responsible Body classes. This, however, was challenged by the Russell Report which declared that though the goodwill was appreciated, public libraries should not be expected to undertake the task because ordinary borrowers should be protected against such undue demands from adult classes wanting long-term borrowing.[5] Similarly, the use of public libraries as accommodation for adult classes and other educational activities – a practice often preferred by both teachers and students – has been held to be full of difficulty. Should library authorities spend valuable resources on making accommodation available and with it appropriate equipment including not only chairs and tables, but perhaps blackboard, projector and screen? Some authorities are doubtful, though many groups of adult students continue to find a congenial meeting place in their local library, and many librarians argue that their library is the 'natural place' for adult classes.

A much more serious controversy concerns the question whether a public library should be actively involved in the education of adults as the 'cultural centre' of the community and the direct provider of educational activities. Some librarians, notably Edward Sydney of Leyton in the 1930s and 1940s were pioneers of 'library extension work' which included the provision of lectures, short courses, readings, film shows, exhibitions, music recitals, debates and discussion groups. In the nineteenth century some public libraries had experimented with this kind of activity but in the twentieth century many librarians are sceptical, feeling, as the Library Association declared in 1943, that 'it is the function of the public library to provide books . . . for the organizing of formal educational activities the responsibility lies with the education authority and other agencies'.[6] At the present time librarians seem divided in their opinions, and how much direct provision is undertaken depends upon local circumstances and the personal views of the librarian, together with the willingness of his or her committee to provide the necessary funds. Some libraries manage arts centres, Manchester has a library theatre and many other libraries provide lectures and exhibitions. Some co-operate in joint courses with the WEA or an extra-mural department, and in one or two areas special joint committees have been established between the public libraries and the various organizations for adult education.[7] As a minimum contribution, most librarians help with publicity in the form of posters, bookmarks and displays of reading matter relevant to courses and lectures arranged by other agencies.

Shortage of finance and other resources has long been a serious problem even before the reductions of the 1980s. In the older libraries there are few rooms suitable for small group work and there are often shortcomings in the amount of available equipment. Perhaps the main problem, however, lies in the type of training which most librarians have received; on the whole this has been limited to the traditional care of the printed works and to ways of making the collection both adequate and easily accessible to the public. Very few librarians have been trained as educators although a few have now begun to take the advanced diplomas and higher degrees in adult education offered by some universities. The Schools of Librarianship are also extending the range of the courses they provide. Most librarians seem to consider that they can be fully occupied assisting the individual reader and that there should be limits to direct involvement in the provision of more formal education for adults. Otherwise, they argue, money and resources will be drained away from the central services of the public libraries. One solution to the problem was offered by the Alexander Committee; it recommended that 'each library authority should appoint appropriate members of staff to maintain close liaison with those concerned with adult education in their area, so that the full resources of the library service may be used in the interests of adult education'.[8] Difficult though the attitudes of some librarians may be, a greater problem is the attitude of about two-thirds of the population who are not members of public libraries. A few may have private collections or borrow via other members of the family, but many are indifferent and perhaps hostile. As already suggested, some statistics indicate that nearly 30% of the population never read books at all which seems a high proportion, though it is lower than in France or Germany. Possibly the special attention now being given to the relationship between children and the libraries may change this situation; through readings, play activities and other enterprises, the rising generation may come to view the public library as a less forbidding place. An increase in literacy may also help although this could be offset by non-book forms of communication. Many British libraries, however, are still a long way from the imaginative centres on the continent and from the concept, put forward by Denis Howell in 1967, of libraries as 'cultural centres in the widest sense . . . where there is a multiplicity of activity — record recitals, discussion groups, poetry and play readings, exhibitions — reflecting the work of local cultural and social organizations'. Even where an outgoing policy is

154

adopted successive librarians and changing committees may cause wide fluctuations in what is actually done. There may also be lingering suspicions about reading as a vehicle for indoctrination and escapism — a suspicion voiced by Shaw when he declared that 'what we call education and culture is for the most part nothing but the substitution of reading for experience, of literature for life, of the obsolete fictitious for the contemporary real'.[9] The established national library advisory councils for England and for Wales attempt to solve existing problems and improve the general quality of the service but perhaps what is most needed is more clarity about the role of the public library in the education of adults.

Museums and Art Galleries

Originally museums were used solely for the conservation of objects and only a few people — usually amateur antiquarians and some scientists — took any interest in them. Most originated in collections made by those with wealth and power, sometimes as an investment but often for private display.[10] Some remain in private hands, as in the collections held in old aristocratic homes such as Chatsworth in Derbyshire, while others have come into the possession of Trusts or universities, an example being the possession by Manchester University of the Manchester Museum and the Whitworth Art Gallery. Others have passed into public ownership, either central or local. All of them depend, however, on the ideas and resources of those in control, and their educational role is subject to much the same arguments as that of the public libraries, with which it is sometimes felt desirable they should be combined. The central argument is whether they should be essentially places where material is collected and conserved, a source of reference and an adjunct to education, or whether they should be a 'most valuable public educational service'[11] for those with the least specialist knowledge, and centres of community educational activity. Some have stressed the reference value of a museum in which all objects are severely ordered and carefully and concisely registered and annotated. Others have stated bluntly that: 'Education and Museums — museums *are* education ... They exist to further it, they can be neither provided, maintained nor utilized without it'.[12] On the whole, many of the 700 or so museums and art galleries in the United Kingdom remain essentially reference collections, despite recent changes and the pressure of bodies such as the Advisory Council on Education in Scotland which, in its excellent 1951 *Report on Libraries, Museums and Art Galleries,* urged the development of a positive educational role. Some were lost during the Second World War although fewer than in the continent of Europe where there has been a rebirth of remarkable quality in terms of display and architecture in the new museums and art galleries.

Those who wish to exploit the educational potential of museums and art galleries for adults have developed courses of lectures and guided tours, as well as providing publications of all kinds including reproductions. They also offer advisory services and have developed links with local societies, as well as in some instances creating their own clubs and associations. Some produce travelling exhibitions and have developed loan schemes, a particular example being the Derbyshire Museum Service, which has been willing to lend considerable amounts of material, either originals or well-produced replicas to adult voluntary organizations as well as to schools. Popular television programmes have resulted in an apparently ever-increasing interest in archaeology, local history, art history and antiques, and some museums in co-operation with education authorities have encouraged the use of their premises for organized adult classes, or have established outreach centres under their control. Publicity through the mass media has sometimes resulted in large crowds for specialist exhibitions such as that of the Tutankhamun treasures which toured the national museums in the 1970s.

Educationally there are obvious opportunities, which some curators have seized upon, but there are many problems, of which the usual shortage of resources is perhaps the most important. The Alexander Report noted that most of the local museums and art galleries in Scotland had very limited means and that the majority were not in the hands of local authorities, which in 1975 for example had only thirty-eight of the ninety in existence in Scotland. In general, museums tend to operate in isolation despite the Council for Museums and Galleries in Scotland which advises museum authorities on the planning and operating of the services. This council is aided by central government funds and grant aid is offered for specific projects of improvement. The total amount of money, particularly for the small local museums, however, contrasts greatly with expenditure elsewhere in the world and some museums have had to close because of financial difficulties. Further problems are inadequate staffing, poor facilities for training and general support services. Only a minority have education officers, and hard-pressed curators, however enthusiastic, find it difficult to extend the range of their offering, especially if they have a vigorous committee devoted to the idea of conservation of museum objects, paintings and sculpture, rather than to their educational use. This latter attitude has been described as 'object-centred' in contrast to 'man-centred', and rests basically on a strong belief in the value of preserving the cultural heritage and of protecting it from possible depradation by a public not thought to be convinced of its value. Some curators, indeed, have been described as 'possessive old hoarders' and a certain reservation, even hostility, to the public still persists among some museum officials. Until recently this has to a large extent been reciprocated by the mass of the public who have shown indifference to the fate of museums and reluctance to enter buildings which they felt were not for them. The conventional public image of a museum still seems to be that of a rather dismal building with large and lofty rooms full of objects arranged in a way people cannot understand and clearly marked 'Do not Touch'. As a 1971 Department of Education and Science Survey put it: 'The word 'Museum' is perhaps in part responsible for the present unsatisfactory state of affairs. Does it not suggest a depressing decaying institution, the last resting place of travellers' mementoes, and of fossils which have undeservedly survived from ages long ago?'[13]

The better museums have countered this image by stimulating, imaginative displays, encouraging activity, perhaps with the aid of gadgets, allowing people to handle all but the rarest or most delicate material, and giving attention to restaurant and toilet facilities, rest rooms with comfortable chairs, and aids such as ramps for the physically disabled. They have also built strong connections with members of the public in classes and voluntary organizations, particularly those concerned with art and archaeology, and have often developed their own groups, perhaps known as 'Friends of the Museum'. All of this seeks to increase public interest and support and to remove the bad image. Some museum and art gallery staff conduct courses for the WEA or university extra-mural departments, as in Sheffield, although it is clear that many more adult educational organizations could make much more use of the staff and facilities on offer. Some in fact argue that members of the public need some training in how to make the best use of the museums and galleries, if only to check the general tendency of those who do enter to try and see all the exhibits in one rapid tour. Given more resources, most curators now seem likely to develop the educational possibilities of which they have become aware. The larger museums and art galleries are already providing much supportive material such as easily-assimilated explanations, films, tapes, photographs and transparencies, and there is an increasing tendency to provide specialist exhibitions of a limited duration which have proved attractive to many who otherwise would not have entered. There has also been a development of single subject museums, such as the railway museums in York and Glossop, the motor museum at Beaulieu, the doll museum in Blackpool and costume museums in various parts of the country. Some museums have particular themes such as the science and industry museums in Bradford, Manchester and elsewhere, the historical street in York and craft museums such as the Lhaidhays Croft Museum near Wick. There are also some devoted to a particular industry such as Pilkington's Glass Museum in St Helens, the Wedgwood pottery museum and the Quarry Bank Mill in Styal, Cheshire which focuses on the textile industry. Many manor houses, especially National Trust properties, have also taken definite steps to provide historically suitable furniture and fittings as well as competent guides to help public understanding. Alternatively, if the architecture is the special feature, as at Little Moreton Hall in Cheshire, the rooms may be left relatively bare in order to concentrate attention on the building. Rather more slowly than in Scandinavia, some folk museums have been created, sometimes using country estates as the home for open air exhibits, somewhat on the lines of the Skansen Museum in Sweden or the 'Heritage Parks' found in various parts of North America. One example is the North of England Open Air Museum set up at Beamish in Durham in 1970 on a 200-acre site. This includes a pithead and miners' cottages, a railway area with steam trains, a tramway, a home farm with equipment of the eighteenth century or earlier, a 100-ton steam shovel and a growing range of other examples of machinery and materials related to life in the region. Old buildings are brought from all areas, rebuilt on a site and equipped with the kind of furniture or machinery they once held. Other examples are the Highland Museum at Kingussie in Scotland, the Welsh Folk Museum at St Fagans near Cardiff which was established in 1947 and the Ulster Folk and Transport Museum set up at Cultra Manor near Belfast in 1958. Besides attention to the past, some museums have mounted displays on contemporary science or art, themes once considered outside their brief.

There is little doubt than an infusion of finance would produce very considerable developments. A more abundant, well-trained, professional staff, paid reasonable salaries instead of the inadequate amounts usual in the smaller museums, would build a service much more comparable with that elsewhere in Europe. Like the Library Association, the Museums Association continues to press for better conditions and remuneration for its Fellows and Associates so that they can serve the public more adequately. There are encouraging examples in various parts of the country but too much still depends on charity and upon the overwork of devoted members of staff. Perhaps more could be done to link the various museums and art galleries more closely; the Alexander Report suggested, for example, that the national and large town museums might provide support services for the educational work undertaken by museums in the more thinly populated areas. Similarly, they might arrange touring exhibitions to the smaller towns and rural areas in general. At present it seems that many people lack even the knowledge that some museums and art galleries exist;[14] though statistics show some increases in the annual number of visitors to the major public art galleries and museums most of these are in London and it is likely that many of the visitors are from overseas. The major question is that of role. Those who wish the galleries and museums to exist essentially for preservation purposes often consider that the necessary finance could be raised by high admission charges. Those who stress the educational potential, and those who think of cultural development, want to bring the public in as cheaply as possible and extend considerably the activities as well as the range of exhibits in a statutory government supported service. If the latter view is taken, then more efforts are needed to provide more congenial surroundings, to adjust location as well as opening times to meet local needs and to secure more training both for museum and gallery staff and for members of the public, including those who as 'museum volunteers' often undertake supportive responsibilities.

The Arts Council and Societies concerned with the arts and culture

The Arts Council of Great Britain had its origins in the provision of travelling art exhibitions. In 1935, the British Institute of Adult Education began an experiment in 'Art for the People' in which collections of pictures, lent by private collectors, were sent out for a month to places where there were very few opportunities to see paintings and sculptures. Two of the first places to be chosen were Swindon and Barnsley. The exhibitions were accompanied by talks by experts and by observers who initiated informal discussions with visitors. The scheme was a success[15] and during the war it was transmuted into the Council for the Encouragement of Music and the Arts (CEMA) and in 1945 into the Arts Council, the former Secretary of the BIAE, Mr. W.E. Williams, becoming its secretary in 1951. The Arts Council charter makes it clear that the original idea of increasing knowledge and understanding of the arts is kept much in mind, as well as the aims of making the arts more widely accessible and of attempting to get co-operation between all concerned. The close connection with adult education is also exemplified by the appointment in 1975 of Sir Roy Shaw, former professor of adult education in Keele University, to be its secretary general. There are now separate Arts Councils, each with its own Director, in Scotland, Wales and Northern Ireland, but all have the same type of objectives.

The Councils are some of the principal channels of central government funding of the Arts although the national museums and galleries receive separate government grants. They give aid mainly for professional arts activities, and hence the bulk of the funds go in subsidies to independent professional arts-promoting organizations. In England these include the Royal Opera and Royal Ballet companies, the National Theatre, the Royal Shakespeare Company, the National Opera and eight symphony orchestras. About sixty regional theatres and various smaller drama companies, dance organizations and music and arts festivals receive aid as well as a few local arts centres. Arts centres have been systematically encouraged since the 1960s and in offering opportunities for the practice and enjoyment of the arts, they are valuable ancillaries to organized education for adults. Each arts centre and local arts council is unique with its own developing tradition, but, using the 'centre idea', each tries to provide a focus in which the local community can try to improve the general status of the arts within its area.[16] Inevitably, like all voluntary organizations, they tend to wax and wane as membership and personal enthusiasms change, but at their best they constitute a vital part of non-formal education for adults. Regional Arts Associations (at present twelve in England) have also developed and these work in partnership with the national Arts Councils from which they obtain financial assistance. They also attempt to work with the local authorities but the quality of this relationship depends upon the policies of the latter. The national Arts Councils also support individual artists, administer training schemes and directly present some art exhibitions as well as arranging tours by ballet, drama and opera companies. Further aid comes from the publication of references books and information bulletins.

Financial restrictions prevent the Arts Councils from carrying out all that they would like to do. Perhaps inevitably they tend to support in the main the major national orchestras and opera, ballet and theatre companies. In Scotland in 1979—80 some 43% of the budget of the Scottish Arts Council was spent on the four major companies — Scottish Opera, the Scottish National Orchestra, the Scottish Philharmonic Society and the Scottish Ballet — leaving only just over 50% for the other 800 clients and 6% for operating costs. Not infrequently, therefore, they are accused of neglecting the provinces, and also of élitism and lack of attention to the needs of the masses. As suggested earlier, defining the 'arts' and 'culture' is a difficult problem but it is one which the Arts Councils have to face when distributing funds. The most persistent problem remains the amount of these funds; central government appears determined to reduce rather than increase its grants and the local authorities in general fail to provide even a fraction of the financial support regularly given by most medium-sized towns in Europe. As a Conservative Discussion Paper on the Arts commented in 1978, spending on the arts is 'not an optional extra, but is as vital in its contribution to the quality of life and the promotion of human happiness as expenditure on health and education'. Yet the amount per head from central government is minimal, an example being the £1.40 per annum in Scotland in 1979—80. Perhaps the public, and through them the elected councillors and members of parliament, need more educational help in developing interest and appreciation of the value of cultural arts in the modern world. Certainly so far there has been little sign of the creation of public support represented for example, in the theatre-audience organization of the *Volksbühne* in Germany.[17] As with museums and art galleries, much depends on relationships with the public and the organized visits of many voluntary societies may be helpful if well received, and provided with adequate guidance. The women's organizations, such as the Townswomen's Guilds and the Women's Institutes, are good examples of the way in which some have taken parties not only to British institutions but overseas to Salzburg, Paris, Florence, Rome and other 'cultural centres'.

The educational potential of voluntary societies concerned with music and the arts seems to be considerable as well as varied. Some groups tend to concentrate on public performances but many, such as the Lancaster Community Arts Group, declare their intention to establish positive links with various sectors of the community with workshops in places such as hospitals and youth clubs. With a membership of people already reasonably accomplished in some branch of the arts, many societies think of themselves more as fostering the appreciation of music, drama or art among the public than as being personally involved in their own learning process. Thus most members of art societies can already paint, and in the various philharmonic choirs and amateur operatic societies most can already sing. Nevertheless it is unwise to discount the improvements in proficiency and knowledge gained by members through society meetings. The use of residential colleges and adult education centres for the display of artistic or dramatic productions by voluntary amateur societies is also of educational importance both to the students who attend and to the amateurs whose confidence is developed in this way.

Supporting the large number of local societies are national voluntary organizations each concerned with a particular aspect of the arts. An example is the Scottish Community Drama Association founded in 1926, which, as the principal amateur theatre organization in Scotland, organizes an annual national Drama Festival and has a professional, trained staff who are available to all local centres as providers of advice, lectures and practical instruction on all aspects of theatre. It also organizes short courses in drama from time to time, and maintains five libraries from which copies of plays and other books on drama may be borrowed. There is also the British Theatre Association, which organizes drama schools and festivals, and arranges local pageants and touring companies as well as helping in the selection and circulation of plays and costumes. In music the Rural Music Schools Association has given much aid to the organization and professional development of village orchestras as well as assisting individuals with their knowledge and skills. Founded by Miss Mary Ibberson in Hertfordshire in 1929, the schools are independent centres from which teachers go out to groups and to which people come to practice and learn more about music. They exist in the rural areas of the southern half of England and have had a somewhat difficult time since the departure of the founder. For dancing the English Folk Dance and Song Society (EFDSS) provides instruction and encourages the formation of local groups, as does the Royal Scottish Country Dance Society. There are also societies concerned with films and more recently with television, such as the British Film Institute based on London which seeks to develop the art of the film and to foster public appreciation, publishing a periodical *Sight and Sound* and a *Film Bulletin*. In Scotland the Scottish Film Council is a grant-aided organization whose purposes are to promote the use of the film and other audio-visual media in education and industry, and to encourage an understanding and appreciation of the cinema. It holds the Scottish Central Film Library, has a Regional Film Theatre and a technical department, as well as working with the Scottish Educational Film Association to help teachers and industrial training officers. It is the headquarters of the Scottish Group of the British Federation of Film Societies, another body concentrating on the study of the cinema as a subject in its own right. There is also a Society for Education in Film and Television, which publishes a quarterly periodical entitled *Screen and Screen Education,* a Society for Education through Arts, various Civic Trusts and the Council for the Preservation of Rural England. In Scotland the Saltire Society, founded in 1936 for the purpose of encouraging a deeper interest in the arts and culture of Scotland, has provided publications, lectures and discussions concerned particularly with art, architecture, music, crafts, literature and social history.

All these organizations try to encourage public interest in aesthetic matters, and a growing belief in the value of creative skills. New developments occur from time to time. A recent example is CETU (the Community Education Training Unit) which arose in the north-west of England in 1976 'to promote and develop aspects of education, community development and community arts in order to help people achieve greater control of their lives and of the structures in society that influence them'.[18] In pursuit of this aim the unit has put much stress on non-formal education and experiential learning, helping groups and local workers to identify needs and use resources. Examples of the help it has given are community self-surveys, the establishment of silk screen and photographic workshops, making available various methods of visual communication and compiling a resources directory. Experimental in conception, it has had various changes of staff, and its survival may well depend upon the continuing initiative of a small group of people, as well as upon securing the necessary funds. So far it has had financial support from the Arts Council, Merseyside Arts Association, North-West Arts Association, Marks and Spencers Ltd, the Manpower Services Commission and the Gulbenkian Foundation, but there is no guarantee that any of this will continue.

How far the sort of provision sketched in this chapter is an essential part of the education of adults is a matter of argument. In a sense it is very ill-defined and it is not surprising that some regard it as being only auxiliary, an aid to the 'real education' elsewhere. So far there have been only sporadic attempts to examine its implications for the more structured forms of education. Should museums, art galleries, libraries and artistic performances all be more closely related to adult classes? Should professional artists, composers and writers be more widely used in teaching work? How far should their work be regarded as central, rather than marginal, in the life of the community? What is the place of the arts in education? At present several different concepts vie for supremacy, and the uncertainty shows in the type of funding, staffing and attitudes. Anxiety about priorities in the use of resources is particularly marked when general cut-backs are threatened. Is it enough just to store the 'cultural heritage', on the grounds that this may be difficult enough because the cost and, for instance, the increasing problems of space to house expanding collections, or should every effort be made, perhaps particularly by imaginative displays, to secure the active involvement of more people? Should more professional *animateurs* be appointed and if so just what should be their duties? Is more advertising and general publicity likely to secure creative activity or will it bring only more passive spectatorship? The active involvement alternative links with the ideas put forward in the Faure Report that the task is to enable people 'to fulfil their potential and to maximise personal satisfaction through the provision of open access to educational opportunities throughout life'.[19] This is, however, still a long way from the ideas and reactions of the majority of people in Britain, in whose lives libraries, museums, art galleries and performances of music, drama and classical dance have little place. At an Arts Council conference in 1979 it was recommended that informal joint adult education and arts working groups should be established on a regional or group basis to look at some of the problems and to promote collaboration. Mutual lack of knowledge on the part of both the educational agencies for adults and of bodies involved in the arts remains a barrier to real co-operation and to the much-needed process of synthesizing practice and appreciation of the arts. New initiatives have been taken in a few areas by Regional Arts Associations, but these have barely touched the problem. What is most needed is a more positive attitude among the educators of adults.

References

1. See SIMPSON, J.A, *Towards Cultural Democracy*, 1976, Council of Europe. Commissioned by the Council for Cultural Co-operation for the Oslo Conference of Ministers with Responsibility for Cultural Affairs. The quotation is given on p. 16.

2. Ibid. The whole of chapter 1 is relevant.

3. Figures for 1975 show an expenditure over the age of sixteen of $9.7, as compared to 8.4 in Belgium and Denmark, 6.5 in West Germany and 6 in France. See *Social Trends* No. 9 (1979 edition) HMSO. Table 12.11.

4. See TRENAMAN, J, *Communication and Comprehension*, 1967. Longmans.

5. Russell Report, paras 349 and 354. See also an earlier discussion in *Library Association Record*, 58 (12), Dec. 1956, pp. 471–474, on 'The provision of books to adult classes', and the Ministry of Education *Standards of Public Library Service in England and Wales*, (the Bourdillon Report), 1962, pp. 25–26.

6. Library Association. *Proposals for the Post-War Development of the Public Library Service*, 1943, LA, pp. 14–15.

7. For example, the Public Libraries and Adult Education Committee for the North-West formed in 1960.

8. Alexander Report, para 199.

9. SHAW, G.B. Preface to *Man and Superman*.

10. A good brief historical survey is given in CHADWICK, A.F. *The Role of the Museum and Art Gallery in Community Education*, 1980, University of Nottingham Dept. of Adult Education, pp. 3–12.

11. ALLEN, D, *Papers on the Role of Museums in Education*, 1954, UNESCO, Introduction.

12. ALLEN, D. Paper read in 1949 to the Royal Society of Arts. Quoted in NIAE *Museums and Adult Education,* 1956.

13. Department of Education and Science, *Museums in Education,* Education Survey, No. 12, 1971, HMSO, p. 49.

14. See CHADWICK, Op. cit.

15. For a brief history see the account written by SIR WILLIAM E. WILLIAMS on 'The pre-history of the Arts Council' in *Aims and Action in Adult Education, 1921–1971,* published by the NIAE in 1971.

16. See, for example, HUTCHINSON, R. *Three Arts Centres: a Study of South Hill Park, the Gardner Centre and Chapter,* 1977, Arts Council.

17. See DAVIES, C.W. *Theatre Audience Organization: the example of Germany,* 1972.

18. CETU booklet, *Statement of Aims.*

19. FAURE, E. (Ed.) *Learning to Be: the World of Education Today and Tomorrow,* 1972, UNESCO and Harrap.

CHAPTER 10

Education with a social dimension

Despite the marked stress on education for personal development, especially in the second half of the twentieth century, the education of adults has always had social or community connotations. Its social importance is publicly acknowledged but with varying interpretations and varying emphases. Of the many asserted social purposes, three broad groups seem particularly worth consideration and these may be described as 'good citizenship', 'social well-being', and 'social caring'. These titles are somewhat arbitrary but represent interpretations of considerable importance in determining policies, the allocation of resources and the general organization of the provision.

Education and 'Good Citizenship'

As noted earlier, definitions of 'good citizenship' depend upon political view-points. From the point of view of a dictator or an oligarchy, or even of those who believe that once elected a government should 'rule with firmness', 'good citizens' are those who accept the ideas and practices of those in power, and the ways of life at home and at work which are judged by the rulers to be of most benefit to that society. Education in this light is an instrument of conditioning, of producing acceptance and as much conformity as possible. A dominant theme in nineteenth century Britain, particularly to secure a disciplined workforce, it can be seen today in the objectives of socialization and acculturalization which seem to characterize the more traditional schools of thought. Certain values, attitudes and behaviour patterns are advanced as being desirable in society and efforts are made to secure adherence to these. Television has been accused of being the great guardian of the status quo, and a medium which not only reflects middle-class ideals and aspirations but sets out to secure their acceptance.[1] Other bodies said to use 'education' for the propagation of doctrines or ideologies are, of course, the political parties and the churches, but many other organizations use educational methods to try to get acceptance of their ideas. Often associated with this approach is the concept that for most people only a limited, or one-sided, education is desirable if social discipline is to be secured. This 'education' is to be carefully selected by those in power to ensure that each individual can fit into a particular niche, an often-quoted example being that of job-related education with its processes of sorting out, filtering and grading. Education stops for those who cannot pass the next test, and those who drop out early are deemed to have had enough to equip them for jobs at the lowest level. It will be noted that this interpretation is also a utilitarian one, a belief that education is concerned primarily with vocational ends designed to aid 'productivity'.

The alternative view of the 'good citizen' is that of a person who is democratically active, who thinks for himself and acts in ways which he has decided are good for the community to which he belongs. Robert Peers declared that 'men and women should learn how to use knowledge; how to judge between conflicting ideas; how to use facts in order to reach conclusions". The ideal democracy is one in which all are informed, critical citizens who both produce and control changes in the social order. This view also stresses the rights of minorities and the use of education to help preserve human dignity and identity. Education is seen, therefore, both as personal, developing abilities and capacity to think, and also as socially significant 'because the man whom education liberates is a man in society, and his society will be affected by the change which education creates in him'.[3] In his note on 'Matters peculiar to Wales' at the end of the Russell Report, R.T. Ellis saw adult education 'as a lifeline to the continued vitality of the (Welsh) language and the cultural heritage'[4] and looked with favour upon the 'democratic voluntaryism' of the WEA as the means of providing it. The stress upon the importance of the individual in society is seen in the Alexander Report's support for community education, and in its approval of the comment made in 1955 by Sir Eric Ashby that:

> we live in a society which confers on the worker political responsibility, civic rights and leisure. The contemporary problem in adult education is that among many people . . . the leisure is without purpose, the civic rights are without significance and the political responsibility is assumed without understanding. We are learning the hard way that social emancipation without personal emancipation is of little value. In a world noisy with the organs of mass communication and riddled with propaganda, modern man is hard put to it to preserve his status as an individual. To help preserve this status is the contemporary task for adult education.[5]

For the educator of adults there appear to be several specific problems. How is interest in community affairs to be stimulated among all members of the community? Many do not show any desire for such an interest and, feeling powerless, have retired into a kind of resentful defensiveness, exhibiting only apathy when asked to share in the running of affairs.

Community Projects

The Residential Settlements, the first of which, Toynbee Hall, was established in 1884, encourage the voluntary service of university men and women in neighbourhood centres in urban depressed areas — originally they were to reside or 'settle' for a time in such areas — and although many Settlements have developed as centres of social research, they are still 'schools of citizenship for the education of the electors in the technique of democracy through discussion and social intercourse and practical experience of self government'.[6]

The twelve Community Development Projects of the 1970s also tried to develop citizen initiative and involvement among those who felt politically and economically impotent. These tried to link together local official and unofficial efforts and to get people to make constructive use of their powers.

165

The results were seen in resident-run community groups of various kinds, community newspapers, local environmental improvement work carried out voluntarily, such as the cleaning up of old canals and derelict sites, and very informal adult educational work. The knowledge gained, the confidence and personal development achieved are difficult to quantify but through community development, with its emphasis on 'felt need' and 'self-help' some of those who are normally 'non-joiners' have been stimulated to free some of their latent strengths and potential. 'Community development is an educational process,' said Biddle and Biddle[7] and this kind of non-formal contribution is now being made by community development officers employed by many local authorities. Their work at its best shows a patient, tolerant understanding and an imaginative attempt to stimulate people's confidence to become involved, to feel that change is possible, to identify needs in informal meetings, and to go forward to some kind of action. Much of this is similar to Freire's approach to 'conscientization', although in community development the process is said to be often more important than the end product and it may well be as much concerned with conserving the social fabric as with achieving innovations. The aim is to help people, to work with them rather than for them.[8]

Participation

'Participation' has become a desirable ideal in many quarters, especially since the Skeffington Report[9] with its stress on the need to involve all people in planning. In some areas the WEA has given a lead in trying to stimulate those who do not normally participate, notably for example by the appointment of a tutor-organiser with special responsibility for this in the working class districts of Liverpool. Some universities have also given help, as for example that provided by Southampton University in its New Communities Project.[10] For those who do join organizations, the problem of education for active democratic citizenship seems a little easier. The development of confidence is still needed but to it can be added much-needed information and organizational skills. Perhaps the major contribution to citizenship education in fact is the practical experience gained by many members of voluntary organizations in running their own affairs, making unpaid committees work and carrying out programmes of their own devising. In this way people learn not only the technicalities and organizational skills of democratic government but also something of the value of mutual trust, of weighing the evidence, of trying to make sound judgements, of establishing relationships and of other aspects of the democratic spirit, without which the machinery is barren. They also learn communication skills, how to use language to express ideas, and in general how to make their needs and wishes understood. Traditionally citizenship education has been the major 'social purpose' of the WEA, and some declare that participation in the self-government of the organization is more important than the subject content of the classes. The same could be said of the multitude of other voluntary organizations such as the Townswomen's Guilds with their avowed intention to educate women for citizenship. Further examples are the non-conformist churches' emphasis on lay participation in government and the growing number of informal discussion groups which have elements similar to those of the Swedish study circles.

Civic Education

Providing people with information about democratic government, there is the Hansard Society founded in 1944, which seeks 'to arouse interest in and spread knowledge throughout the world of the proceedings of Parliament', and organizations such as the United Nations Association with its programmes of lectures and debates about international affairs. Like all voluntary organizations, specialist societies concerned with education for citizenship tend to come and go; early examples were the Association for Education in Citizenship of the 1930s and 1940s, and the Bureau of Current Affairs in the 1950s which followed the wartime experiment of the Army Bureau (ABCA). On the whole the LEAs have not entered very much into this area, perhaps because of a dislike of any kind of 'political education' and the fears of elected councillors of the effects it might have. Some LEA adult education centres have included 'civics' courses in their programmes, however, and Goldsmith's College in London has provided 'citizens rights' courses. The broadcasting authorities have also been active, as for example in 1976-7 when the BBC put out a radio course on *'What right have you got?'*, which dealt with the rights and responsibilities of ordinary citizens in contemporary British society. Local radio has also shown itself willing to co-operate with community development workers and adult educators in providing programmes of information and general stimulus, as well as help for local action groups.

Adult Education and Social Change

Participation and active citizenship carry with them a challenge to those in authority in that they are often a means of inducing social change. As John Bennington, the leader of the Coventry Community Development Project team, said, participation 'is ultimately a question of gaining access to the decision making table, i.e. a structural redistribution of power'. Some would question whether this drive towards political activity and perhaps to militant protest is in fact education at all, although many others believe it to be a quite vital sector. If a university stimulates a study group which undertakes a survey of attitudes and preferences towards alternative policies of house demolition and rebuilding, or modernization, and sends the results to the local councillors who are about to take action on such matters, this can be seen as gross interference and a threat, or alternatively as an important learning experience.[11] Similarly, adult educational organizations are open to challenge when they associate themselves with pleas for more industrial democracy on the lines suggested by the Bullock Committee and attempt to equip workers for the exercise of their 'democratic rights and responsibilities'. 'Knowledge is power' has long been a watchword of the WEA, the Co-operative Movement and many working class organizations, but those in power in political or economic life may think that acquiescence and acceptance is easier than encouraging independent ideas and feelings. Adult educators using a non-formal community development approach may therefore find themselves in a conflict situation as well as face to face with the dilemma of trying to reconcile demands for community involvement with the maintenance of traditional academic standards. The 'education of the citizen' may seem safe enough if contemplated in academic isolation but dangerous when it leads to action groups and responses to problems in modern society such as violence, the impact of new motorways, local housing, immigration and power sharing. The relationship between education and 'good' citizenship is complex and subject to a good deal of emotional response despite the agreed basic statement of the 1976 International Conference on Adult Education that this kind of education 'incorporates anything which enlarges men's understanding, activiates them and helps them to make their own decisions and to implement those decisions for themselves'.[12]

Education for 'Social Well Being'

Similar questions arise over interpretations of 'social well-being'. Is it the sum of the well-being of all individuals or does the good of the whole community transcend the welfare of individuals? Of what does 'well-being' consist? Who determines it, or should determine it? Are there differences between what people want and what they need? The educational responses to this kind of question again show much variety; at one extreme education seems to be used for purposes of indoctrination while at the other education seems designed to stimulate individual responsibility for decisions. On the whole 'well-being' tends to be viewed in terms of health and safety, adequacy of food and housing, satisfaction in relationships, the quality of the environment and sometimes moral behaviour.

Health and Safety

Health and safety education is often concentrated in particular campaigns, such as those concerned with personal hygiene, anti-smoking, smoke control, and the wearing of seat belts in cars or crash helmets on motorcycles. They may be supported by laws passed by the central government, but frequently rely only on persuasion and the pressures of the audio-visual media. These national campaigns are often translated into local action by local voluntary organizations or by local units of national bodies. In the anti-smokiing campaign, for example, new local groups as well as branches of ASH (Action on Smoking and Health) have endeavoured to secure a ban on smoking in shops, hotels and various public places, and to develop public pressure by talks and discussions arranged either independently or with voluntary organizations. Local authorities may assist with finance or with special displays in libraries, and they may directly contribute to general health and home safety education in regular adult courses dealing with subjects such as car maintenance, beauty culture, cookery and electrical installations as well as through keep fit and sport. Informal health education, often on an individual one-to-one basis is also given by industrial health officers, district and community nurses and indeed general practitioners and dentists. Similarly, much information is handed on in health clubs and keep fit societies, as well as by the press and broad-casting in phone-in programmes such as the regular medical spots on the Jimmy Young programme on Radio 2. Industry and the trade unions also contribute to safety education in factories and elsewhere. For sports clubs and all the many national associations for particular sports, as well as for the Sports Council, health and safety is, of course, part of the general activity designed to stimulate the provision and use of better facilities.

Promoting and encouraging health education are the Scottish Health Education Unit and the Scottish Council for Health Education, and the equivalent Health Education Council for the rest of Britain, Northern Ireland as well as England and Wales. These bodies were set up in 1968 after the Cohen Committee had reported in 1964. They provide some courses them-selves but are also sources of information and advice, issuing publications from time to time, both booklets and newsletters, as well as lists of what other people provide. In association with the BBC, for example, they issued a booklet in 1979 on *Feeling Great* in support of a national keep fit campaign backed by a television series. In some parts of the country, there are special types of provision such as that of the regional committees for cancer edu-cation in Manchester and Liverpool. These are concerned with ways of in-forming the public, and with reducing the emotional tension about the subject of cancer, so that people can come to a better understanding of diagnosis and treatment. Undertaking educational as well as therapeutic tasks are organ-izations such as Alcoholics Anonymous whose meetings are designed to re-educate people so that they can acquire a new value system through sharing experiences in an atmosphere of trust and respect.

Family Planning and Marriage Guidance

Much of this can be regarded as teaching people what to think and believe and it is said to be justified because of the degree of certainty involved. There are, however, perennial arguments about safety measures such as seat belts in cars, and about health matters such as inoculation or the virtues of 'jogging'. Similarly, questions are raised about education concerned with human relationships, especially with family planning, marriage guidance and parent education. Information about methods of family planning is given in welfare clinics, and individually by members of the medical service, but this is frowned upon by some religious organizations, and the main issues may be seen to be not so much the supply of information as the discussion of attitudes and behaviour patterns which condition its use. 'Social well-being' in these terms may be seen to require either education for individual moral values and attitudes, *or* education to secure a restriction of population growth in an overcrowded world, *or* education in personal relationships. The provision of education concerned with marriage guidance is a similar area in which the churches seem to have lost their supremacy, and just as there is a secular Family Planning Association so there is a secular National Marriage Guidance Council which has a network of local councils and counsellors, some of whom arrange special courses, sometimes in association with other voluntary organ-izations or with LEAs. The rapid changes in community life have produced a series of conflicts within society which people find increasingly difficult to resolve as individuals. These include increasing family mobility, the dispersal of the larger family unit and increasing isolation, as well as the challenges to moral and cultural standards to which the National Marriage Guidance Council drew attention in its evidence to the Russell Committee. Sometimes members of the Council tutor courses for those about to be married or newly married. Perhaps more often the approach is through informal discussions about the family and family life, organized by community groups or by the churches which in many areas still play a considerable part. Education to promote well-being through helping an individual to meet family and social needs can in some circumstances become therapy and the borderline between education and therapy then is undoubtedly thin.

Parent Education

With marriage guidance may be linked parent education which tries to help parents to be better informed about children and to cultivate judgement in bringing up their own children. As Janet Hall said in a National Marriage Guidance Council booklet: 'it seeks to promote a search for family stability in a society of flux, and to focus on the need to comprehend differences in the status, values and points of view of the various members of the family.'[13] This is a complex process, however, and the approach to it may come from many different angles. Many parents acquire their attitudes and information about how to bring up children from their own parents, peer groups, news-papers and broadcasting, with results which are not always consistent. There is an increasing awareness that co-operation between parents and schools will help children to obtain maximum benefit but a barrier still exists in the traditional working-class attitude of keeping out of the schools. Value-judgements condition the quality of family life, and parent education is thus not solely concerned with information about child development and the physical welfare of children, but must include a search for understanding of the parental role, communication skills and the development of confidence. In a sense, therefore, almost every type of education for adults may be part of parent education. Special courses are provided by a number of LEAs such as Ealing, however, in association with local Parent-Teacher Associations (PTAs) in which are included a fairly wide range of topics concerned with the organization of the education service, child learning and the help parents can give. PTAs also operate independently but so far include only a minority of parents, generally middle class, despite the efforts of the National Federation of Parent-Teacher Associations. There are also a small number of separate Associations for Parents, as in Halifax, and some linkage with the International Federation for Parent Education. Regular information for parents is provided by the Confederation for the Advancement of State Education, and by the Advisory Centre for Education (ACE). Sheffield University's Division of Continuing Education has also organized experimental Mothers' Group programmes since 1971, similar to those in some of the settlements and adult education centres, in which informal discussion is the vehicle for the transmission of a good deal of information about child psychology. Moreover, the pre-school playgroups movement has been well supported by the adult education agencies.

Consumer Education

Educational help is also suggested for consumers. Although protected to some extent by legislation, especially that concerned with food hygiene, quality control and correct description, consumers, it is believed, need to develop a more critical approach and a sounder understanding of buying and selling so that they can make a more rational selection of goods instead of being mere victims of modern sales methods. 'Consumer education' though defined in several different ways, is seen as a requirement for all citizens, both for their own protection and as a way of creating a more satisfactory society.[14] It is asserted that some manufacturers talk of 'educating' the public but mean just persuasion to buy their products. Part of consumer education is carried out in evening classes in cookery, home furnishing and home management where there are discussions about wise buying and budgeting, but it may also be seen as a function of 'citizenship' courses of many kinds, especially those concerned with the law. Information about quality is available from many sources including local design centres and the Council of Industrial Design as well as programmes on the mass media, but perhaps the main need is to develop discrimination. Reports in journals and newspapers about consumer tests, and the provision of exhibitions concerned with this aspect of life, help to widen the consumer's knowledge but the critical weighing of the evidence is seen to be more vital. In this the Consumers' Association has taken a lead, particularly through its publications such as *Which*, and the consumer groups which have resulted from its work continue to have influence over a growing proportion of the population. Besides a Research Institute for Consumer Affairs, there is a National Federation of Consumer Groups, which was formed in 1963 to co-ordinate and assist the development of local groups. It remains true, however, that those most concerned are the middle classes and that the movement is dominated by the already better educated. Since 1972, a National Consumer Project (NCP) has been attempting to remedy this situation. Jointly organized by the Education Department of the Co-operative Union Ltd, the WEA, the National Federation of Consumer Groups and the TUC Education Department, the NCP sets out to establish informal groups among those not usually involved, which discuss the local situation and feed back findings and opinions to a national consumer conference each summer. These groups have volunteer leaders and are assisted by centrally-produced material in packs which provide discussion notes, work data-sheets for activities, and items for completion. The aim is to indicate 'areas of difficulty, interest of dispute rather than to provide specific answers or information'.[15]

Environmental Education

A further area of social well-being is seen in general concern to improve the environment. Besides the work of local authority environmental health officers, there are many voluntary agencies which set out to inform the public and to involve them in the preservation of amenities and the creation of new ones. Many counties have Conservation Societies or Trusts, whose volunteer members undertake activities as varied as the clearance of lakes, ponds and canals, the removal of overgrown shrubs, attention to fencing and replanting and the creation and maintenance of nature reserves and nature trails. For them 'learning by doing' is a constant reality. The National Trusts in Scotland and in England and Wales, both independent charities, have developed over a hundred centres in many parts of Britain since the foundation of the first one in the Manchester region in 1948. There are also ten National Parks and a growing number of smaller Country Parks, each with a small staff, together with a Heritage Education Group, established by the Department of the Environment and administered by the Civic Trust, itself set up to further the quality of the environment. In all these organizations, talks, discussions, organized visits, exhibitions and film shows are regular features and from them comes a flow of information in the form of magazines, books and leaflets. Finally, in terms of the broader world environment, there are organizations such as Christian Aid which seek 'to educate the public at large to the needs of the third world'.

Education for 'social caring'

The Disadvantaged

The way in which a country looks after its minorities is said to be a test of its civilization, and this would seem particularly true of the treatment of citizens disadvantaged in some way or another. In a fully just society, no doubt every effort would be made to provide everyone, however handicapped, with all opportunities for educational development as well as the right to play as full a part as possible in the life of the community. The temptation of the better educated and non-disadvantaged sectors however is to forget the handicapped,[16] to sweep them out of sight and in some instances physically to shut them away. Those who are handicapped do not easily find a place in a society that demands high productivity and they may be relegated to the most menial jobs. The general community tends to be indifferent and some educators have been accused of patronizing attitudes with their invention of polysyllables such as 'underprivileged' and 'disadvantaged', although there are now some signs that the size of the problem is becoming more recognized. At an earlier data attention to the 'disadvantaged' resulted partly in an 'irregular drip of conscience money' and more than an echo of the old conscience-salving philanthropy can still be seen in the attitude of many people in Britain today. Some of those who examine the problem draw distinctions between 'disadvantage' and 'deprivation', while others, as in the Russell Report, tentatively distinguish between physical, social and educational disadvantage.[17] Such distinctions in practice may often become blurred, however, and the following pages therefore merely select some examples of the educational provision which has been made for particular groups in order to show the general problems and the degree to which needs are not being met.

A simple listing of the main types of handicap indicates immediately the great variety. Besides the mentally ill and the mentally handicapped, there are all those with physical handicaps of many different kinds — crippled limbs, breathing problems, heart troubles, epilepsy etc., as well as the deaf and the hard of hearing, the blind and the partially sighted, and those with speech defects or dyslexia. There are also those who are socially handicapped, perhaps because of drug addiction or alcoholism, those who are socially isolated, perhaps because of ignorance of the imagery and vocabulary which make communication possible, and those who are economically disadvantaged. Even with this limited list it is clear that many different needs exist and that there are many variations, quite apart from multiple disadvantage, so that it is quite inadequate to put them all together in an undifferentiated mass. If society is really to 'care' for these minorities, the need is for sensitive individual treatment in which education, therapy and welfare are likely to be closely interwoven.

The Mentally III and Mentally Handicapped

For the mentally ill and the mentally handicapped, provision is usually made in institutions provided by the health or social service agencies such as hospitals, day centres and hostels, the major objectives being to help people learn skills which will enable them to participate more fully in ordinary life, especially skills of communication and social 'know-how', to develop initiative and stimulate curiosity and indeed to develop all their latent abilities.[18] Some help in this is given by the WEA and other voluntary educational organizations and in some LEA areas there exist part-time and occasionally full-time courses in a few colleges of further education. Progress in this kind of development, however, has been slow, despite the growing interest which followed the Warnock Report,[19] and it has been hampered by a general shortage of staff. A voluntary organization, the Psychiatric Rehabilitation Association, has used education as a therapy, introducing those discharged from hospitals 'to ways of seeing life as a larger, more interesting, less frightening place'[20] and has brought together the various agencies in education, health and welfare to further its objectives. The National Association for Mental Health (MIND) issues publications and stimulates interest by short courses and conferences, while particularly noteworthy are the informal educational services provided for mentally retarded people by the Gateway Clubs. These are linked together in a National Federation and by 1979 there were between 400 and 500 clubs providing for about 25,000 members. The clubs provide facilities for lesisure and recreation and in organized programmes of activities try to promote the emotional, mental and physical development of members. A special Gateway Award Scheme has been set up to help develop self-confidence, perserverance and initiative, and, though remaining a voluntary organization, the Federation has received some grants from the Department of Education and Science.[21]

The Physically Handicapped

Most physically handicapped adults have difficulty in attending the normal provision in centres and institutes. Too many educational buildings are virtually inaccessible to the person in a wheelchair, and the provision of ramps, wider doors and suitable toilets has developed very slowly, only a minority of buildings still being so equipped. Similarly, only a few LEAs make provision of mechanical aids to communication, such as typewriters and cassette recorders for those whose disability restricts their note-taking. A special exception is Hereward College in Coventry, the first LEA college for the further education of the physically handicapped, which opened in 1971. Another exception is the Open University which provides scripts for the deaf, tapes for the blind and personal 'helpers' at its Summer Schools. It admits over a thousand handicapped students to its courses each year. From time to time there has been pressure on libraries to adopt a code of practice concerning access, aids and advice, but financial restrictions have so far prevented its acceptance on a large scale. Those handicapped later in life seem to have greater difficulty in adjustment than those born with the disability, and are often over-sensitive to patronizing treatment and the sometimes changed attitudes of the family. Psychological help to build a new image and a new confidence is provided in some areas by advisory services and by informal social and educational activities in clubs and societies such as those of the British Legion, the Multiple Sclerosis Society, and the British Epilepsy Society. In some areas, classes have been organized jointly by the LEAs and voluntary agencies; these include coaching for paraplegic sports, art, keep fit, liberal studies and crafts such as dressmaking for spastics. The British Council for Rehabilitation of the Disabled (REHAB) has helped with correspondence courses as well as with vocational classes, and the British Red Cross Society has been particularly helpful to long-stay hospital patients. In general, however, as a 1977 report indicated, most handicapped adults in Britain do not find the opportunities for education which they clearly want, and often they are not reached by the publicity for the limited amount of provision which does exist.[22]

The Blind and the Deaf

The unevenness of the provision is also seen in education for the blind and the deaf. Peter Clyne noted that in 1970 only 11% of LEAs in England and Wales made any specific educational provision for blind adults, and that only 28% provided for the deaf adult, most of it being for the deafened adult, not for the born deaf. The most active of these Authorities provide classes for blind people in pottery and crafts, dancing, cookery, woodwork, swimming, audio-typing, and beauty care and make-up, often equipped with specially adapted tools and machines. Special provision for the deafened adult tends to be concerned with new skills of communication, such as lip-reading, or with changes in recreational interests, whereas the limited amount available for the born deaf tends to stress the further attainment of linguistic proficiency begun in childhood. Whether the two groups should be separated is a matter of controversy and what arrangements do exist are generally haphazard and variable in quality. The City Lit., however, with its special Department of Further Education for the Deaf, together with the Royal National Institute for the Deaf, has been very active in trying to meet the needs, both vocational and non-vocational, of adults of all ages and all degrees of deafness. Brixton College of Further Education also offers a full-time course for young people educated as children at special schools for the deaf.

A group which has attracted much concern since the early 1970s is that of people who are in need of basic education. At first the problem was conceived as being that of literacy but later this was extended to numeracy and 'coping' skills. As an ACACE Report put it, adult basic education means 'the fundamental skills and knowledge to plug into any system to continuing education'. These include 'literacy and other verbal skills, including English as a second language; basic skills in number; and a body of general knowledge relevant to the day-to-day lives of adults in society; together with those other elements of education, both formal and informal, without which an adult might find himself cut off from continuing education, vocational preparation, or cultural and recreational activity.'[23] After early work in the British Army during the Second World War, with the establishment of its Basic Education Centres, and in voluntary organizations such as Cambridge House in London which culminated in a conference mounted by the British Association of Settlements in 1973 on 'Status Illiterate, Prospects Zero', the campaign for adequate literacy teaching – the 'Right to Read' – acquired more urgency. The BBC announced a three-year project of television and radio programmes, beginning with a series called *'On the Move',* and in 1975 the Adult Literacy Resources Unit (ALRA) was set up with government funding of £1 million for the first year. After three years this was superseded by the Adult Literacy Unit (ALU) with only £300,000 a year, and in 1980 this was followed by the Adult Literacy and Basic Skills Unit (ALBSU) with £500,000 per year for two years. Similar agencies were established in Scotland although no schemes there were really operative until 1975, and the agencies have been felt to be 'poor relations in the field of community education'. Even so, the Scottish Adult Basic Education Unit in its first year (1980-81) received £60,000 from the Scottish Education Department. 'In a literate society, being illiterate is a massive handicap,' said Shirley Williams, and it was estimated that perhaps two million people in Britain had a reading age of less than nine years. So far it would seem that only a few hundred thousand have been reached despite an initial considerable development of provision by the LEAs which more recently have tended to integrate the work into the general adult education provision in centres and colleges and to reduce its amount. A range of voluntary organizations, including Cambridge House and Beauchamp Lodge in London and some sections of the WEA, continue to co-operate and to experiment, while the Training Services Division of the Manpower Services Commission has provided funds for LEA basic general education courses in preparation for TOPs courses. There are also many agencies outside the education service which contribute to basic education. These include the Area Health Authorities through hospitals, occupational therapy units and community nursing services; local authority departments of social service through, for example, day centres, old people's homes, training centres and workshops; and all the various local counselling and advisory services, unevenly spread though they are. In the early part of the literacy campaign there was a great deal of one-to-one teaching and an extensive use of volunteer tutors, at one time about 60,000 in number, and although much of the work has developed into group tuition with paid professional teachers there still remains a case for some individual tuition and volunteer but trained help. The overall plan to co-ordinate all types of provision, however, still seems a long way off in most parts of the country and even without financial stringency there are problems of obtaining collaboration in place of competition between the contributors. Some special material has been produced, for example, the Resource Pack *Moving Ahead* of the Scottish Adult Literacy Unit, with associated videotapes, or the Yorkshire Television/National Extension College manuals, workbooks and card games for *Make it Count*, but much more is needed. As will be discussed in a later chapter, the development of basic education also emphasizes the need for more training to secure adequate teaching and skilled counselling. There are also particular problems in rural areas where the population is isolated and scattered as in parts of Wales and Scotland. Insecurity about resources has been a constant source of worry even though the special schemes have managed to attract more government support than many other aspects of education for adults.[24]

Ethnic Minorities

Other groups for which the need for special educational opportunities has been recognized are immigrants and ethnic minorities. In some cases general basic education is required but more usually the need is for English language skills if serious social and economic disadvantages are to be overcome. Just how many potential students there are seems not to be known, although in 1978 the Commission for Racial Equality suggested that there were over 200,000 adults in Britain who could speak English only slightly or not at all. Some provision is made by agencies such as the Community Relations Councils as well as by LEAs in some areas. Classes may be held in the day-time or evening and there are considerable variations in the fees paid and in the duration of the tuition. The accommodation may also be very varied: the range extends from adult education centres and colleges of further education to health clinics, mosques, temples, and indeed any building thought to be appropriate. There is also some home tuition. Some ethnic minority organizations provide courses, an example being *Ente Nazionale Acli Istruzione Professionale (ENAIP)* which provides tuition for Italian workers. Since 1975, industrial language training units have also helped immigrants at their place of work both through training them in English language skills, and through training designed to help native British supervisors and trade unionists understand the problem; an approach which has TUC support.[25] These units have operated with a good deal of autonomy in various urban centres with high levels of immigrant populations, such as Bradford, Leicester, Walsall and London. There is a National Centre for Industrial Language Training (NCILT) which has provided teaching materials, information and advice, and some in-service training programmes for staff, as well as making some attempt to secure co-ordination. There are also a few projects in basic trade unionism for immigrant workers, as in Manchester, where, with MSC funding and LEA support, a five-year programme for the inner city is being carried out. A special problem is that of many Asian women who are prevented by social and religious conventions from enrolling in usual education classes, although in some places it has been possible to arrange informal education in welfare clinics and private homes. Some attempts by the broadcasting authorities to reach the ethnic minority and immigrant groups have met with a mixed reception, a noted example being *'Parosi'*, a series put out in 1977 by the BBC.

As always, voluntary organizations are active in this field although in varying degrees. Few concern themselves with the whole range of immigrants, who include European and Philippine au pair girls, Cypriot, Chinese, Italian and Spanish workers, refugees from Vietnam and elsewhere, as well as those from India, Pakistan, Bangladesh, East Africa, and the West Indies. If variations of cultural background, beliefs, customs and languages are of vital importance in the world, it seems essential that there should be very full educational opportunities both for the new communities and for the established host community for the benefit of both. It is perhaps particularly important to arrange education which will take the native community away from ignorance, misunderstanding and negative attitudes. Some beginnings have been made by the promotion of Asian and African music, drama and dancing for the general public and by attempts to provide information and understanding about these and about different religions and customs. At an earlier date there was a Centre for Information and Advice on Educational Disadvantage (CED) concerned particularly with ethnic minorities but this was closed in November 1979 by the withdrawal of government grants. Sporadically there have been attempts to provide special educational opportunities for the gypsies, and there is an Advisory Council for the Education of Romany and other Travellers (ACERT).

The Aged

Attention has also been paid to the needs of older groups in the population. In general terms the greatest need would seem to be adjustment to changed circumstances, possibly to loss of competence and independence, but older people need to develop new interests as well as maintain old ones if a satisfactory life is to be achieved. In an attempt to help, pre-retirement courses are now organized in many places, both in adult education centres and in industrial works, though there are more for men than for women. These courses usually provide both relevant information and opportunities to explore possible ways of using the extra 'leisure' time expected to be available. There is also a Pre-Retirement Association which publishes a monthly magazine called *Choice* as well as paperback books, and organizes several types of course, directed particularly at groups in industry. It is estimated that about 1,500 workers in Britain reach retirement age each day and, for those who are retired, most local authorities, through either their education or social service departments, and many voluntary organizations, provide courses and other activities. Old People's Welfare Centres teach subjects such as dressmaking and woodwork, and the various Senior Citizens Clubs often have programmes of talks, discussions, visits, choral singing, etc., as well as purely recreational activities. Most of this type of programme is, however, for the relatively able bodied; for those who are incapacitated, there is only a small amount of provision in residential homes for the elderly. This again is for the few: more bedridden old people are cared for in their own or in their children's homes than in old people's establishments. Elderly people living alone may present a considerable problem and it is estimated that about twenty per cent of old people in Britain do not have living descendants. Even so, if they choose to use it, assistance for all old people is available from organizations such as Age Concern (National Old People's Welfare Council), Help the Aged, the Centre for Policy on Ageing (formerly the National Corporation of the Care of Old People) and the Women's Royal Voluntary Services. It is argued that more programmes of self-help would be useful and that these could be organized at little cost.

Post-Prison Education

Reference has been made earlier to work-related education for prisoners and to the importance of basic education for them, as well as to the variable amount of hobby education and liberal studies. It would seem, however, that although almost half the adult prisoners participate in education while in prison, very few do so after release. There seems to be scope, in fact, for a combined effort by the probation service and the LEAs as well as more assistance to the National Association for Care and Resettlement of Offenders (NACRO) which is involved in this task as a voluntary organization. NACRO has a special Education Advisory Service which tries to help offenders by assessing their needs and abilities, providing information and advice about their choice of educational and other aids, and giving general support, in, for example, study methods or adjustment to college life.

Education for Social Caring — some general problems

Education for social caring in Britain might perhaps be described as rich in variety but lacking any cohesion. Behind it is a persistent strong tradition of voluntary effort although some local authorities have also become deeply involved. One of the major problems is how to get co-operation and effectiveness in the relationship between the contributors. In some places there would seem to be very little communication, while in others contact seems to lead to real disputes because of different analyses of needs and of the action required. Local associations and local councils find it difficult to agree and it seems almost impossible to determine their respective functions. Voluntary organizations are a great mixture. They include old established agencies such as the Residential Settlements and much newer pressure groups and local action groups. Some churches look upon education for the disadvantaged as part of their pastoral care and the network of adult educational organizations such as the WEA and the ECA hold conferences on urban problems and urban renewal. Employers and trade unions play a part, as do the broadcasters in both the BBC and the IBA. But each tends to work too much in isolation and liaison is weak. A second problem is how to marry adequate help from statutory authorities which plan 'what the people need' with the initiatives implied in 'citizen participation'. As one person put it, can 'big brother' work with the 'radical activist'? At present there is much untidiness, in some places overlapping provision and in others gross inadequacy. A third problem, seen in the provision of urban aid, the work of the Manpower Services Commission and various programmes of citizenship education, is how to preserve decentralized control in local areas against, on the one hand, overall rigid planning by central government and, on the other, the powerful impact of the mass media.

Fourth, but of great importance, is the question whether disadvantaged groups in need of social care should be isolated in a narrow-based type of provision. Literacy was selected for special treatment on its own and only after some years have there been strong moves to integrate it with general programmes of education for all adults. Segregation is still seen in the special programmes for the blind, the deaf, the physically handicapped, the unemployed, the old and the women. There is obviously a need for separate treatment in some instances but not necessarily for the whole provision. Some groups, indeed, greatly resent segregation, preferring to mix with the rest of the population and to be treated as 'normal'. Many of the old, for example, prefer the company of younger people, and the physically handicapped may gain a necessary stimulus from contact with, as well as providing a helpful challenge to, able-bodied colleagues. On the other hand, some disadvantaged may well need supportive care in a supportive environment and may feel suspicious, isolationist or defeatist in a strange institution not designed for their needs, and with people not particularly sympathetic or tolerant towards them. They may also desire special administrative arrangements if they are to use existing types of provision even if these are no more than minor matters concerned with the timing of classes, and regulations about minimum numbers. Examples of both the integrative and separatist approaches can be seen in various parts of the country and neighbouring Authorities may pursue quite different policies, despite the strong support given to integration by the Russell Report. Perhaps the major need is for the development of a continuum along which groups can pass from segregation to integration as they gain more skills and self-confidence. For some it will be difficult to move away from segregation but for others it may be just a temporary staging post.

Whatever the form of provision, a growing case has been made for a measure of positive discrimination in the provision of resources. At present many of the disadvantaged are neglected and the resources are inadequate, whether they are material resources such as equipment, adaptation of buildings, transport and accessible advertising, or human resources in terms of teachers, counsellors, advisers, research workers and helpers of all kinds. Only by special efforts, it is argued, can the disadvantaged groups have free and full opportunities for education in a system which is somewhat inflexible and primarily organized for the rest of the population. In turn it is suggested that people outside the special groups need a particular education which alerts them to the social problems that exist, helps them to modify unsympathetic attitudes, and stimulates them to be active in trying to secure more adequate solutions to the problems. Education for social caring in Britain has so far exhibited a process of muddling through, in which some outstanding achievements are surrounded by ignorance and wide areas of non-provision. Too often the problems are regarded as peripheral.

References

1. See, for example, HOGGART, R, *On the Nature and Quality of Mass Communications,* 1959, William F. Harvey Memorial Lecture.

2. PEERS, R. *Adult Education: a Comparative Study,* 1953, Routledge and Kegan Paul. Revised 3rd edition 1972, p. 129.

3. JULIUS NYERERE in his opening address to the International Adult Education Conference, sponsored by the International Council for Adult Education, Dar es Salaam, June 1976.

4. Russell Report, p. 171. Para 72 in the Supplement on Wales.

5. ASHBY, E, *The Pathology of Adult Education,* 1955, William F. Harvey Memorial Lecture. Boyd, Belfast. (Quoted in para. 95 of the Alexander Report).

6. PIMLOTT, J.A.R. *Toynbee Hall: Fifty Years of Social Progress, 1884–1934,* 1935, Dent & Sons, p. 265.

7. BIDDLE, W.W. and BIDDLE, L.J. *The Community Development Process,* 1966, Holt, Rinehart and Winston.

8. For the development of this theme see BATTEN, T.R. *Communities and their Development,* 1957, OUP, and LOVETT, T. *Adult Education, Community Development and the Working Class.* 1975, Ward Lock Educational.

9. *People and Planning* – Report of the Committee on Public Participation in Planning, 1969, HMSO.

10. See FORDHAM, P., POULTON, G. and RANDLE, L. *Learning Networks in Adult Education,* 1979, Routledge and Kegan Paul.

11. An interesting article on Manchester University's entry into this field is by BRYAN LUCKHAM: 'An enlargement of vision: the university response' in *New Universities Quarterly,* 34/1, Winter, 1979/80 pp. 108-119, from which this example is taken.

12. ICAE International Conference, 1976. Agreed manifesto.

13. National Marriage Guidance Council *Sex education in perspective Part II,* 1972, NMGC.

14. For further information see *Consumer Education* produced in 1964 by the Research Institute for Consumer Affairs in association with the NIAE.

15. See leaflets available from the Co-operative Union Education Department, Stanford Hall, Loughborough.

16. The Final Report of the Third UNESCO International Conference on Adult Education held in 1972 referred to them as the 'forgotten people'.

17. Russell Report, paras 277-279 discuss this point.

18. See MITTLER, P.J. and GITTINS, S.G. (Eds) *The Educational Needs of Mentally Handicapped Adults.*

19. Report of the Committee of Enquiry chaired by Mary Warnock into *the Education of Handicapped Children and Young People,* 1978, HMSO.

20. Director of the Psychiatric Rehabilitation Association, quoted in CLYNE, P. *The Disadvantaged Adult,* p. 59.

21. See article by FRANCIS STUART: 'Informal educational services for the mentally handicapped: the role of Gateway Clubs', *Adult Education,*

51/5, Jan. 1979, pp. 297-300. PHAB is a word made up from the initial letters of Physically Handicapped and Able Bodied. It seeks to encourage integration and therefore to break down barriers of prejudice and insecurity as well as to develop interests and social contacts. PHAB began in association with the National Association of Youth Clubs but now has older adult groups as well as those for the 14-25 age group.

22. MOHR, DIANA H. *Adult Education and the Physically Handicapped Person*, 1977, The Disabled Living Foundation.

23. ACACE *A Strategy for the Basic Education of Adults*, 1979. (Report commissioned by the Secretary of State for Education and Science.)

24. For further information about the literacy campaigns see the reports of ALRA, ALU and ALBSU for England and Wales, and SCALRA, SCALU and SABEU for Scotland.

25. See TUC Statement on *Priorities in Continuing Education*, 1978, TUC. By 1980 there were 26 Units.

CHAPTER 11

Co-operation and co-ordination between providing agencies

There is freedom and vitality in the uncontrolled growth or decline of a multitude of separate, unrelated activities and organizations, and often to them co-operation is surrounded by suspicion and 'co-ordination' is anathema. In particular, co-operation with government, central or local, seems to be viewed as full of danger by some supporters of voluntary organizations who fear a loss of freedom. Indeed, in Britain there are long-standing traditions of suspicion of government as well as of decentralized independence. Other people, while not so opposed, feel that the education of adults is too heterogeneous for satisfactory co-operation, and that it is much too difficult to find a basis for useful contact. On the other hand, for a long time there have been advocates of co-operation urging that it would not deaden new activities, and that it would greatly strengthen the public case for the education of adults. 'I would myself rather use the word partnership than the word co-ordination,' said Principal Nicholson in 1943[1] at the first wartime conference of the British Institute of Adult Education, and many since then have stressed the need to develop consultative machinery to bring a little order to the large patchwork of the multifarious activities which constitute the education of adults in Britain. Only then, they urge, will it be possible to develop an adequate provision, a broad spectrum of services, with satisfactory resources and a clear avoidance of unnecessary duplication. Committees 'to study the possibilities of co-operation' have been fairly common in some parts of the country since the support given by the 1919 Report to Adult Education Joint Committees for non-university education as well as for extra-mural education,[2] and the advocacy was continued in the Russell and Alexander Reports. The problem, however, is that though 'partnership' has gained in popularity, the provision of actual machinery for consultation and co-operation is still undeveloped and unevenly spread, especially at local level. Support for co-operation is strong in some areas but extremely weak in others, if it can be seen to exist at all.

A greater degree of success can be claimed at national level. Organizations with similar interests, or a particular subject area in common, have for a long time seen some virtue in coming together nationally, and national organizations already noted include university bodies such as the UCAE and SCUTREA, voluntary organizations with central federations such as the WEA, the NFWI, the NUTG, the ECA and the NFCA, and agencies in the mainly work-related field such as the MSC, BEC, TEC and their Scottish equivalents.

To these may be added the trade union national bodies, including the Civil Service Council for Further Education, as well as the TUC, and the central committees concerned with civilian assistance to the education of the army, navy and air force. The list is a long one and other examples are all the various church national organizations concerned with the education of adults and the various Standing Conferences of Voluntary Youth Organizations. For the LEAs there is the Council of LEAs (CLEA) which links the Association of County Councils (ACC) and the Association of Metropolitan Authorities (AMA) in attempts to get some common policy and solutions to problems. In terms of single subject interests, attempts to get some overall national co-operation over basic education have been noted as well as the organizations concerned with drama, music, a language or a craft, while almost all sports organizations have national bodies, themselves linked in the Sports Council, the Scottish Sports Council or the Sports Council of Northern Ireland. These exist to foster the development of sport and to stimulate a greater and better-used provision of facilities. Among the newer national organizations is the Christian Association for Adult and Continuing Education, founded in 1979 which brings together 'those working in and outside the churches of all denominations, concerned with sharing concerns and expertise in local net-works and at national level'. It holds conferences and issues a quarterly bulletin entitled *Collage*.

Institutes at National Level

On the whole, all the organizations just mentioned believe that partnership gives strength, despite the occasional break away of one of their component units. Each national body has a basis of common ground in terms of either type of organization or special interests, and any friction therefore is likely to be 'within the family'. The main part of this chapter, however, is concerned with attempts to secure consultation and co-operation between organizations which are dissimilar except that in one way or another they are concerned with the education of adults. In Britain, the oldest of these is the National Institute of Adult Education (England and Wales) (NIAE) which was formed in 1949 by the merger of the National Foundation for Adult Education, founded in 1946, with the much older British Institute of Adult Education (BIAE), founded in 1921 by Albert Mansbridge and Lord Haldane as a branch of the World Associ-ation of Adult Education which they had created in 1919.[3] Seen by the Russell Committee as 'a major non-governmental force in the development of the adult education service', the NIAE has the object of promoting 'the study and the general advancement of adult education'.[4] It seeks to achieve this in four main ways. First, it facilitates the exchange of experiences by conferences and meetings, especially by an annual study conference, which focus public attention on the achievements and problems of the work. It also helps indi-viduals and organizations throughout the year to make contact with other facilities existing in Britain. Second, it serves as a clearing house for the col-lection and dissemination of information about the education of adults and as a centre for advice. Over the years the Institute and its predecessors have built up a sizeable collection of books and other publications and although this is not yet the national resource centre of documentary material which some would like to see it become, it has been considerably strengthened in recent years by the appointment of a qualified librarian. The Institute also publishes books, pamphlets, journals and articles concerning adult education. These include important regular publications such as *Adult Education,* the longest established journal in the field which began life in 1926, the twice yearly *Studies in Adult Education, Teaching Adults* and the *Calendar of Residential Short Courses,* and the annual *Yearbook.* Among the books published have been the *Select Bibliographies of Adult Education in Great Britain* and *Research in Adult Education in the British Isles,* while from time to time monographs and special pamphlets are issued. A third function of the NIAE is to 'encourage, initiate and conduct enquiry, experiment, research and training in adult education', and this too leads to publications, notable examples being *Provision of Adult Education* in 1970 and the report on *Accommodation and Staffing* in 1963. Joint enquiries have led to reports as diverse as the important *New Ventures in Broadcasting* in 1927, *Liberal Education in a Technical Age* in 1955 and *Paid Educational Leave* in 1975. Despite its small staff and inadequate resources, the Institute has made a substantial contribution to thought and action about the education of adults, as is evidenced for example by its pre-war work in the 'Art for the People' scheme which led to the Arts Council, and by its more recent responsibilities in the various literacy agancies which have been put under its wing. This contribution is also reflected in its fourth major function, that of developing 'co-operative relations with organisations, institutions and individuals promoting adult education in other countries and with appropriate international organisations'. It has, in fact, become the major English and Welsh institution in this work especially through its contacts with UNESCO, the International Council of Adult Education, the British Council and the European Bureau of Adult Education. From time to time questions have been asked about a possible separate Welsh Institute of Adult Education but so far there seems to be little support for this in Wales.

It has been held that 'a large part of the Institute's usefulness derives from its status as an independent consultative and advisory body, whose objects are not competitive with the operating functions of any of its constituents'.[5] Its membership is wide, including local education authorities, universities, adult colleges, all the major voluntary organizations concerned with the practice of education for adults, representatives of the educational branches of the Services, of the Prison Department of the Home Office and of the Council for Educational Technology, and representatives of the Committee of Vice-Chancellors and Principals and of the Committee of Directors of Polytechnics together with an increasing number of individual members with a strong interest in the education of adults. It includes regional bodies and local institutions providing education for adults as well as the national professional, consultative or advisory bodies. The government of this 'umbrella' body for all types of education for adults is a council elected triennially by the members and this in turn elects a smaller executive committee. The executive appoints sub-committees, working parties and special project committees as required, a long-standing example being the important publication sub-committee. The Institute has unpaid honorary officers — a president who is chairman of the council, up to three vice-presidents, the chairman and vice-chairman of the executive committee and the treasurer — with only a relatively small paid staff of director, deputy director, senior research officer, publications officer and librarian together with a few capable administrative and clerical assistants. In view of the wide range of activities and functions nowadays carried by the Institute, and of its general importance in the field, it is clear that it could achieve even more with more adequate resources. The main sources of finance are annual contributions from members, particularly those from the LEAs on agreed scales, earnings from publications and other activities, and a grant in aid from the Department of Education and Science. Finance from a variety of sources may well ensure the 'qualities of independence, expansion of role and flexibility' so praised by the Russell Report[6] but does not guarantee a secure and adequate financial basis for desirable development.

Left out in the merger of 1949, the Scottish branch of the British Institute of Adult Education quickly became the independent Scottish Institute of Adult Education (SIAE). Its declared aim is 'to advance education amongst adult members of the community and to co-ordinate the efforts of organisations, institutions and individuals in obtaining that aim'.[7] Like the NIAE, with which it maintains close association, it serves as an information and documentation centre, keeping adult educators in Scotland in touch with new ideas and new developments through reports, newsletters, a yearbook and a journal, the *Scottish Journal of Adult Education*. It also organizes conferences, promotes new projects and seeks to formulate policy, often with the aid of working parties. An example was the important publication in 1968 of a report on the finance, administration and physical provision of adult education in Scotland.[8] A central problem for the SIAE, however, has always been its very limited resources. Coming mainly from the education authorities in membership and from a grant by the Scottish Education Department, these restrict the function of the Institute as the main forum in Scotland for all educators of adults. With a small headquarters office, it usually has finance only for one full-time executive director and for minimum clerical support. Even so, it has in corporate membership most of the regional and other education authorities, Scottish universities and Districts of the WEA, together with the Scottish TUC, the broadcasting authorities, a wide range of voluntary organizations in associate membership, and individuals 'concerned with and interested in the education of adults in Scotland'. In government, it has a council and executive committee, similar in essentials to those of the NIAE, and for much of its work it depends on the voluntary efforts of the honorary officers and committee members. It maintains links with many organizations both in Britian and overseas, notably with the European Bureau of Adult Education and the International Council of Adult Education, and, like the NIAE in southern Britain, it has looked after the successive separate Scottish literacy agencies. Some changes of constitution and perhaps of function have been envisaged for the 1980s but the Institute is clearly viewed as an essential association which because of its independence can freely put forward the views of all agencies.

Northern Ireland has no exact equivalent, but the Irish National Association of Adult Education, AONTAS, was established in 1969 as 'an advisory and consultative body, reflecting nationally the interests, hopes and anxieties of all groups, agencies and individuals' in the whole of Ireland and it has a membership in the North. Like the other national bodies, it is 'a clearing house for ideas and information', a 'reference centre', a creator of 'positive public awareness of the needs and opportunities of lifelong learning' and 'a medium of communication and co-operation between all those involved in adult education in Ireland'.[9] It holds major conferences, issues policy statements from time to time on subjects such as paid educational leave, and the function of radio and television in adult education, and gives help to individuals. Perhaps a special feature is its role as a co-operator 'with other agencies, seeking the development, adequate appreciation and understanding of Irish culture'. Membership is open to individuals, organizations and institutions interested or involved in adult education, and these elect a council which in turn elects an executive committee in the usual pattern of government. AONTAS has a full-time director and clerical staff based in Dublin, but also has honorary officers and committee members. It, too is linked to the European Bureau and the International Council of Adult Education and it publishes *Newsletters* and a *Review of Adult Education*.

While recognizing the general value of these organizations, some question whether they achieve enough co-operation and co-ordination. From time to time there are also declarations that the annual conferences are unwieldy and unproductive, gaining too little national publicity. It seems clear, however, that they are an important means whereby different agencies and individuals come together, and this is even more apparent in the Executive Committees where much constructive work is done. The directors in their many visits to other organizations and meetings are able also to facilitate contact and understanding, and to develop links within the overall pattern of provision, as well as to disseminate ideas of good practice. There are, of course, weaknesses in that some bodies whose work is clearly educational, are underrepresented if seen at all. Largely because of the problems of the old 'limited' definition, work-related education for adults is often underrepresented, although the situation is changing and bodies such as the MSC are now more in evidence. Similarly, there seems little collaboration with some professional bodies, such as the Joint Board for Clinical Nursing, or with sports agencies such as the Sports Councils. Links with Art Centres and the public library and museum service are also tenuous, although the major national organizations are now coming into membership. The Institutes in recent decades have done much to extend the interpretation of 'adult education' in their titles but there are still plenty of gaps to be filled. As they stand, however, they provide a positive answer to a situation in which almost everyone seems in favour of co-operation but few have a clear view of ways of achieving it. In this they are well ahead of the various government departments concerned with the education of adults; at present there seems to be little if any co-ordination between these and much dispute about the sort of structures which might bring it about.

National Advisory Councils

In the 1970s under the pressure particularly of the Russell and Alexander Reports, national advisory councils were established in the United Kingdom under government auspices and finance, in addition to the independent Institutes. The first of these was the Northern Ireland Council for Continuing Education (NICCE) which came into being in October 1974 with the Permanent Secretary of the Northern Ireland Department of Education as its Chairman. 'Continuing education' was chosen with some care as a title 'considered to embrace all forms of further education' and 'in the very broadest sense' to be 'any educational activity which enriches the life of the individual'.[10] The Council found that there were 'virtually no mechanisms for formal co-operation between the various providers of courses and those responsible for educational resources' and therefore set out to act as a forum for the exchange of information and ideas. In this way it brings together the Area Education and Library Boards, the universities, including the Open University, the Polytechnics, the WEA and many other bodies such as the Ulster Folk and Transport Museum, the Arts Council of Northern Ireland, the Armagh Planetarium, the agricultural colleges of the Department of Agriculture, the Public Record Office, the BBC and Ulster Television, the Prison Education Service and the public libraries. The Council has the task of advising the Department of Education on 'the framework and development of continuing education in Northern Ireland' and on the co-ordination of programmes and facilities offered by the various providing agencies, and to this end it has established a series of specialist panels. Some of these such as the publicity panel and the programme co-ordinating panel have become virtually permanent committees, while others have been more transient. The resources panel produced a report on what was available and this was published[11] as being of general interest and relevance. Besides members of the Council, the panels may co-opt people from outside with particular knowledge or expertise.

The second advisory council came into being in October 1977, after the pressure of the Venables Report had been added to that of the Russell Report. This was the Advisory Council for Adult and Continuing Education (ACACE), charged by the Secretary of State with the task of advising 'generally on matters relevant to the provision of education for adults in England and Wales' [14] and given the particular remit:

(a) to promote co-operation between the various bodies in adult education and review current practice, organisation and priorities, with a view to the most effective deployment of the available resources; and

(b) to promote the development of future policies and priorities, with full regard to the concept of education as a process continuing throughout life.

The Council began with twenty-two members appointed by the Secretary of State 'in a personal rather than a representative capacity' but between them having experience in a wide range of provision including that of being a student. There are also assessors appointed from the MSC and the NIAE as well as from the DES and the Welsh Office Education Department. In contrast to Northern Ireland, it has an independent chairman, the first being Dr Richard Hoggart, and an independent secretariat. Appointed in the first instance for three years, ACACE had its life extended in 1980 for a further three years with some changes of membership, but it remains to be seen if it will become a permanent feature. In the meantime it works vigorously through two major committees and a considerable number of other committees each with a particular task. Some individual Council members also undertake 'watching briefs' to look at special features. Reports resulting from this activity are published as available, notable issues being those on adult basic education, advisory and counselling services for adults, and adult students and higher education. Discussion papers are issued from time to time such as *Present Imperfect* on current trends in adult education and the questions to be faced, and there are also 'occasional papers', usually personal contributions by members of Council. In general the Council wishes to conduct its business as openly as possible and therefore issues an *Information Release* after each Council meeting. It sees itself as a clearing house for ideas and information — as both a collector and vigorous disseminator not unlike the NIAE — and also as an authoritative voice for the education of adults which is able to make itself heard at the highest levels of policy making. With a broad remit, it has investigated a range of matters, including the training of adult educators, education for retirement, adult education and ethnic minorities, accommodation for adult education, and ways of improving the national statistics on adult education. Sharing office accommodation with the NIAE in Leicester seems to have helped both by maintaining close relationships and by using the information resources available there.

The Scottish Council for Community Education (SCCE) was established by the Secretary of State for Scotland in January, 1979 with the following terms of reference:

> To advise the Secretary of State on matters relating to community education; to promote the development of community education; and to foster co-operation among the statutory and voluntary organisations concerned.

The Council has twenty-three members and an independent chairman, at first the vice-chancellor of the university of Aberdeen, but in contrast to ACACE its secretariat is from within the Scottish Education Department, and its 'chief adviser' is the Chief Inspector (Informal Further Education) in Scotland. 'Community education' came directly from the recommendations of the Alexander Committee.[12] One of the early tasks it was given was to examine the relationships between the various national bodies, in particular the Scottish Community Education Centre, the SIAE and the Scottish Standing Conference of Voluntary Youth Organizations, but it seems to have found considerable problems in trying to get cohesion in this somewhat disparate area. The matter is further complicated by the existence of the Council for Tertiary Education in Scotland which has so far concentrated on the education of the 16-19 age group but is beginning to look at the structure and management of tertiary education widely interpreted. As in all the advisory councils, much activity takes place in working groups which then report to the main Council. In Scotland early attention has been paid to the training of all workers in community education, whether full-time, part-time or voluntary, and to the gathering of statistics, a special study costing up to £5,000 being commissioned for this purpose. The SCCE publishes *Occasional Papers, Discussion Papers* and *Information Releases,* and members of the Council are active in visiting various parts of Scotland to meet those working in the field. A danger seen by several Scottish adult educators is that the better-developed youth and community service might well dominate or even swallow up the rather weak adult education service. The former had in fact made great progress under the Standing Consultative Council on Youth and Community Service, members of which are most active in the new Council.

Some would like these Councils to have more power — to be more the 'development' councils of the Russell Report than the advisory bodies they are in fact set up to be — and complain that they are not as vigorous as they ought to be in challenging government policy when it threatens the education of adults. Others believe that the steady pressure of memoranda, reports and publications is more valuable in the long run, and feel that the Councils are steps in the right direction, useful focal points for debates and perhaps campaigns on continuing education. Whether the Councils will be allowed to continue for more than a few years remains uncertain, but they stand out as examples of what is possible even in times of financial stringency. With their unpaid membership and small full-time staffs they are relatively cheap to run and they could have a vital influence on future policy.

Co-operation at Regional Level

Although co-operation between the departments of central government at national level is hardly existent, there are often very good relationships at regional level. Much, of course, depends on the personalities of those in regional offices, but informal co-operation stemming from good personal relationships is an important factor in the whole of the provision of education for adults. In this way, at regional level, officers of the MSC and the DES come together, university staffs join with trade union educators and industrial trainers, and voluntary workers link their activities with those of full-time workers in social and community work as well as in more formal education. As noted earlier, the structure of most national organizations has a regional tier, such as a District of the WEA, and it is relatively easy for the full-time educators of adults at this level to establish contact with those in other organizations. *Ad hoc* bodies also come into being to serve particular purposes such as planning a particular course or conference and sometimes these acquire more durability. An informal meeting of three full-time educators of adults in Lancashire in 1947 has now developed into the 'North-West Adult Education Conference' with an annual meeting attended by about 200 people, although it still has little formal structure and receives no grant aid. It is organized by a group of volunteers who are interested in encouraging everyone in the north-west of England associated with the education of adults to come together once a year to share experiences and discuss developments. A similar organization was formed in the north-east of England in 1980. Examples of other informal bodies designed to promote co-operation at a regional level are the Public Libraries Adult Education Committee of the North-West (PLAEC) which brings together the libraries, the LEAs and the Responsible Bodies, and the Adult Educators' Seminars in Manchester and Nottingham. A similar body in Liverpool led to the Merseyside and District Institute of Adult Education which was formed in 1973, with a formal constitution and serviced by Liverpool University Institute of Extension Studies. Besides its regular meetings, it established working parties from time to time to examine aspects of the work such as adult literacy, the mentally disordered adult, and prison education, and it has issued various publications. Like the others it, too, has no grant aid and depends upon voluntary subscriptions and voluntary officers.

An older body of a similar kind is the East Midlands Regional Institute of Adult Education with a base in Nottingham and drawing much on the work of the Adult Educators' Seminar there. Its general aim is defined as that of providing 'a forum for the exchange of experience and ideas, to stimulate and widen interest in adult education, to help and encourage newcomers to the field, and in all these ways to contribute to the development of adult education within the Region'. Independent, it is supported and controlled by its members, who may be full or part-time workers and students, or corporate members such as local authorities, universities, libraries and voluntary organizations. Viewed essentially as a way of bringing people into contact with each other across the whole range of adult educational provision, the Institute also took the lead in campaigning against the cuts proposed for the late 1970s and early 1980s.

Regional Advisory Councils

Some would like such organizations to be concerned only with areas of provision which are not work-related, whereas others would like regional bodies to collaborate in all aspects of education for adults. For this purpose they tend to look towards the Regional Advisory Councils (RACs) which were founded mostly after 1946 in order to develop the regional planning which at the time was felt to be essential if undue duplication of vocational courses was to be prevented in the post-war expansion. A few areas had attempted to meet the problem of wasteful overlaps in the provision by the establishment of regional councils before the Second World War — the Yorkshire Council for Further Education, for example, was founded in 1929 and the West Midlands Council in 1935 — and by 1947 nine Regional Advisory Councils for Further Education had been established in England, while in Wales, the Welsh Joint Education Committee (WJEC) was created with similar functions. In Scotland five Regional Advisory Councils for Technical Education were set up by 1949, each reflecting the very different characteristics of their areas. There is, for example, a great contrast between the industrial regions of Glasgow and the south-west, where there had been a Joint Committee as early as 1901, and the Highlands and Islands region which has no tradition of technical education.

The organization pattern of the Councils is also varied but in most of the English and Welsh ones, at least one-third of the members are representatives of the constituent local education authorities (usually the chief education officers), about a dozen or so are principals and sometimes other staff of major establishments, including the polytechnics, a smaller number represent the universities in the region and there are representatives from industry and commerce (both employers and employees), with perhaps some from sectors of non-vocational education for adults. An HMI, usually the Regional Staff Inspector, acts as assessor and makes known the views of the Department of Education and Science. In Scotland, the Councils have a somewhat similar membership, but, reflecting the different organization of higher technological education, they must include representatives of the direct grant central institutions, usually a governor and the principal. These representative Councils are, of course, too large for detailed work — the average size is ninety people — and responsibilities are normally devolved to an executive committee and various standing committees, advisory committess, and working groups. To these, additional specialists and experts are co-opted, either permanently or on an *ad hoc* basis, their advice therefore being available before policies are determined. The Councils in fact have become the principal regional machinery for work-related education for adults and although officially they are advisory, in practice their advice is accepted.

Financed by the LEAs in their region, their central function is to provide a meeting point in which representatives of industry, commerce and the education authorities can examine, plan and co-ordinate the provision of 'further education' within the region, assessing needs and to some extent controlling resources. In addition, they may promote and advise on developments, issue memoranda, reports and publicity matter, promote training opportunities, conferences and general co-operation, and in some cases act as validating and examining bodies. Each Council has evolved in its own way and in both constitutions and activities there are many variations, Most still concentrate their attention on technical education but since the late 1960s, some of the English Advisory Councils have become more active in the non work-related sector. Some have pioneered new developments, as in the East Midlands scheme for the training of part-time teachers of adults, or in the early courses for executives in industry. Much depends upon staffing: most Councils have a permanent secretary and staff but the latter is usually small in number.

In recent years, it has been said that the RACs have become outdated, that their multitude of committees wastes the time of a large number of people, that they have become bureaucratic and unadventurous instead of being dynamic and forward-looking, and that they are ineffective because theoretically they are largely powerless. These views are not always consistent, but the many changes in provision which have taken place since the RACs were created has inevitably led to questions about their structure and functions and to suggestions that the new situation requires new machinery. In 1979 the Oakes Report[13] suggested the establishment of new regional bodies to be called Regional Advisory and Consultative Councils for Further Education (RACCsFE) which would have broader functions, including the oversight of teacher education which up to 1975 had been mainly carried out by the twenty-three Area Training Organisations (ATOs) in England and Wales. These had been responsible for the co-ordination of teacher training facilities in their area, and for validation, but their existence was terminated by decision of central government. For the new Regional Councils it was thought that only minor modifications in the areas of the old RACs would be required in England and Wales, but to date the various other problems remain unresolved, especially those concerning the extension of function to include all 'non-advanced further education', the exact relationship with the polytechnics and the perennial difficulty of determining the amount of financial commitment the LEAs are willing to undertake. Though the Council of LEAs has paid attention to these matters, no decisions have yet been taken by central government over the new machinery required. In some areas, however, financial restraints have considerably reduced RAC work and the machinery for co-operation seems likely to be weakened rather than strengthened. In Scotland and Northern Ireland the issues are perhaps a little less under discussion, while in Wales the WJEC has devised its own new committees to develop its concern with non-vocational education for adults.

Rural Community Councils

In the countryside a good deal of pioneer work has been carried out by the Rural Community Councils which at county level try to bring together every-one interested in improving the conditions of rural life. The first was formed in Oxfordshire in 1921 as the result of the work of a joint committee of the Women's Institutes, the YWCA, The Village Clubs Association, the WEA, the Oxford Tutorial Classes Committee, the County Director of Education, the County Director of Agriculture and a member of the County Council Com-mittee on Rural Industries. Conferences of the National Council of Social Service, (now the National Council for Voluntary Organizations) then advo-cated the establishment of a Rural Community Council in each county, and they have come into existence in most parts of England and Wales. Their activities are many and varied and depend very much on the interests of the Council members, the officials and the organizations in membership. Not infrequently after the pioneer work has been successful, it is then handed on to other organizations, rural planning for example going to the Council for the Preservation of Rural England and much music and drama activity being handed over to the LEA. In particular, they promote the welfare of people living in rural areas by the provision of amenities for social life, fostering rural crafts and customs, stimulating interest in the Parish Councils, arranging weekend schools and conferences, encouraging self-help programmes and above all by campaigns for the erection of village halls. Autonomous, these organs of non-formal education tend to be underfinanced and their few salaried officials are overworked and underpaid.

Co-operation at the Local, Sub-regional Level

The Russell Report firmly recommended 'the establishment in every local education authority area of a Local Development Council for Adult Edu-cation' [14] and the Alexander Report recommended 'regional advisory councils' with much the same objectives.[15] According to Russell these councils were to be *ad hoc* bodies:

> widely representative of those who have an interest in adult education as providers or users or students. Representatives might be drawn from the major providing bodies, the educational and quasi-educational institutions, asssociations of tutors and teachers, industry, voluntary, social and com-munity organisations, associations for the disadvantaged, local radio, local societies, students' councils of adult education institutions and similar bodies.

The Alexander Report envisaged 'a widely representative body' in the larger regions but in the islands probably 'a more simple form of consultative machinery'. Membership was to be of the major providers, including sports centres, art centres, libraries and museums, of 'organisations with a "consumer interest", including trade unions and community associations', and of 'organ-isations in a position to identify community needs' such as social work departments, councils of social service and the youth and community services. In no part of Britain, however, were the Councils to have financial or other powers. Their functions would be to 'facilitate discussion and consultation' so as to influence the planning of adult education in the area, to identify needs and inadequacies of provision, to advise on methods of informing the adult public and to sponsor or suggest experiments. Both Committees left the details of the machinery to local decision, merely emphasizing that 'it is vital that there should be co-operation, goodwill and mutual understanding'. The Russell Committee, however, clearly thought of a large body, with detailed work being carried out in sub-committees, while the Alexander Committee believed that 'for effective working . . . the membership should not normally exceed 30 at any time'. It added that 'this suggests that in certain cases there may be a need for some form of rotating membership in order to secure the involvement of all relevant local organisations'.

The central government has not directly implemented these recommendations, but some LEAs have taken action and have established local development councils, although with many variations, some near to the criteria suggested, but some with wide differences. In an ACACE survey of 1980[16] it was noted that twenty-one LEAs in England and Wales 'have organised local development councils along the lines recommended in the report and that six more have plans to establish them'. Another nineteen have bodies resembling those recommended but not identical, and twenty-six have other kinds of established consultative procedures. It seems clear that a third of the LEAs in England and Wales have no established channels of consultation and that another third have only restricted means. The position is perhaps slightly worse in Scotland. None of the existing local development councils, it would appear, are really consulted before policy decisions are made, but some seem to be valuable as a forum and as a means of helping collaboration and perhaps co-ordination. A few examples which indicate this are the Humberside Development Council which has about fifty representatives and has tried to establish co-operative discussion leading to a development plan, and Manchester Central Development Council for Community Education which has reviewed needs, made representations to local government and organized working parties and one-day conferences. In the Bristol area, there are joint county committees on adult education as well as 'standing conferences', but these have only a limited consultative role.

Local development councils in practice have a number of unresolved problems. Within the broad spectrum of the education of adults, there are sectional rivalries and suspicions which make co-operation difficult. There is little evidence to suggest the LEAs would like to take over all the work of voluntary organizations, but many of the latter seem to have this fear and are cautious in their relationships, especially when told that the LEAs are to give 'leadership in the co-operative enterprise of community education'.[17] 'He who walks with the tiger, may end up inside.' The suspicion is long standing and hard to eradicate; it was seen, for example, early in the century when it killed proposals from the Board of Education, the predecessor of the DES, for the establishment of 'local committees for further education' with a wide membership. Some agencies do not wish to co-operate but merely to carry out their own activities regardless of others. Some believe in competition rather than co-operation, fight for their own power and position and are not worried by questions about possible waste and overlapping. They tend to keep away from local development councils of any kind, and either ignore or denounce any suggestions about co-operation which emanate from the meetings.

The size of the council may present difficulties. If it is to be representative of all interests then in many towns this would mean a membership of well over a hundred; even in relatively small places there are likely to be forty or fifty agencies concerned with the education of adults. In these circumstances, real discussion and consultation becomes difficult if not impossible and the council may appear remote and ineffectual. On the other hand, small councils which do not include representatives of all bodies can lead to endless battles with unrepresented minorities and sometimes to manipulation by officials anxious to retain and wield such powers as they think they possess. It has been suggested that an LEA area is too large just for one development council and that, therefore, a series of neighbourhood participative groups should be formed which could then feed ideas to a central council. Overworked officials of voluntary organizations concerned with the larger area, however, are likely to protest at the size of the load of too many meetings. Most authorities have still to devise a satisfactory structure which would allow both for a wide and equitable distribution of membership and for general usefulness and efficiency.

Related to this are questions concerning the purposes of local development councils, their role, powers and responsibilities. Some of the existing councils appear to be weak and time-wasting because their purposes are unclear, at least to the members, and they therefore lose the support of busy representatives. More important is the question of power. If local development councils are given real power, are the elected members of the Authority, or the professional adult educators, likely to be willing to accept their decisions, and what is to happen if the recommendations of the development council conflict with LEA policy, tangle in political controversy, and seek to exert unwelcome pressure on the Authority? On the other hand if local development councils have no power, how can interest, attendance and support be maintained? So far the evidence suggests that local development councils work best when they have clear-cut, specific tasks, such as the planning of local conferences or exhibitions, the provision of joint advertising, survey work, community projects and the joint servicing of adult organizations by providing lists of teachers, lecturers and organizers. It may be argued, however, that these tasks can be carried out better by informal consultations rather than by a formal council or committee, especially if the latter costs money. Even so, the ACACE Enquiry of 1980 revealed that most LEAs with local development councils would recommend other Authorities to follow their example.

Despite the problems at all levels a strong case can be made out for organized formal consultation as well as informal friendly contacts, if a democratically controlled and adequate provision of education for adults is to be obtained, and current needs met, throughout the whole country. Without a structure contact may disappear by default in some areas, especially if officials are overworked and immersed in detailed administration. The mere existence of consultative machinery makes sure that the opportunities for communication and collaboration are present and that people are reminded of them at regular intervals. In general, liaison and the exchange of ideas would seem to be helpful both to the providing agencies and to the bodies which have need of educational assistance from time to time; it can retain flexibility while leading to a more planned use of resources. The problems of poor communication, poor human relationships and weak finances exist, of course, in many countries, as can be seen in the deliberations of the international organizations such as the International Council for Adult Education and the European Bureau of Adult Education.[18] Some think, however, that the relative homogeneity of interests in Britain ought to make the solutions more easy to achieve.

References

1. See the Report of the conference given in *Adult Education*, XVI/2, Dec. 1943, p. 45.
2. See 1919 Report, para 334f, page 171.
3. See the *World Association for Adult Education Bulletin*, No. 1, July 1919, and E.M. HUTCHINSON 'From British Institute to National Institute, 1921-71', in *Aims and Action in Adult Education, 1921-1971*, (NIAE 1971).
4. Quotation from the revised *Constitution* of 1979 which became operative in 1980. Many of the phrases used in this paragraph are from the same source.
5. Russell Report, para 429, p. 142.
6. Russell Report, also para 429.
7. See *Constitution* of 1973, amended up to 1978 and quoted in full in the 1978 Yearbook of the SIAE.
8. *Scottish Adult Education* — Report of the Working Party on Adult Education in Scotland, 1968, SIAE.
9. All quotations from the *Constitution* of AONTAS.
10. See the Terms of Reference, the Background Note issued by the NICCE, and the foreword to the *Report of the Resources Panel* issued in 1979.
11. Department of Education for Northern Ireland, *Resources available for Continuing Education in Northern Ireland* — the Report of the Resources Panel of the CCE, 1977, HMSO.
12. Alexander Report, paras 161-166.
13. Department of Education and Science *Report of the Working Group on the management of higher education in the maintained sector*, 1978, HMSO (Cmd 7130). (The Oakes Report.)
14. Russell Report, paras. 170-172.
15. Alexander Report, paras 209-210.
16. See ACACE, *Secretariat's Report on Local Development Councils for Adult Education* Feb. 1980, ACACE-CD/143R.
17. Ministry of Education, *Further Education*, Pamphlet No. 8, 1947, HMSO, para 20.
18. See for example the report of a conference of the European Bureau of Adult Education in 1978 on *The Development of Local Educational Networks*.

CHAPTER 12

Staffing and training

'The provision of staff of good quality, in sufficient numbers, with necessary training and wisely and economically deployed, is critical to all the developments in adult education which we recommend'.[1] These comments at the beginning of the section on 'Staff' in the Russell Report are paralleled in the Alexander Report by the statement: 'the expanded and efficient service we wish to see in Scotland can be achieved only by staff whose personal qualities are matched by the relevance and thoroughness of their training'.[2] Although a few still cling to the earlier view that training is unnecessary and undesirable, and that successful adult educators are 'born not made', the idea of training on the whole now has general acceptance in Britain and providers have given it more and more attention. Few people in Britain, however, have attempted to plan for the whole range of training needs which have to be taken into account if the education of adults is to be adequately staffed. Existing plans and projects tend to be embryonic, *ad hoc,* limited and directed only to small areas of need, while some parts of the country offer little practical evidence of a real concern, even if the authorities approve in principle. Staffing and training are, in fact, much like the provision of education for adults as a whole – largely unplanned, somewhat disorganized and often inconsistent. This chapter, therefore, only picks out some of the main features and raises questions which ought to be faced.

Staffing

Part of the problem of planning is the great diversity of the provision. The most obvious staffing requirement would appear to be that of teachers of adults but even this raises a number of questions. Are teachers of children a satisfactory source of supply or are there too many differences between the teaching of children and the teaching of adults to make this really viable? For technical and vocational subjects is the right source of teachers those working in industry or the professions? Are new young graduates to be recruited or is 'experience of life' a first essential? For art and music should one turn to artists and musicians? In some subject areas is it better to look to the enthusiastic amateur with a strong hobby interest? If learning exchanges are to be developed, should the whole population be regarded as a teaching resource and ways be devised of ensuring an easy and effective use of this potential? How realistic is the view that each person should be both teacher and student?

There are similar awkward questions about organizers, advisers and administrators of educational work with adults. Should they be recruited only from those with experience of teaching adults? Should their role be multipurpose or specialist? Is there a case for a separate profession of educational managers? Can the same person organize work with both adults and youths? How far can there be a 'comprehensive, community education service' as recommended by the Alexander Committee? A strong case can be made for the provision of counsellors and advisers but how far should these be integrated with other staff, rather than developed as separate specialists? What should be the ratio between full-time and part-time staff, and how best can voluntary workers be used, if at all? It may be useful to think of the staffing of education for adults as a sort of pyramid, as suggested long ago by Professor Houle in Chicago:

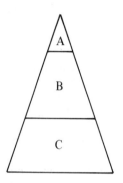

Those whose primary concern is with the education of adults.

Those who, as part of their paid employment, combine the function of adult educator with other duties.

Voluntary unpaid 'lay leaders' who help to plan, organize or contact adult education activities.

Houle suggested that librarians and museum curators should be included in B, but the list could easily be extended by personnel officers, social workers, clergymen, those in the health service, internal university staff and the multitude of teachers of children who also serve as teachers of adults. As for the volunteers who take part in organized provision of all kinds, 'their number is legion and their influence is enormous'. Some might want to add a fourth tier of everyone else if the argument is accepted that all are self-educators as well as potential teachers of others. Even in the more formal classes, 'the principle which gave most life and vigour', said Mansbridge, 'was that each student was held to be a teacher and each teacher held to be a student'.[3] Supporters of experiential learning, now popular in some areas, should perhaps contemplate the need to train all who participate in any way.

At the present time it is not easy to obtain accurate statistics even about the number of paid educators of adults, and variant figures are often quoted. Much depends upon the bases for these, the time at which they were obtained and, of course, upon the chosen definition of 'adult educator'. In 1973, the Russell Report suggested that in England and Wales the total staff employed full-time in non-vocational adult education in all its forms amounted to something like 1,300 individuals while the number of part-time tutors in all sectors probably approached 100,000.[4] For Scotland in 1975 the Alexander Report talked of the 'poor staffing position' which had 'persisted for years', and declared that there were 'only about 130 people for whom adult education is a major part of their full-time work and only some 90 of these are concerned to a substantial extent with administration or organisation'.[5] It noted, however, that over 500 people were employed full-time by education authorities in youth and community service as organizers, wardens and leaders. The Haycocks Second Report on *Training* issued in 1978 suggested that in England and Wales in terms of the whole range of educational work with adults, there were about 76,000 full-time staff and about 140,000 part-time teachers, including about 10,000 part-time teachers employed by the Responsible Bodies.[6] The Third Report suggested the slightly higher figures of 77,000 full-time and 145,000 part-time. Most of the full-time teachers are employed in the work-related sector, the colleges of further and higher education, and the polytechnics, and the position is similar in Scotland and Northern Ireland. The Carnegy Report[7] suggested that for 'community education' in Scotland there were 600 or so full-time workers and perhaps 12,000 paid part-time workers in 1976. There were, however, no full-time employees in non work-related education for adults until 1965 when Fife recruited 'tutor-organizers' and Edinburgh 'principal tutors'. The Alexander Report recommended the appointment of 200 new staff in Scotland in the period 1975-80 but this has not been implemented and, except for literacy and basic education staff, there has been little change in the general situation. One of the many statistical problems, of course, is that of trying to separate teaching from organizing, administering and advising, especially in the non work-related sector where a combination of duties is often a marked feature. Whereas in the vocationally oriented colleges there is a fairly clear structure indicating who teaches and who administers, the position in the non work-related sector is more confused with, for instance, heads of centres, organizers, advisers, tutor-organizers and adult or further education officers, who may or may not combine some teaching with organization and administration and who are all likely to undertake counselling work from time to time. In practice they are often more generalists than specialists. Elsdon in the early 1970s thought that this type of education for adults employed perhaps 2,300 full-time or shared appointments of administrators, advisers, organizers and teachers, and probably about 100,000 part-time teachers, a figure more than double the number of part-timers in the work-related sector. At an earlier date, a survey by the NIAE in 1963 gave the figures as 954 full-time workers and about 60,000 part-timers in England and Wales while three years later the NIAE Secretary estimated 1,150 full-time and 58,500 part-time.[8] In comparison the number of full-time staff in the adult education centres (*Volkshochschule*) of the German Federal Republic was reported in 1979 to be between 1,200 and 1,500 with 500 to 700 administrative workers and 88,000 part-time teachers.[9]

These figures all reflect what has been called 'mainstream' education for adults and to them must be added teachers, administrators and organizers employed full-time or part-time by the correspondence colleges, commercial and private institutions of various kinds, field study centres and all the many voluntary organizations. Harris[10] in 1975 estimated that there were six or seven thousand correspondence tutors and drew attention to the employment by the Open University at that time of 4,500 part-time tutors. Williams and Woodhall pointed out in 1979 how difficult it was to make a reliable estimate of the total number of teachers employed in the private sector as a whole but suggested that over 99% of correspondence course teachers were part-time and probably about 44% of the rest.[11] No one so far has felt able to count accurately the numbers of organizers and administrators employed by voluntary agencies.[12] Problems of terminology often obscure the contribution made by 'coaches' and 'instructors', especially important in areas such as sports, health, driving and many crafts. The total number also grows considerably if among educators of adults are included doctors and nurses, social workers and clergymen, and indeed anyone in the 'caring' professions who help adults to learn. It seems likely that potentially there are thousands of volunteer teachers, as shown by the 80,000 who came forward for the adult literacy schemes, and besides the unpaid 'lay leaders' who do so much to aid the development of education for adults, there is the uncounted multitude of voluntary members of committees and informal groups which aid and abet them. As G.D.H. Cole once said 'odd jobs are the essence of working class education'.

There has been a great expansion in the number of full-time educators of adults in the second half of the twentieth century. In 1945 full-time teachers of adults in all sectors numbered little more than 4,500 in England and Wales, and less than 500 in Scotland and Northern Ireland. Much of the expansion has taken place in the colleges of further education to cope with a rising tide of full-time students on work-related courses and has been aided by various White Papers and Reports as well as by the increase in the number and type of awards. The full-time teaching strength has increased to about 70,000 and has been matched by a considerable expansion in the provision of administrators both within the colleges and at LEA offices. In the non work-related sector many LEAs did not appoint full-time principals, organizers and advisers until the 1960s, or even the 1970s. In the university extra-mural departments and the WEA a rapid expansion just after the Second World War took the number of full-time teachers and organizers from about 80 to 250, followed by a slower increase to nearly 500 by 1980. The expansion in all sectors has been uneven, however, developing in fits and starts, and showing great differences between the various parts of Britain. In the late 1970s expansion seems to have come to a half and despite union opposition, there may now be contraction of staff of all kinds.

There is considerable turnover among the part-time teachers, and to a lesser extent among the full-time staff. Some estimates suggest that in some areas the turnover of part-time teachers may be as high as 30%, and probably overall it is between 10 and 20%.[13] Mobility, involving perhaps new job responsibilities, as well as a change in the place of residence, is one factor; another may be some disenchantment after hard experiences of evening classes on winter evenings; and some may feel that there is too much discrepancy between effort and financial reward. Some appear to teach intermittently with sometimes long gaps between classes. Others in the full-time ranks have used work in adult education as a stepping stone to posts elsewhere, sometimes to internal posts in universities, sometimes to jobs in industry or politics and sometimes to other branches of education. On the other hand there are some devoted educators of adults who have given years of endeavour to help develop the work, sometimes in an unpaid or underpaid capacity. Among these should be placed the voluntary officers in, for example, the WEA, who have been known to spend ten or more hours a week in helping to solve the problems faced by the organization. It can be argued that this type of enthusiasm and self-sacrifice is needed among all types of educators as much now as in more pioneer days, but that there is also a great need for a better professional career structure for a full-time cadre on whom the army of part-timers should be able to rely. For a period the position looked more hopeful in that some LEAs were establishing posts at senior levels which combined organizing, advisory and in-service training functions, but only a minority have done so and the future seems doubtful. The general question of professionalism is discussed later in this chapter.

Training of educators of adults

The provision of training opportunities for those concerned with the education of adults has, therefore, to be set against a background of uncertainty over numbers, turnover, the type of posts available and resources in general. Moreover, there are still those who view training with some hostility as a useless expenditure of resources, fearing rigidity and formalism instead of the spontaneity and enthusiasm they see in voluntaryism. Possibly the word 'training' should be changed to 'education' or 'professional development', if only to get rid of the idea that the process involves the production of a standard stereotype labelled 'adult educator'. 'Training', however, is the word in common use and here it is used for the processes whereby educators of adults acquire and develop both professional skills and knowledge and their own personal capabilities which together enable them to function more helpfully and efficiently. As Elsdon has pointed out, some have managed to train themselves by weighing up their own experiences — such perhaps are 'born teachers' — but most seem to require some outside help. A sad feature of the present position is that the opportunities to get such help are still relatively few, despite the support of the 1919 Report, the 1928 Report on *The Tutor in Adult Education,*[14] Pamphlet No. 8 in 1947 and the subsequent Russell, Alexander and Carnegy Reports. Most of those engaged in the education of adults, either full-time or part-time, are still professionally untrained in any organized way. The ATCDE evidence to the James enquiry in 1972 suggested that two-thirds of the full-time teachers in further education were without training, and this is approximately the same position described earlier in the 1966 Report on the *Supply and Training of Teachers for Further Education*[15] and again later in the 1975 Haycocks Report,[16] although the latter pointed out that some of the 'untrained' have undertaken part-time courses leading to qualifications other than professional teacher training. Of the part-time teachers some, perhaps 40% but probably less, are school teachers trained for work with children, but the others are drawn from a wide range of occupations. Those working with university extra-mural departments, the WEA and other voluntary agencies are perhaps even more diverse and less trained as educators of adults. So far, in contrast to children's education, there has been no requirement of 'qualified teacher status' in the adult sector and, despite the excellence of some teachers of adults, it is not surprising that there have been somewhat severe criticisms of the general quality of the teaching in some classes.

Most of the teachers in the field have subject knowledge, and are usually appointed on the basis of some recognized subject qualification, possibly a degree, a craft certificate or a technical award. A view which still prevails in some quarters is that subject competence is the main essential and that training should consist largely of an extension, undating and deepening of subject knowledge. This idea was reflected, for example, in the courses arranged for Responsible Body tutors in the 1950s by the Central Joint Advisory Committee and in some LEA short in-service courses in 'women's subjects'. It is still seen in the appointment of staff to universities, colleges and centres where it is still comparatively rare to have questions asked about teaching competence. To subject knowledge, the addition of a few hints and tips on teaching may be thought desirable for adequate 'training'; a not uncommon approach seen in talks to new teachers by LEA centre heads or college heads of departments, and in the visits to classes by extra-mural administrators, WEA district secretaries and others. Some have believed in a kind of apprenticeship system whereby the new teacher would learn by being attached to a practising established teacher. Examples of this could be seen in the early training work of the old London County Council and of the West Riding of Yorkshire, and in the Oxford Extension Delegacy scheme for 'apprentice tutors' which ran from 1946 to 1968. Supporters of this approach believe that it enables new teachers somehow to pick up the essentials of their craft, the basic ideas and approach, and knowledge of administrative regulations and similar matters. In some parts of the country, however, even this is regarded as unnecessary and there is an assumption that knowledge of a subject is equivalent to ability to teach it and that 'experience is the best kind of training'. Similarly administrators and organizers are thought to need only the application of a little 'common sense' and some imitation of predecessors and precedents. Only relatively recently has training for educational management appeared as a possible alternative to 'learning on the job'.

There is a parallel opposition to any kind of formal training for university teachers or administrators, despite pioneer work in Manchester from the early 1950s onwards and the development of more organized schemes in the 1970s. Nevertheless in the 1960s and 1970s, across the whole field of educational work with adults and young people, there was increasing recognition that however valuable 'hints and tips' might be as part of training, something more was needed. In some parts of the country training courses have thus developed which are concerned more with the development of teaching competence than with subject updating. Partly these echo some experiments in Forces' education during the war years, work in Chicago on the training of adult educators and the growing concern in Europe which was seen in conferences on training such as that organized by the European Bureau of Adult Education in 1961, and the 1965 meeting under the auspices of the Council of Europe.[17] The whole of the first issue of the international journal *Convergence* in March, 1968, was devoted to the training of adult educators, and more recently there have been the three Haycocks reports[18] from the Advisory Committee on the Supply and Training of Teachers. The need for training was particularly marked during the literacy campaign from 1975 onwards. Actual progress, however, has been slow even for adult work-related education, as is shown by the weak responses to the various reports which came out almost regularly at five year intervals from about 1956 onwards.[19] Lack of clarity about objectives and about levels of training has also contributed to the failure to develop a fully adequate training programme and there have been numerous arguments about the relative merits of pre-service, 'initial', 'in-service' and 'advanced' training. Should training be given in regular recurrent periods? Do particular types of work have differing training needs? Should training be institutionalized? If so, are existing institutions such as teacher training establishments and universities appropriate or are special institutions required? Or should training be carried out where the classes are held? What part can be played by distance learning? Who should be the trainers, and how much training do they require? Should there be some form of certification and if so, of what kind? Who should finance training?

Training of full-time teachers

For the training of full-time teachers in the mainly work-related sector in England, there has been a concentration of resources in four specialist colleges of education – Bolton, Huddersfield, Wolverhampton and Garnett (London) – two of which are now part of the neighbouring polytechnics. On the whole, these have mostly provided courses of initial training leading to a certificate in education. Besides one year full-time pre-service courses, which are similar to the courses for the training of graduates as schoolteachers, the colleges have also developed four-term sandwich courses and two-year part-time courses for serving teachers which incorporate periods of full-time attendance. Thus the sandwich course may be one of two terms in college and two in the teacher's own establishment with the teaching supervised by specialist tutors. In Wales there is a rather shorter sandwich course or a one year full-time course run jointly by the University College of Cardiff and the University of Wales Institute of Science and Technology. The main growth in recent years has been in part-time courses, and following the 1966 Report some of the colleges developed 'extra-mural' centres to make these more readily available, staff of the colleges going out to colleges of further education to organize day courses of teacher training which are made available to all teachers within travelling distance. Problems concerning the full-time in-service courses have been the reluctance of establishments and LEAs to release teachers, and of individual teachers to be away from home without adequate subsistence and travelling grants. In 1974 the numbers of students taking courses of initial training at the English colleges of education and at University College, Cardiff were 1,288 full-time, 383 four-term sandwich, and 902 two-year part-time, i.e., a total of 2,573 including both full-time and part-time. Those taking these courses tend to be over the age of 30. In 1977 the first B.Ed. degree course for teachers in further education began at Wolverhampton. This was validated by CNAA and was intended to replace the certificate in education. There are, however, questions being raised about the future of training provided separately for the adult sector, some declaring that all teachers should study a 'common core' in the same institutions with an opportunity to specialize in terms of particular age groups. Similarly with the coming of an entirely graduate profession of teachers in schools, there is also advocacy that those working with adults should be offered degrees rather than certificates or diplomas. Some of the colleges provide a range of short courses, conferences, workshops and study groups designed as a form of in-service training for those working in a wide range of provision, including the hospital service and industrial organizations as well as the colleges of further and higher education. Some, too, have moved to the provision of advanced studies; Bolton College, for example, provides courses leading to a Diploma in Advanced Study in Technical Education and to a Master's degree with special reference to technical education.

In Scotland, full-time courses in youth and community service are provided in four colleges of education: Moray House since 1960, Jordanhill since 1964 and Aberdeen and Dundee since 1971. These lead either to a Diploma after two or three years, or to a Certificate after one year. The latter is open only to graduates, qualified teachers and certain special categories of teachers, and, allowing for qualifications and experience on entry, students are expected to acquire the same knowledge, practical work experience and expertise as in the Diploma course. Each college has tended to vary the content and approach within agreed broad guidelines and the total number of students in training reached just over 340 in 1975–6. Regional courses have been developed for the in-service training of staff by, for example, the collaboration of Moray House College with the Lothian and Border Regions, or that of Aberdeen College of Education with the Grampian Region. Following the Carnegy Report of 1977, there have been moves to establish a modular system and in 1980 an Interim National Training Group was established to consider the organization of training opportunities in Scotland. In the meantime some of the Colleges of Education provide a two-term pre-service course for further education teachers recruited from industry and commerce, or a sandwich course soon after their appointment. But, as elsewhere, most teachers of adults in Scotland continue to serve without training.

A growing number of universities are making a contribution by advanced courses designed in the main for experienced full-time educators of adults. Nottingham had launched a Diploma in Adult Education in the 1920s but it attracted only a handful of candidates, and post-war developments were pioneered by Manchester as from 1949 when a new department was established. A full-time certificate course there began in 1955, to be converted to an advanced diploma in 1961, which Nottingham followed in 1966, both universities attracting students from a broad spectrum of educators of adults including those in work-related and non work-related LEA provision, in community work, in the churches, in industry and in the voluntary agencies. Later Manchester provided a separate diploma for community development workers though still regarding them as part of the adult educational scene, and similarly, after the Industrial Training Act of 1964, it established a separate diploma in industrial education and training. Other universities have joined in the provision and by 1980 advanced awards in the education of adults were provided by fourteen universities, including the Universities of Edinburgh and Glasgow and the New University of Ulster. Most of these universities provide opportunities for further study beyond the advanced diploma level, in the form of Master's courses (both research and 'taught') and of Ph.D. courses in the education of adults. The more senior experienced full-time educators of adults, for whom this provision is designed, find it difficult to obtain secondment and hence most take the part-time options. It can be argued, of course, that they need periods away from the constant preoccupation with day-to-day problems so that they have a chance to consider the wider aims and implications of the work they are doing. At their best, these courses provide full library facilities, opportunities for experiment and study, together with organized opportunities for contact with other educators of adults and with a wide range of educational activities. The content of the courses varies but most include reference to the philosophy, psychology and history of the education of adults, and to methods and evaluation. In some, great emphasis is placed on experiential learning and upon students following their own interests under tutorial guidance, while in others there is more insistence on a controlled curriculum. To some extent these stresses reflect differences of opinion about objectives: should the purpose be the exploration of academic knowledge, or should the course seek to have a direct impact on the quality of the contribution the student makes in his job? The type of staff also has an effect: some departments prefer to appoint academic specialists in some aspect of study, for example the psychology of adult learning, while others believe that only those with much practical experience in the education of adults should undertake the work of training. Without this experience it is felt that there is a danger of theory becoming remote from practice.

Training of part-time teachers

For both full-time and part-time teachers who are qualified in their subject but lack teaching qualifications, the City and Guilds of London Institute (CGLI) provides a Further Education Teacher's Certificate, Course No. 730 as it is often known. This requires a part-time attendance of about 150 hours, usually at a college of further or higher education, and a minimum of 30 hours teaching practice. The course may be held in the daytime or evening, and provides for a study of the principles and methods of teaching adults. The Institute provides a broad syllabus and area assessors who co-ordinate the standards of assessment, but the exact content, organization and methods of the courses are the responsibility of the colleges. This can provide a very flexible way in which further education teachers can undertake professional training and obtain a certificate, but it allows for possibly too much variation in approach and standards. For those who possess a Teacher's Certificate, the Institute also provides a Further Education Teacher's Advanced Certificate requiring some 200 hours of attendance. The content of this is a study of the aims and organization of 'further and adult' education, and one special subject chosen from a range of options. Since the 1970s the CGLI has paid more attention to the needs of teachers working in the non work-related sector and some pioneer courses with special variations have developed. Some voluntary organizations are also using the course; in Essex, for example the County Pre-School Playgroups Association has linked the in-service training of its part-time tutors to Course 730. There have also been experiments with methods of assessment other than the traditional final written examination, and it seems possible that considerable modifications in the whole scheme may take place in the future. In the meantime, an average of some 3,000 students are attending per year, and it has clearly become a valued route for those unable to attend full-time courses, or any other course provided by the specialist colleges. The 730 course attracts candidates from H.M. Forces, the health service and industrial training establishments as well as from teachers in LEA colleges and centres.

Over the years other courses have developed. The Royal Society of Arts (RSA) offers three teacher's certificates, one in shorthand, one in typewriting and one in office practice, all of which are organized on a two-part basis, one concerned with appropriate skills and the other with principles of teaching. Courses leading to the awards may be offered at regional and local levels, and, except for the office practice scheme, by correspondence. The RSA examines and validates the awards and colleges are required to register with it. Periods of supervised teaching practice or probationary teaching are also required. The College of Preceptors provides a Further Education Staff Training Course (Alternative D) within its Associateship (ACP) from which candidates may proceed by part-time day or evening modular courses to the Licentiateship qualification (LCP) which is recognized as equivalent to a university first degree for salary purposes for full-time teachers. The candidates so far have been mainly full-time staff, but some part-timers have been allowed on condition that they have at least 700 hours of teaching experience by the end of the course. The course content is prescribed and includes general theories of education, the psychology of learning, and methods of teaching as well as the organization and administration of education for adults. Courses are held within further education institutions and the trainers are usually senior members of staff. Some of the colleges which are thought to have an adequate staff and library resources are now permitted to put forward proposals for an internal scheme of training for newly appointed full-. time staff which after external validation can lead to the award of the ACP.

Some, but not all, the Regional Advisory Councils in England and Wales have shown an interest in the training of part-time teachers of adults over a long period of time. Conferences and other meetings concerned particularly with subject updating were an early feature, and in the 1970s full schemes of training concerned with teaching competence were developed, the first being in the East Midlands. Courses of basic training were also provided in Yorkshire and Humberside by the mid-1970s, and the work of some LEAs in the north-west has had to the establishment of a very full scheme of training for part-time teachers on a modular basis as well as to a scheme of training for full-time teachers based on the first Haycocks Report. Somewhat in accord with the proposals of the second Haycocks Report, these schemes for part-time teachers normally have three stages, the first being a 'brief initiation into basic teaching skills' usually of about 36 or 40 hours in length, the second a more substantial in-service series of modules designed to enhance the teachers' skills and understanding and to extend their sensitivity to students' learning needs, and the third seeking to develop greater teaching competence by studies in depth. In the areas where the RACs are most active provision has been made for training the trainers and for elaborate systems of validation. Some individual LEAs have been active in developing their own schemes, as for example those of the ILEA and the provision at the regular Glamorgan Summer School at Barry. Schemes of training for literacy teachers have been in evidence in recent years and the City Lit. has a special course for teachers of lip reading to adults. The pattern is very varied and the provision is beset by problems of finance and staffing, but a general move forward has been seen in some parts of the country and this could be intensified by more leadership from the central government.

Independent voluntary organizations are also playing some part in the provision of training. The Keep Fit Association Teacher's Award has some degree of parity with the City and Guilds Advanced 730, although it includes only a limited amount of teaching practice. Most of the voluntary organizations tend to stress subject competence, however, and include only a few hints and tips on teaching. At present this is particularly true of the various awards for teachers of dancing and of the courses for coaches and instructors in the sports organizations such as the Amateur Swimming Association, the Lawn Tennis Association, the Football Association and the Badminton Association. Rather more attention to teaching competence, however, is given in the courses for teachers and instructors organized by the British Red Cross Society, the National Marriage Guidance Council and the British Theatre Association. This is also true of the short craft instructors courses organized for their own members by the National Federation of Women's Institutes and held at Denman College. Very many voluntary organizations seem in fact to be concerned with the provision of training for part-time teachers of adults, but most of them seem to work in isolation and tend to have very limited views of training, though there are signs of some change in this. For full-time teachers there are also independent courses offering fairly substantial training opportunities such as the Associateship schemes of the College of Craft Education and those leading to the Approved Driving Instructors's Award of the National Joint Council. The Pre-retirement Association is also active and play-leadership courses have been organized in association with LEAs such as the Greater London Council and the ILEA. Other important agencies are those responsible for the training of instructors in the armed forces and in the police service, and for that of groups such as nurse tutors. The course for Metropolitan Police Officers as trainers, for example, is one of 400 hours, after which successful students are posted to the staff of the Training School for three years, during which time they are encouraged to obtain the City and Guilds Teachers Certificate or other formal teaching qualifications. The Institute of Advanced Nursing Education also has a substantial course leading to the award in clinical teaching.

Training of organizers and administrators

Most of the training described in previous paragraphs has been concerned with the training of teachers, rather than organizers and administrators, with the exception of that provided by the College of Preceptors and the advanced City and Guilds 730. The third Haycocks Report of 1978[20] noted the great variety of levels at which 'management' takes place in the adult sector and the wide variety of appointments with management functions. These include not only principals and directors, administrative officers and heads of departments but also course tutors, those responsible for libraries etc. and some part-time workers in the non work-related sector. The Report suggested that 'even in the most favourable economic conditions effective management is important; in conditions of economic stringency it is doubly so'. Yet though a number of bodies are interested in training for this kind of work, and a variety of courses exist, no coherent total scheme has come into being. The only institution exclusively concerned with training for educational management in further education is the Further Education Staff College which was set up at Coombe Lodge, Somerset, in 1962. The typical method there has been the residential study conference in which key people in industry meet the senior staff of the colleges, or where principals, vice-principals and heads of departments can come together to discuss problems of management. Examples of the subjects of these conferences are 'The management of engineering education', 'The work of the college principal', 'The relationships between schools and colleges in the education of the 16–19 year old', 'The management of polytechnics' and 'The management of colleges in Scotland'. Meeting with a rather apathetic response in the early days, the college now seems well established despite threats to its finances which are a direct charge on every local authority. It has been suggested that given more resources the Staff College could provide a more useful link with Western Europe, feeding ideas both ways.

The Centre for Extension Studies in Loughborough University of Technology has developed a training programme in management for adult education intended for principals and vice-principals in the non work-related centres, together with those occupying similar positions in the general studies or adult education departments of the colleges of further and higher education. The programme consists mainly of linked one-week residential courses organized as seminars examining the range of problems experienced by the members. Some polytechnics and the larger colleges have developed their own management training programmes for their staff and a few colleges have given special attention to the training of all members of staff in administrative and organizational skills and methods. So far little has been provided for the volunteers or part-time organizers in voluntary organizations, although some WEA branch officers come together each session in half-day or full-day meetings to discuss organizational problems, and there have been a small number of special short courses for voluntary workers. More definite guidance and training is also given to members of the Women's Institutes and Townswomens Guilds in their *Handbooks* and in the short courses provided for members undertaking special roles as financial advisers to the local units or as organizers of new developments. In the many hundreds of voluntary organizations, however, the opportunities are spread very thinly, and are often non-existent, so that the voluntary worker struggles alone with the task of being a committee member, secretary or chairman, often undertaking managerial roles at short notice.

Training of counsellors

Advice and counselling for adults in educational matters is a relatively neglected area and little has been done to secure adequate staffing and training. All teachers of adults are likely to be involved in this aspect of the work which, in its simplest form, may be helping people to find relevant information and then to use it. Students often need advice or guidance on the options open to them, and it can be argued that many require counselling which will help them to articulate their needs, even perhaps the sort of diagnostic counselling which is evident in other sectors of education. As the ACACE Report on existing services[21] pointed out in 1979, there is a considerable overlap in practice between the functions of information, advice and counselling, however desirable in theory it may be to draw distinctions. In recent years there have been some interesting experiments but they have tended to be isolated, to be spread unevenly throughout the country and to be considerably under-financed. Even the most common type of provision, that of supplying information about adult opportunities for education, is uncoordinated and often bewildering to potential students. Thus information is provided separately by the institutions offering courses, by the LEAs or voluntary bodies which give them support, by public libraries, by Citizens Advice Bureaux and some-times neighbourhood centres, by local newspapers and local radio, by Job Centres and by the Manpower Services Commission, by the private Careers Research and Advisory Centre (CRAC), by professional associations, by the Open University, by the Institutes of Adult Education and by many other agencies. Careers guidance has a similar number of providers including especially the MSC and voluntary agencies such as the National Advisory Centre on Careers for Women and the National Association for the Care and Resettlement of Offenders (NACRO). Educational guidance for adults on the whole is a recent development, although the Educational Guidance Service for Adults in Belfast (EGSA) was set up in 1967, surviving under a variety of auspices. Other examples have been the Educational Guidance Services for Adults in Hatfield, and a similar organization in Merseyside (MEGSA), Leisure and Educational Opportunities in Lancaster, and various advisory services and advisory centres in Tower Hamlets, London, in Malvern and in West Sussex. Others are planned but the position is so fluid that some named above have already ceased to exist.

In some areas volunteers man the whole service, in others full-time teachers and organizers of education for adults are drawn into the work and in a few there are professional full-time counsellors. Much depends on the funds available, usually uncertain and insecure, and upon decisions about the objectives of the service. Should guidance be mainly directed to the disadvantaged or educationally less self-reliant, or should it be for the assistance of everyone? The methods used, although often of considerable value to clients, tend to be *ad hoc* and unassessed, and, perhaps inevitably in an understaffed service, record keeping is often minimal. There are also differing opinions about the desirability of professional training as well as about the type of staff required. Most agencies seem to accept the need for some training in counselling, at least in theory, in order to develop necessary skills and greater sensitivity to client problems but there are doubts about the need for a separate cadre of professionally trained and accredited counsellors. The result is that most staff have had no initial training, although some may draw upon experience in other fields, and open courses such as those of the National Marriage Guidance Council or the Careers Service. Open University tutor counsellors often draw upon a variety of experience and some have been occupational psychologists. Occasionally there are one-day meetings and workshops, as organized by the University of Lancaster in 1977, and even short courses in further education colleges but for most of the country such opportunities are rare, a situation which contrasts sharply with the sort of training given for example to those in educational 'brokering' in the United States. The main developments in Britain, in fact, have been in the training of social and community workers and other 'caring' professions. In Scotland no educational advisory services for adults were operational in

1979 although a number of proposals had come forward in the late 1970s recommending local advisory services as a minimum base, and suggesting a *Compendium of Scottish Continuing Education* which would draw together information about all formal education for adults. It has been suggested that a counselling component should be included in all the various training courses for educators of adults, but so far where it does exist it appears to be optional and often superficial. In contrast 'Counselling theories and techniques' is a core subject in the Diploma course in adult and continuing education in Maynooth, Ireland. In a conference in Los Angeles in 1977, Paul Bertelsen of UNESCO, while commenting that 'it cannot be desirable to have a "closed shop" of adult education counsellors', strongly supported 'the professional development of this field to provide the necessary back-up to the non-professional counsellors'.[22]

Conferences, seminars and short courses

To the variety of courses leading to awards can be added a range of non award-bearing courses, conferences, seminars and other activities, all of which contribute to the training of those educators of adults who choose to participate, although it would seem that unfortunately only a small proportion do so. One example of the less formal course is the annual residential one-week school which for many years has been organized by HM Inspectorate and the DES for a wide range of adult educators, community workers, youth workers and teachers of general studies who are employed by the LEAs, the Responsible Bodies and various voluntary organizations. Often called the 'Salisbury courses' from their most frequent location in the early days, these have helped to strengthen the common interests of the profession and to provide a good deal of experimental training material. Training, of course, should be viewed not just in terms of courses but as including the many more informal and more incidental opportunities. Short opportunities are offered from time to time by WEA Districts and the more active LEAs in the form of induction meetings for new teachers, one-day meetings, and conferences, and by some university extra-mural departments which hold weekend courses for tutors as well as including in their summer school programmes special one-week courses for teachers of adults. Recent examples of the latter are those offered by Nottingham and Oxford. As already noted, a few universities such as Manchester and Nottingham have taken the lead in establishing adult educators' seminars or regular meetings of full-time staff drawn from all branches of the work. These have programmes devised by the members and have not only provided much-needed contacts between the various agencies but have given a considerable stimulus to the development of expertise and co-operation. Often each meeting has a different topic but a seminar may devote a year to one theme such as literacy or the training of part-time teachers of adults. Very occasionally a university department has experimented, too, with short courses for voluntary workers, and with one-day meetings for the office staffs and caretakers in establishments of education for adults, those front-line staff who are often the first contacts made by the enquiring public. Stimulus and informal training may also be regarded as part of the task of staff meetings in all sectors of the work, especially if such meetings are planned as regular seminars. In some areas, however, such meetings are a rarity, although there may be valuable incidental consultation and discussion between the more and the less experienced.

Professional associations

Important incidental training work is also carried out by the numerous professional associations. Besides attention to professional conditions and salaries, most of these organize conferences and other meetings in which discussions may range over all aspects of educational work with adults and provide a considerable stimulus to understanding. From time to time they may arrange a series of meetings to discuss particular problems. For instance, the Society of Industrial Tutors has had a programme of regular seminar-conferences on the teaching of industrial relations. The Welsh Association, which is in associate membership with the NUT, has also encouraged training courses at national level, as well as single meetings. Many of the professional associations have a local and regional structure as well as national headquarters, with meetings at all levels, and despite rising costs some issue regular journals or newsletters. Examples are the *NATFHE Journal* and the *Journal of Further and Higher Education,* the *Bulletins* of the AUT and of the ACW, and the *Newsletters* of the ARE. All of these provide both information and stimulus to their members and seek to improve both the quality of the work and professional conditions. Similar training influences are the publications of the National Institutes of Adult Education, the regular series on *Teaching Adults* of the NIAE (England and Wales) being of particular value to part-time teachers. The colleges of education (technical) have also sponsored a journal to assist those working in the field, entitled *The Vocational Aspect of Education,* issued three times a year.

A question of professionalism

To some extent this situation reflects an attitude to the general staffing of education for adults which still prevails in some quarters as a kind of hand-over from the days of amateurism and part-time transient employment on the road to some other work. No doubt all professions have had to struggle for recognition but that of the educator of adults seems to have been particularly beset with problems. Naturally there are some difficulties associated with professionalism, for instance, the problem of restricted entry which would threaten the valuable role of voluntary workers. Moreover, in view of the great diversity of activities within the educational provision for adults some adults find it difficult to conceive of a single profession. What, it is asked, are the unifying factors between teachers of the wide range of subjects in very different institutions, teachers in distance learning, organizers, advisers, administrators and others linked to the provision. Is there a single body of knowledge relevant to the education of adults? As noted earlier, there has been a rapid expansion during recent decades in the number of those who are full-time educators of adults; but there have been only a few signs of insistence by employers on professional criteria, although in some places the demand has grown for training as a condition of employment. Part of the problem is the loose, flexible, career structure which has emerged. Although this flexibility can be advantageous there could also be benefits in a more coherent structure. As in other professions, however, educators of adults can expect the obsolescence of some types of post and the need to change jobs several times in a working lifetime. It is easy to speculate, for example, about the effects on traditional posts of the advent of teaching machines, learning laboratories, computers, educational television and all the other technological devices for learning which may emerge in the age of the microchip. Movement from one type of post to another has already been a feature of life for many educators of adults. Thus lecturers in colleges of further education have become industrial trainers, prison education officers and community workers have become adult education centre heads, WEA tutor—organizers turn into LEA area organizers and further education officers into principals of colleges. Partly, there has been a sideways movement, with no change of level or remuneration, but there has also been some increase in the number of senior posts through which a more adequate promotional structure can emerge. Professionalism, however, in part implies status within society and this depends on the value given to the work by other members of the community. It is therefore essential to get away from the image of an activity which is sometimes declared to be 'under-valued, unprestigious, under-funded and under-resourced'.[23] Full-time competent, professional leadership is needed to promote the quality of the work but a sense of professional commitment is also needed from the part-time teachers, organizers, and volunteers. The evidence suggests that these will continue to be needed and that they are of vital importance, but that they require suitable management and training provided through the expertise of a full-time staff.

Despite financial restraints there seems to be a strong case for the more extensive and sustained development of training facilities for all engaged in the work. Initial and in-service training is perhaps of particular importance in the immediate future, but recurrent education and training is needed throughout the service life of all educators just as much as for the population as a whole. The education of adults is likely to remain in a state of flux and those working in the field need constantly to rethink their role and to take the initiative in developing new enterprises. One example to be considered is the impact of changes which enable students to manage their own learning. At present in Britian there is a patchwork of training possibilities, largely unco-ordinated, despite some progress towards overall planning in the late 1970s. Similarly in this pluralist type of provision there are anomalies in the remuneration of those employed either full-time or part-time. One of the many problems is how to create a salary structure and career expectations which will both attract and retain suitable persons and yet allow for some flexibility of growth. The general position is a considerable improvement on that of the early 1960s but as in so much of the rest of Europe 'the present situation as regards status, qualification and training is anarchical and defective'.[24] Britain could give a clear lead in creating a properly structured and articulated profession of educators of adults.

References

1. Russell Report, para 355.

2. Alexander Report, para 228.

3. MANSBRIDGE, A. *Adventure in Working Class Education,* 1920, Longmans.

4. Russell Report, para 395. See also Table 28 on p. 246.

5. Alexander Report, para 225. The 130 seem to be made up of 30+ employed by university extra-mural departments, 20 by education authorities, 20 by voluntary agencies and about 60 in the community service with a major responsibility for organizing adult education classes.

6. ACSTT. Second Haycocks Report 1978.

7. Scottish Education Department. *Professional Education and Training for Community Education.*

8. See ELSDON, K.T. *Training for Adult Education,* 1975 and NIAE Reports on 'Accommodation and staffing' in *Adult Education,* XXV/5, Jan. 1963, and on 'Recruitment and training' in *Adult Education,* XXVIII/6, March, 1966.

9. Figures given by Helmuth Dolff, Director of the Deutscher Volkshochschul Verband in Dec. 1979.

10. HARRIS, W.J.A. *The Distance Tutor.*

11. WILLIAMS, G. and WOODHALL, M. *Independent Further Education,* 1979, PSI Studies, Especially pp. 56—59.

12. Although attempted in part in the NIAE 1963 Report (op. cit.) — see pp. 252—3.

13. See NIAE 1963 Report, p. 259 and ELSDON (op. cit.) p. 10.

14. *The Tutor in Adult Education: an Enquiry into the Problems of Supply and Training.* A Report of a Joint Committee of the British Institute of Adult Education and the Tutors' Association, 1928, Carnegie U.K. Trustees.

15. DES, *The Supply and Training of Teachers for Further Education,* 1966, HMSO. (Report for ACSTT of working party under chairmanship of Sir Lionel Russell.)

16. ACSTT. First Haycocks Report 1975.

17. See EBAE *Report of Conference on Training,* 1961 and Council of Europe, CCC, Report on *Workers in Adult Education — their Status, Recruitment and Training,* 1966, Council of Europe.

18. ACSTT op. cit.

19. Thus 1956 the Willis Jackson Report on *The Supply and Training of Teachers for Technical Colleges;* 1961 ACSTT Report *Teachers for Further Education* and 1966 Russell Report (op. cit.) on *The Supply and Training of Teachers for Further Education.* At an earlier date the McNair Report of 1944 on *Teachers and Youth Leaders* had had to argue a case for any kind of distinctive professional training for those working in further education.

20. ACSTT. Third Haycocks Report.

21. ACACE, *Links to Learning,* 1979, The Council. This reviews the position,

lists the services as known, and makes recommendations. See also: the *Bibliography of Educational Information, Advisory and Counselling Services for Adults in the United Kingdom,* prepared by HAROLD MARKS and published by London Association for Continuing Education in 1979 and *Information Advisory and Counselling Services Newsletter,* Issue no. 1, 1978, edited by M. REDMOND and S. SLIPMAN.

22. Paper prepared for the International Symposium on 'Ways and means of strengthening information and counselling services for adult learners' held by the College of Continuing Education, University of Southern California and UNESCO, May 1977.

23. HETHERINGTON, JULIE, 'Professionalism and part-time staff in adult education', *Adult Education,* 52/5, Jan. 1980, pp. 324–328.

24. SIMPSON, J.A. *Today and Tomorrow in European Adult Education,* 1972, Council of Europe. p. 179.

CHAPTER 13

Present trends and the future: policies, needs and possibilities

The challenge

One of the many paradoxes at the beginning of the 1980s is that although rapid change in all aspects of life is occurring, most people cling to ideas and attitudes which belong to an earlier age and which they believe are permanent. There is both a knowledge explosion and knowledge obsolescence, but many people continue to act as though the 'package' of knowledge gained in childhood is adequate for the rest of their lives. The micro-electronic revolution is rapidly reducing the demand for labour in the manufacturing industries and in those service industries, such as banking and insurance, which depend heavily on clerical and information handling skills: yet people still tend to look to them to provide mass employment, just as earlier people looked to agriculture. The hope that the displaced employees will be able to transfer to perhaps more interesting jobs looks increasingly thin and it seems more likely that many will remain out of work for the rest of their lives. Yet the work ethic persists with all its implications for status and self-respect, and most people are very ill prepared for the leisure and longer periods of non-work which are likely. Western society, it has been said, is *for* work and *against* leisure, or at any rate what appears to be 'idle' leisure. There are also considerable changes in the population structure and it seems clear that by the mid 1980s probably one-sixth of the population will be over the age of 65. Moreover, it is becoming almost realistic to think or retirement as lasting longer than 'working life'. The implications of this trend are little considered. A massive shift in thinking is needed but so far there are few signs of this happening.

A vital factor in the required change of attitudes is education, and the logic of developments in a rapidly-changing world implies the central significance of recurrent education for adults. Looking back, it is clear that the provision of the latter made considerable strides forward in the third quarter of the twentieth century and that it now serves a significant percentage of the population, perhaps 40% participating at some period of their lives. The growth, however, has been accompanied by a more or less permanent theme of government under-financing and relative neglect, much more support being given, for example, to sport. So far it seems, too, that those who have been most assisted are those who were already in a position of advantage, a situation intensified by the recent pressures of inflation and generally rising costs. Furthermore, some non-attenders still seem to view the education of adults as something odd, and though their views may be losing strength, they may be reinforced by an undue emphasis on remedial education.

The possible policies

In policy terms, the major question is not the central significance of education for adults, which internationally has received world-wide acknowledgement, but who should enjoy it, and with this the attendant question of how it should be organized. The answers depend essentially on political attitudes and beliefs, on concepts of justice and on ideas about the importance of the individual and the nature of man. Broadly speaking two distinct, though perhaps extreme, policies can be observed, both logically tenable though very different in character.

In essence the first policy assumes that the 'good' society is, or should be, hierarchical, élitist and competitive, individuals within it being free to struggle for status and power or other rewards. The second policy assumes that the 'good' society is, or should be, more egalitarian and democratic, with individuals co-operating for the common good. Education in the first society would be the responsibility of the individual, not of the state, and available either as a commodity to be purchased or as a privilege awarded only to a meritocracy. Recurrent work-related education, for example, might be thought essential for managers, scientists and directors of all types of human activity so that they could keep up to date with changing developments and probable work reorientation. These would be likely to be the same people who had passed the early examinations and other 'hurdles' as children and adolescents. Those who had failed to surmount earlier hurdles but who were lucky enough to be in the few remaining 'essential' low-level jobs might be granted just enough recurrent work-related retraining to ensure their efficiency. Education which is not work-related would be available as a luxury provision on sale to all who could afford to buy it at full cost, and as a commercial commodity it would be expected to be profit making. In an unequal society, therefore, it would be available in practice only to an élite. The policy would not allow for special provision for the disadvantaged or other 'lame ducks' who had 'failed' in the race for success. In the early nineteenth century, the exponents of this kind of policy expressed the view that the education of the mass of ordinary people was anyway undesirable and probably dangerous to the stability of society; as poverty was caused by moral weakness and ineptitude, the poor might well misinterpret, or be 'led astray' by, education. The more it was reserved for those who could afford to pay for it, the better. Though not directly voiced so far, there are some signs of a re-emergence of this view.

The only exception to this general policy of laying the onus on the individual, with education as something to be 'won', would be the possibility of using it either to assist the economy or to secure discipline and conformity. In these terms the task of childhood education is seen to be mainly that of securing adjustment to existing society and of sorting out and grading. That of the limited adult sector would be a continuation of the same process. If the education of the ordinary adult in these terms should seem to fail, however, then it would be thought better to transfer the resources to 'sedation', especially for the probably large numbers of the unemployed, by providing more recreations of a passive kind. If these still did not prevent unrest, then the resources would be given instead to increasing the forces of law and order. Otherwise government should intervene as little as possible, and education would be not a public service but provided mainly by commercial entrepreneurs, and perhaps in part by employers in industry, commerce or the services. These would be expected to provide whatever accommodation and equipment was needed and employ whatever staff was required. Although education of any kind would be of little importance in the lives of most people, the education of children being as restricted as that of the adult, it would be of major value for the successful élite, duly acknowledged by their willingness to pay the full cost of a service rightly held to be precious. The attraction of the policy lies in its supposed removal of an expensive educational burden from government both central and local, but its philosophy depends on a particular interpretation of the place of the State, the value of private enterprise and 'freedom of choice'.

Few politicians of any party seem likely at present to risk the direct application of such a policy with its open attack on the value of education for all and its reversal of the trends in educational provision which have developed over the past century or so. Until recently no one in Britain since the early nineteenth century has held the view that all the costs of education, child as well as adult, should be charged to the consumer, and all politicians apparently still give lip service to 'equal educational opportunities' even if they differ in the interpretation.

However, most seem equally reluctant to adopt the logical alternative policy, that of a comprehensive service of education for children and adults, publicly financed and freely available to the whole community. This second policy argues that social justice requires full and continuing educational opportunities throughout life for everyone in all walks of life. This is regarded as essential because only in this way can each individual develop his or her abilities and capacity to the full and obtain a greater control over the quality of the environment. Everyone should have the opportunity to acquire the skills and technical competence necessary to be able to contribute fully to the welfare of the community, but, acknowledging the likelihood of more leisure time, this opportunity should include the development of creativity, imagination and self-awareness through which to find meaning and purpose in life.

This kind of education for personal development is seen not as a luxury or a privilege but as a basic human right, to be enjoyed by all members of the community. Instead of thoughts of 'sedation' or repression, it is believed that human beings would improve the quality of their lives by purposeful activity as well as by freely chosen relaxation. Envisaging a forthcoming world, Harold Entwistle suggests that it would be one in which 'we undertake activities we like while machines do what we don't like'. Education would also help all people to exercise their rights and responsibilities as democratic citizens in a socially responsible community. In terms of organization, the policy holds that it should be the responsibility of government to ensure that education throughout life is available to everyone; it must play the major part because only then can the community ensure both adequate resources and the kind of distribution which makes education freely

216

accessible to all. Although special provision would be made to help those handicapped in any way, education would be a normal part of the lives of all adults as well as of all children; as Ruskin commented: 'You do not learn that you may live; you live that you may learn.' Behind this policy is a belief in the value of each human being and in the power of education to release unrealized potential. It suggests a certain equality of status as well as of access to education, and it emphasizes the role of government in ensuring this, while using voluntary agencies as part of the available resources. Essentially it has a deep distrust of 'hurdles' of any kind, of tests which people must pass before moving further, and it rejects any thought of barriers, whether financial or otherwise. As Arthur Jones has noted, 'the educational highway should be a public road open freely to all and not a turnpike exacting tolls'.[1]

Supporters of this policy view the élitist policy as a prescription for disaster, creating so much frustration, boredom and disillusionment among the majority that it could lead only to upheaval. Yet there is no great willingness to activate the major switch of resources which is implicit in the alternative policy. Instead, for instance, there are moves to self-financing education for adults, while retaining it under the LEA wing; expressions of disapproval for commercial entrepreneurs being accompanied by ingenious methods of payment and by differential fees. Similarly, lip service is paid to the value of voluntary organizations but their existence is threatened by the removal of subsidies and their real activities weakened by admonitions to put more effort into money raising. Consciences then tend to be salved by declarations that their members are anyway 'non-joiners' and not worth helping. On the other hand there are those who are willing to subsidize basic education and perhaps technical education even while criticizing both as outdated and not really related enough to 'practical needs', however unclearly defined. It would seem, in fact, that unless there is a determined resistance, the élitist policy of leaving it simply to 'market forces' might well be achieved in some sectors, especially that of non work-related education for adults. There are, moreover, some signs that it could be followed in work-related education by making it the responsibility entirely of private employers.

This trend is quite unacceptable to most adult educators and to all who feel with the Brandt Commissioners that the only road to a less dangerous world is to ensure the preservation and acceptance of 'a belief in man, in human dignity, in basic human rights; a belief in the values of justice, freedom, peace, mutual respect, in love and generosity, in reason rather than force.[2]

The image of 'the education of adults'

To make progress on the road to these ideals we must first improve the general image of 'the education of adults'. There may be no image problem for the minority who are already convinced of its value and have a personal awareness of the need for its extension. Most people, however, still regard education as essentially something for children and see no point in anything more, except perhaps supposed vocational training for the 16—18 year olds. They also tend to think of education as only cognitive learning, the absorption of 'useful' facts and information, and to feel that any inadequacies revealed in adult life are caused by educational failure as children. The blame for such 'failure' is laid on schoolteachers, and thought to be quite irredeemable. The first task, therefore, is to help the majority of people to change these outdated views and attitudes, and to see the value and place of education in adult life. Vague generalizations, however, will not suffice, and the problem is to define with great clarity the objectives and results of education for adults and to interpret its value in ways which can be understood and accepted by ordinary people. Most people are accustomed to giving value to tangible results such as those seen, for example, in craft classes or in the acquisition of new skills leading to a change of job, but it is frequently difficult to indicate the value to the individual of a good generalized lifelong education, or 'personal enrichment' or 'adaptability' until he or she has experienced it. The world is clearly moving away from the old structures and values, but human beings tend to cling to what they know and to fear change to the unknown. Similarly, it is by no means easy to energize people to protect democracy by greater participation, unless they feel personally threatened; many are conditioned to passivity except perhaps at election time, and feel a sense of powerlessness. It has been said that 'to provide education for participation is itself a political statement in favour of a participatory rather than a hierarchical society, but not to provide it cannot be considered a position of neutrality'.[3] Balancing those who fear that mass unemployment in inner city areas will create cynicism, alienation and violence, are those who fear that participation would reduce their own power, and indeed there are many vested interests behind what Arthur Stock has called 'the enormous inertia' of the formal 'front end' model of education. Even some educators of adults appear not to want change, almost to enjoy the 'poor relation' image and the view of their work as 'marginal'. Perhaps a first essential is to educate some of the educators to perceive a new image.

Flexibility and co-operation

Second, we need far greater flexibility in the provision and with it co-operation between all agencies to produce an integrated service. The general public is quite unmoved by battles over old issues such as the vocational/non-vocational division and the relative merits of practical or theoretical studies, or of examination and non-examination based courses. Flexibility implies that the provision should be designed for adults instead of adults being fitted into courses thought convenient by the providers. This may lead to mixtures of full-time and part-time courses despite all the prestige of the former and the fatigue problems of the latter. It will almost certainly mean adjustments in matters such as the timing and length of courses, the liberalization of entry requirements, credit transfers and probably alternating 'work' and study periods. Changes to a less rigid format no doubt would threaten organizational structures such as measurement by student-hours, and staff—student ratios, especially if newer methods of self-learning and flexi-study were included as part of the programme as well as learning networks and teacherless groups. To move forward requires a focus on the 'client', the adult needs must be paramount, and inevitably this must allow for considerable local variations not only between urban and rural areas, but also for the achievement of different goals at different stages of human development. Many issues thus suggest planning based on local knowledge and research and upon student participation in devising the arrangements. In place of the 'jungle' and the battleground, supportive and stimulating co-operation between all sectors and all personnel is required to get effective deployment of resources over the whole of the educational field to meet the extensive needs of all adults. Otherwise the rate of change may outpace the adaptability of the educational service.

The adult educator

Third, we must secure more resources and in particular more adequate staffing. The flexibility just outlined should provide no threat to the security of staff if they too are willing to be less rigid. The central case for the full-time educator of adults rests upon the need for professional help, if people are to be able to diagnose and clarify their own requirements. The interpretation of these needs is a difficult process and only likely to be fruitful if there is a partnership in which the full-time educator works *with* people and nor *for* them. Attention has been drawn earlier to the need for a good counselling service, and this may well be thought central to a comprehensive provision. In simple terms, most adults require advice over the choice of educational methods and activities, encouragement through difficult periods and stimulus to go forward. This kind of assistance requires a high degree of sensitivity and expertise supported by recurrent personal and professional education for the educator. This kind of role, however, differs from the more usually accepted view of an 'educator'; most people have been led to think that 'educator' means 'teacher' and that 'teacher' in turn implies someone who carries out didactic and direct 'teaching'. They tend, therefore, to be bewildered by the view of an educator as someone who, perhaps indirectly, facilitates learning. The image of the teacher has been changing in the primary schools and is well understood in some parts of the adult sector, but perhaps the most important step forward would be change in most secondary schools. The adult should then become less inhibited, more sophisticated in the approach to learning and more able to cope with new methods. At present many adults even if they come to educational activities, expect to be 'taught' and have little idea of the virtues of self-directed enquiry.

No doubt changes in the concept of an 'educator' will take time and, in the meantime, many standard-type classes with a teacher can be expected to continue on traditional lines. If the demand for a subject area is regular and consistent over a fairly long period of time some of the teachers can be expected to be full-time, but in other areas where there are considerable fluctuations in demand it is likely that many will be part-time. Adequacy of staffing implies a stress on quality, without which there is not only likely to be demoralization but also a damaging reduction in esteem. This suggests, as already indicated, a constant need to extend the training programmes for part-time teachers which at the present time are limited to only a few areas. One of the problems is a partial failure to apply in practical situations the knowledge about how to educate adults which has been derived from research;

and both part-time and full-time teachers need to explore further the wide spectrum of methods and techniques which are available. The adult sector has an experimental tradition and this could provide a base on which to build. Professionalism should not imply bureaucracy and one of the features of a comprehensive democratic policy would be the use of all the 'untapped reservoir of talent'[4] which is available. As advocated by the Volunteer Centre[5] there is a strong case for the greater involvement of volunteers in the provision – both as service-givers and as *animateurs* of self-help – but equally this demands efforts to improve their effectiveness by training, in which the full-time educators of adults should play a full role.

Discussions about future possibilities reveal differences between the pessimistic and the optimistic educators of adults. The pessimists see little hope of real change in the provision and think that the majority of people will continue to exhibit a lack of interest. They tend, therefore, to accept an indefinite continuation of the unplanned and uncertain nature of the provision, blown about more by emotional responses to problems than by a clear understanding of them. They are likely not to show any firm opposition to élitist policies but to drift and concentrate their attention on surviving in whatever system emerges. Others, also pessimists, feel that the élitist approach deepens divisions in society rather than heals them, but believe that little can be done about it, and therefore, with foreboding, envisage increased divisiveness, impersonality and violence. At worst they fear that it will result in ultimate destruction and perhaps even think that this is inevitable. The optimist may have the same fears but feels that survival is possible and that the key to a brighter future is education. A long while ago H.G. Wells noted the race between education and catastrophe, and more recently the Montreal Declaration which emerged from the UNESCO Second World Conference of 1960 pointed out that:

> Our first problem is to survive. It is not a question of the survival of the fittest. Either we survive together or we perish together. Survival requires that the countries of the world must learn to live together in peace. 'Learn' is the operative word. Mutual respect, understanding, sympathy, are qualities that are destroyed by ignorance and fostered by knowledge.

The optimists believe that there is yet time.

They also understand that attitude change is a slow process and that the effort required has to be long term. The concept of lifelong education is still a novelty to most people in Britain although more and more have come to accept that adult education has great value to them and that without it there is a vast waste of human resources. The case is a good one. As Julius Nyerere has said, the purpose is the 'liberation of man',[6] or as Percy Lord put it, it is 'the process by which we are taught the art of living . . . a search for fulfilment, for happiness, for a sense of proportion, for understanding and sympathy, for a sense of humour, for contentment and for a sense of purpose'.[7] The first question is whether the educational assets which Britain has accumulated will now be fatally undermined. The second question, assuming survival, is whether they will be used for just a small meritocracy or other form of élite, or whether they will be used for the benefit of all. So far the education of adults in Britain has not been granted the status it has been given elsewhere in the world, and British expenditure on it, as a percentage of the gross national product, falls far short of that of other countries in the European Community. The third question, therefore, asks if Britain can continue in this way, if indeed it can afford *not* to provide. The Venables Report suggested that the provision is 'vital to the well-being of this country – not only for the personal lives of innumerable individual citizens, but because *their* understanding of the issues involved and *their* willingness to co-operate are vital to the future economic recovery and social well-being of this country'.[8] The optimist, therefore, hopes to lead public opinion to a change of attitude, to a wider educational perspective and to a redeployment of resources. There is no doubt that Britain has fully adequate resources with which to build the finest public service of education for all adults and children if it so wishes. The optimist thinks of the better world which could be possible, and hopes to reduce the gap between the ideal and current practice. 'Education', said Henry Morris, 'is committed to the view that the ideal order and the actual order can ultimately be one'.[9] If the road to the education of all adults is to be a long one, then it is important to make haste. It is also important to keep the ideal in mind for it is our only chance of securing the just society and the better life for all which democracy demands. Nor may we ignore the international context: the Brandt Report[10] has argued for a 'global consensus on the moral plane that the basis of any world or national order must be people and respect for their essential rights', going on to state that 'this requires an intensive process of education to bring home to public opinion in every country the vital need to defend the values without which there will be no true economic development and above all no justice, freedom or peace'. In that process the education of adults is central.

References

1. JONES, H.A. Analysing the states of mind of field workers in adult education, in review article in *Studies in Adult Education,* 12/1, April, 1980, p. 59.

2. *North-South: a Programme for Survival.* The Report of the Independent Commission on International Development Issues under the Chairmanship of Willy Brandt, 1980, Pan Books, p. 12.

3. HAMPTON, W. 'Adult education for participation – a survey of provision by educational agencies', *Studies in Adult Education,* 12/2, Oct., 1980, pp. 117–126.

4. Russell Report, See 'General statement', para 2.2 and 'A comprehensive service of adult education', paras 59–74.

5. See the Volunteer Centre leaflet *What it stands for and what it does* (n/d). The Centre is a body which believes that 'Increased community involvement in the voluntary and statutory services – health, social, education, probation and prison – will benefit those who use the services, those who work in them and the community as a whole.'

6. NYERERE, J. *Adult Educational Development,* Opening address at the International Adult Education Conference 1976, sponsored by the International Council for Adult Education.

7. LORD, PERCY. *Lancashire Education, 1870–1970,* Lancs. Education Committee.

8. Venables Report, 1976, para 132, p. 83.

9. MORRIS, H. *The Village College,* 1925, Cambridge University Press, p. 23.

10. Brandt Report op. cit. p. 268.

Notes on Further Reading

1. Year books

Current programmes and annual reports are often the quickest way of gaining information about the provision made by existing organizations, and the most valuable sources for the addresses of these are the *Year Books* of the National Institute of Adult Education (England and Wales) and of the Scottish Institute of Adult Education. These should be available in most libraries but if not they can be obtained from:

NIAE 19B, De Montfort Street, Leicester, LE1 7GE, England
SIAE 4 Queensferry Street, Edinburgh, EH2 4PA, Scotland.

The NIAE Year Book contains much invaluable information about the providing agencies such as the LEAs, the universities, the Ministry of Defence, the Home Office Prison Department, the WEA, the broadcasting authorities and the Manpower Services Commission; about professional, consultative or advisory bodies such as the ECA and the AACE; and about other bodies such as the many voluntary organizations, the industrial training boards, the polytechnics, the regional advisory councils and the residential colleges. It also lists the educational journals and education correspondents and has sections on Scotland, Northern Ireland and overseas contacts, together with relevant extracts from legislation and regulations.

2. Bibliographies

The most extensive annotated bibliographies of British education for adults so far are:

KELLY, T. (Ed.) *A Select Bibliography of Adult Education in Great Britain,* third edition 1974, NIAE. (A supplement or new edition is expected to be available from the NIAE by 1983 or 1984.)

PETERS, A.J. *A Guide to the Study of British Further Education: Published Sources on the Contemporary System,* 1967, NFER.

3. General publications:

BURGESS, T. *Education after School,* 1977, Penguin. (A manifesto for further development which asks questions about purposes and organization.)

CANTOR, L.M. and ROBERTS, I.F. *Further Education Today: a Critical Review,* 1979, Routledge and Kegan Paul. (Revised edition of book first issued in 1969.)

FLUDE, R. and PARROTT, A. *Education and the Challenge of Change,* 1979, OU Press. (Discussion of a recurrent education strategy for Britain.)

LOWE, J. *Adult Education in England and Wales: a Critical Study,* 1970, Michael Joseph. (Survey of non-vocational education but now out of print.)

MEE, G. and WILTSHIRE, H. *Structure and Performance in Adult Education,* 1978, Longmans. (Examines non-vocational education provided by LEAs.)

National Institute of Adult Education *Adequacy of provision for Adult Education,* 1970, NIAE (also *Adult Education,* XLII, 6 March 1970). (Report of a survey of seven representative LEAs in England and Wales.)

PEERS, R. *Adult Education: a Comparative Study,* 3rd Edition 1972 (1st 1958), Routledge & Kegan Paul. (Concerned with non-vocational education. See especially Part II, pp. 105–167.)

ROGERS, J. and GROOMBRIDGE, B. *Right to Learn; the Case for Adult Equality,* 1976, Arrow Books. (A campaigning book asserting the importance of adult education and recommending reform in its organization.)

SIMPSON, J. *Today and Tommorrow in European Adult Education,* 1972, Council of Europe. (Contains a good deal of relevant material and some useful comparisons.)

THOMPSON, J.L. (Ed.) *Adult Education for a Change,* 1980, Hutchinson. (Questions many of the current concepts and practices, and includes some first hand accounts of new developments.)

VENABLES, P.F.R. *Technical Education: its Aims, Organisation and Future Development,* 1955, Bell and Sons. (Much outdated in detail but still valuable for its ideas and stimulus.)

4. Historical background

For those who wish to know more about the historical background to the present provision, the following books are recommended:

HARRISON, J.F.C. *Learning and Living, 1790–1960.* 1961, Routledge and Kegan Paul. (Uses the West Riding of Yorkshire as a case study.)

KELLY, T. *A History of Adult Education in Great Britain,* 2nd revised edition, 1970, Liverpool University Press.

LAWSON, J. and SILVER, H. *A Social History of Education in England,* 1973, Methuen. See particularly Chs. VII–XI.

5. Reports

Department of Education and Science, *Adult Education: a Plan for Development,* 1973, HMSO, London. (The 'Russell Report') Report by a Committee of Inquiry appointed by the Secretary of State for Education and Science under the Chairmanship of Sir Lionel Russell, CBE.

Scottish Education Department. *Adult Education: the Challenge of Change,* 1975, HMSO, Edinburgh. (The 'Alexander Report') Report by a Committee of Inquiry into Adult Education in Scotland appointed by the Secretary of State for Scotland under the Chairmanship of Professor J.W. Alexander.

Open University, *Report of the Committee on Continuing Education,* 1976, Open University. (The 'Venables Report')

6. Periodicals

See the list in the NIAE *Year Book;* of the many which touch on the field, the following are particularly recommended:

Adult Education Quarterly journal for British professional adult educators (NIAE).

Studies in Adult Education Twice yearly journal of research and scholarship (NIAE).

Journal of Scottish Adult Education Twice yearly (SIAE).

The Vocational Aspect of Education Three times yearly (Bolton College of Education (Technical).

Times Educational Supplement/Times Higher Educational Supplement, Weekly.

Journal of Further and Higher Education, Three times a year (NATFHE).

Abbreviations (which may be met in reading about the education of adults)

Note:

The organizations marked * are no longer in existence but are included because reference is still made to them. Where an organization has changed title or joined another body, this is indicated in a note.

AACE	Association for Adult and Continuing Education
ABCA*	Army Bureau of Current Affairs
ABCC	Association of British Correspondence Colleges
ABE	Adult basic education
ACACE	Advisory Council for Adult and Continuing Education
ACC	Association of County Councils
ACE	Advisory Centre for Education
ACERT	Advisory Committee for the Education of Romany and other Travellers
ACFHE	Association of Colleges for Further and Higher Education
ACL	Action Centred Leadership (programme of the Industrial Society)
ACP	Associate of the College of Preceptors
ACSET	Advisory Committee on the Supply and Education of Teachers
ACSTT*	Advisory Committee of the Supply and Training of Teachers (now reformed as ACSET)
ACW	Association of Community Workers
ACWW	Associated Country Women of the World
AE	Adult education
AFE	Advanced further education
ALBSU	Adult Literacy and Basic Skills Unit
ALE	Association for Liberal Education
ALRA*	Adult Literacy Resources Unit (became ALU)
ALU*	Adult Literacy Unit (became ALBSU)
AMA	Association of Metropolitan Authorities
APC	Association of Principals of Colleges
APLET	Association for Programmed Learning and Educational Technology

APT	Association of Polytechnic Teachers
ARE	Association for Recurrent Education
ARELS	Association of Recognised English Language Schools
ASH	Action on Smoking and Health
ASIT	Army School of Instructional Technology
ASRO	Association of Social Research Organisations
ATAE	Association of Tutors in Adult Education
ATCDE*	Association of Teachers in Colleges and Departments of Education (with ATTI developed into NATFHE)
ATO*	Area Training Organisation
ATPE	Association of Teachers in Penal Establishments
ATTI*	Association of Teachers in Technical Institutions (With ATCDE developed into NATFHE)
AUT	Association of University Teachers
AVA	Audio-visual aids
AVIP	Association of Viewdata Information Providers
BACIE	British Association for Commercial and Industrial Education
BAS	British Association of Settlements and Social Action Centres
BBC	British Broadcasting Corporation
BCA*	Bureau of Current Affairs
BCC	British Council of Churches
BEC	Business Educational Council
BFI	British Film Institute
BIAE*	British Institute of Adult Education (Joined with the NFAE in 1949 to become the NIAE)
BIM	British Institute of Management
BoE*	Board of Education (now the DES)
BSI	British Standards Institution
CAACE	Christian Association for Adult and Continuing Education
CACC	Council for the Accreditation of Correspondence Colleges
CAM	Communication Advertising and Marketing Education Foundation
CASE	Campaign for the Advancement of State Education
CAT*	College of Advanced Technology (all became technological universities)
CBEVE	Central Bureau for Educational Visits and Exchanges
CBI	Confederation of British Industry
CCETSW	Central Council for Education and Training in Social Work
CCPR	Central Council of Physical Recreation
CCTV	Closed circuit television

CD	Community development
CDP	*Either* Community Development Project
	or Committee of Directors of Polytechnics
CEC	European Council for Education by Correspondence
CED*	Centre for Information and Advice on Educational Disadvantage
CEDEFOP	Centre européen pour le développement de la formation professionelle (European centre for the development of vocational training)
CEMA*	Council for the Encouragement of Music and the Arts (developed into the Arts Council of Great Britian)
CEO	Chief education officer
CET	Council for Educational Technology
CFE	College of further education
CGLI	City and Guilds of London Institute
CICS*	Centre for International Co-operation and Services (of the Open University)
CILT	Centre for Information on Language Teaching
CIU	Working Men's Club and Institute Union
CJAC*	Central Joint Advisory Committee on Tutorial Classes (to 1958)
CLEA	Council of Local Education Authorities
CNAA	Council for National Academic Awards
COI	Central Office of Information
CoSIRA	Council for Small Industries in Rural Areas
CQSW	Certificate of Qualification in Social Work
CRAC	Careers Research and Advisory Centre
CRE	Commission for Racial Equality
CSE	Certificate of Secondary Education
CSV	Community Service Volunteer
CTEB	Council of Technical Examining Bodies
CUA	Committee for University Assistance to Adult Education in HM Forces
CVCP	Committee of Vice-Chancellors and Principals of the Universities of the United Kingdom
CWDE	Centre for World Development Education
CYSA	Community and Youth Service Association
DE	Department of Employment (central government)
DES	Department of Education and Science (central government)
DHSS	Department of Health and Social Security (central government)
EAW	Electrical Association for Women

EBAE	European Bureau of Adult Education
ECA	Educational Centres Association
EDA	Educational Development Association
EFDSS	English Folk Dance and Song Society
EFVA	Educational Foundation for Visual Aids
EMD	Extra-mural department (of a university)
EOC	Equal Opportunities Commission
EPA	Educational Priority Area
EPC	Education Promotion Certificate (Army)
ESA*	Educational Settlements Association (now the ECA)
ESD	Employment Services Division (MSC)
FCCS	Forces Correspondence Courses Scheme
FE	Further education
FELCO	Federation of English Language Course Organisations
FME	Foundation for Management Education
GCE	General Certificate of Education
	'A' level — Advanced
	'O' level — Ordinary
GTC	General Teaching Council (Scotland)
HE	Higher education
HEC	Health Education Council
HMI	Her Majesty's Inspector(s)
HNC	Higher National Certificate
HND	Higher National Diploma
IBA	Independent Broadcasting Authority
ICAE	International Council for Adult Education
ICCE	International Council for Correspondence Education
ILEA	Inner London Education Authority
ILO	International Labour Office
IRT*	Imperial Relations Trust (now the Commonwealth Relations Trust)
ITB	Industrial Training Board
ITV	Independent television (commercial)
ITRU	Industrial Training Research Unit (Cambridge)
JC	Joint committee
LA	Library Association
LCP	Licentiate of the College of Preceptors

LDC	Local Development Council(s)
LEA	Local Education Authority
MEGSA*	Merseyside Educational Guidance Service for Adults
MIND	National Association for Mental Health
MSC	Manpower Services Commission
MSU	Mature Students Union
NACAE	National Advisory Council on Art Education
NACEIC*	National Advisory Council on Education for Industry and Commerce
NACRO	National Association for the Care and Resettlement of Offenders
NAFE	Non-advanced further education
NALGO	National Association of Local Government Officers
NARE	National Association for Remedial Education
NASO/NASU	National Adult School Organisation, formerly Union
NATESLA	National Association for Teaching English as a Second Language to Adults
NATFHE	National Association of Teachers in Further and Higher Education
NAWC	National Association of Women's Clubs
NAYC	National Association of Youth Clubs
NAYCEO	National Association of Youth and Community Education Officers
NCAVAE	National Committee for Audio-Visual Aids in Education
NCEA	National Co-operative Education Association
NCILT	National Centre for Industrial Language Training
NCL*	National Central Library (now the British Library)
NCLC*	National Council of Labour Colleges
NCP	National Consumer Project
NCTA	National Council for Technological Awards
NCVS/NCSS	National Council for Voluntary Organisations, formerly of Social Service
NEAEC	North East Adult Education Conference
NEC	National Extension College
NFAE*	National Foundation for Adult Education (to 1949)
NFCA	National Federation of Community Associations
NFCTA*	National Federation of Continuative Teachers Associations
NFER	National Foundation for Educational Research in England and Wales
NFU	National Farmers Union
NFVLS	National Federation of Voluntary Literacy Schemes

NFWI	National Federation of Women's Institutes
NIAE	National Institute of Adult Education (England and Wales)
NICCE	Northern Ireland Council for Continuing Education
NMGC	National Marriage Guidance Council
NOW	New Opportunities for Women
NPFA	National Playing Fields Association
NUS	National Union of Students
NUT	National Union of Teachers
NUTG	National Union of Townswomen's Guilds
NWAEC	North West Adult Education Conference
OECD	Organisation for Economic Co-operation and Development
ODI	Overseas Development Institute
ODM	Ministry of Overseas Development
OFE	'Other further education'
ONC	Ordinary National Certificate
OND	Ordinary National Diploma
OU	Open University
OUSA	Open University Students Association
PEL	Paid educational leave
PHAB	Physically Handicapped and Able Bodied (groups)
PLAEC	Public Libraries Adult Education Committee of the North West
PPA	Pre-school Playgroups Association
PQS	Progressive Qualification Scheme (army)
PRA	*Either* Pre-Retirement Association
	Or Psychiatric Rehabilitation Association
PT (pt)	Part-time
PTA	Parent–Teacher Association
RAC	Regional advisory council for further education
RB	Responsible Body
RCA	Royal College of Art
RCC	*Either* Residential Colleges Committee
	Or Rural Community Council
REHAB	British Council for the Rehabilitation of the Disabled
RMSA	Rural Music Schools Association
RSA	Royal Society of Arts
RSG	Rate Support Grant
SALPA	Special Adult Learning Programmes Association
SCABEU	Scottish Adult Basic Education Unit

231

SCALRA*	Scottish Adult Literacy Resource Agency (became SCALU)
SCALU*	Scottish Adult Literacy Unit (became SCABEU)
SCCE	Scottish Council for Community Education
SCNVYO	Standing Conference of National Voluntary Youth Organisations of England and Wales
SCOTBEC	Scottish Business Education Council
SCOTEC	Scottish Technical Education Council
SCUTREA	Standing Conference on University Teaching and Research in the Education of Adults
SED	Scottish Education Department (central government)
SEO	Society of Education Officers
SIAE	Scottish Institute of Adult Education
SIT	Society of Industrial Tutors
SPD	Special Programmes Division (MSC)
SRC	Science Research Council
SRHE	Society for Research into Higher Education
SSCVYO	Scottish Standing Conference of Voluntary Youth Organisations
SSRC	Social Science Research Council
STEP	Special Temporary Employment Programme
SWRI	Scottish Women's Rural Institutes
TEC	Technician Education Council
TES/THES	Times Educational Supplement/Higher Education Supplement
TFL	Training for Life (YMCA)
TG	Townswomen's Guild
TOPS	Training Opportunities Scheme
TSD	Training Services Division (MSC)
TU	Trade union
TUC	Trades Union Congress
TWI*	Training within industry
UCAE	Universities Council for Adult Education
UCCA	University Central Council on Admissions
UCET	University Council for the Education of Teachers
UEMCC*	Universities Extra-mural Consultative Committee (now UCAE)
UGC	University Grants Committee
ULCI*	Union of Lancashire and Cheshire Institutes (now incorporated in the North-Western RAC)
UNESCO	United Nations Educational Scientific and Cultural Organisation

UVT	Unified Vocational Preparation
VSU	Voluntary Services Unit (Home Office)
WAAE*	World Association for Adult Education
WAFEYSO	Welsh Association of Further Education and Youth Service Officers (Cymdeithas Swyddogion Addysg Bellach a Gwasanaeth Ieunctid Cymru)
WEA	Workers' Educational Association
WEEP	Work Experience in Employer's Premises
WETUC*	Workers' Educational Trade Union Committee
WI	Women's Institute
WJEC	Welsh Joint Education Committee
WOW	Wider Opportunities for Women (MSC courses)
WRVS	Women's Royal Voluntary Service
YFC	Young Farmers' Clubs
YMCA	Young Men's Christian Association
YOP	Youth Opportunities Programme
YWCA	Young Women's Christian Association

Index

Note: Reports are given their 'popular' titles e.g. 'Haycocks Report', 'Alexander Report', 'Russell Report'.

243